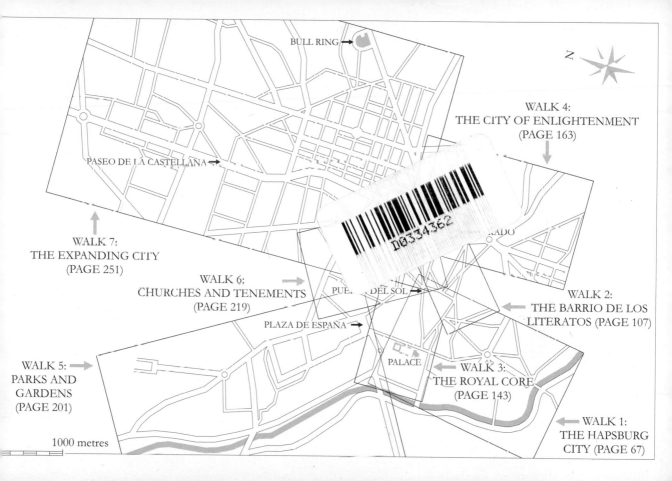

BULL RING

N

WALK 4:
THE CITY OF ENLIGHTENMENT
(PAGE 163)

PASEO DE LA CASTELLANA

...RADO

WALK 7:
THE EXPANDING CITY
(PAGE 251)

WALK 6;
CHURCHES AND TENEMENTS
(PAGE 219)

PUE... DEL SOL

WALK 2:
THE BARRIO DE LOS
LITERATOS (PAGE 107)

PLAZA DE ESPAÑA

WALK 5:
PARKS AND
GARDENS
(PAGE 201)

PALACE

WALK 3:
THE ROYAL CORE
(PAGE 143)

WALK 1:
THE HAPSBURG
CITY (PAGE 67)

1000 metres

Michael Jacobs MADRID

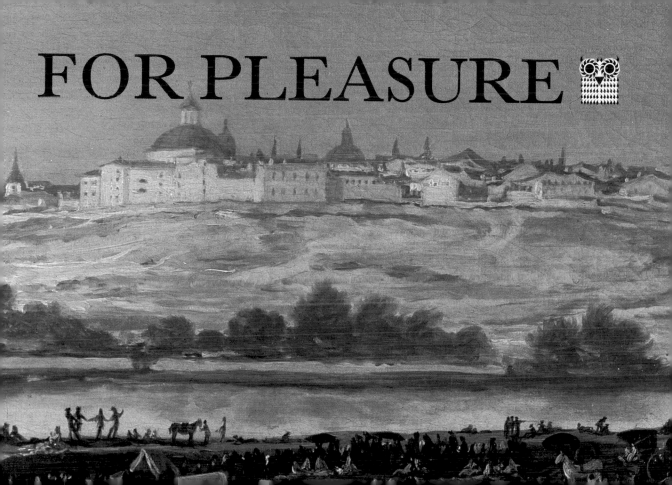

FOR PLEASURE

CONTENTS

Preface and Acknowledgements

Richard Ford, writing in 1845, misled generations of travellers by saying that the 'more Madrid is known the less it will be liked'. The intention of the present book is to show that the very opposite is true, and that those who come here with time to spare and an open mind will encounter not only one of Europe's most exhilarating capitals, but also a wealth of cultural attractions which might surprise those who think of Madrid essentially in terms of the Prado Museum. I have arranged the book as a series of itineraries through areas of Madrid suggestive of different stages in the city's history, but within each of these areas, I have included a wide range of attractions from many different periods. This is not simply an artistic and architectural guide, but a companion to many aspects of the city's culture, a particular emphasis being on Madrid's fascinating literary associations and on its intensive bar and café life.

The staff of numerous Madrid institutions have assisted me in the research for this book, and I would particularly like to thank Lola Baquero of the Ayuntamiento de Madrid, Enrique Benedito of the Fábrica de Tabaco, Vicenta Benedito of the Colección Benedito, María Condor and Juan Antonio Juara Colomer of the Alameda de Osuna, Javier Gutiérrez Marcos of the Comunidad de Madrid, and Santiago Matellano and Alicia Gómez Navarro of the Residencia de Estudiantes. But a book of this kind has been dependant above all on the help, suggestions, companionship and hospitality of my Madrid friends, including Kenny

Armstrong, William and Sonia Chislett, Inma Cuesta, Manuel Fernández Orgil, Danny Garbade, Ian Gibson, Tito de la Guardia, Paco Martínez Moncada, Alfonso, Marco and Miguel Ormaetxea, and Alicia Ríos. For such diverse acts of kindness as driving me around the Madrid cemeteries, providing information on the firm of Capas Seseña, and discussing with me the Madrid of Pérez Galdós, I must thank respectively Jerónimo Hernández, Natacha Seseña and Eduardo Naval. Maite Brik and her mother Lola Matalonga were invaluable accomplices in my investigations of the Madrid tertulias, while Esperanza Flores, on a visit from Seville, introduced me to such personalities of the Malasaña bars as Maria José, Mario, Miguel, Eli, Paloma, 'El Novillo', and the infamous 'Pollo Colorado'. Annie Bennett's flat above the wonderful Sociedad de Autores building has been a second home to me in Madrid, as has that of Carmen de la Guardia and Pepe Llanos in the Barrio de Salamanca. I am indebted to Alexander Fyjis-Walker and Lynette Quinlan for turning the original coffee-table version of this book into a paperback edition. Jackie Rae, with whom I share many happy memories of Madrid, has once again kept up my spirits while I was back at my desk in London.

M. J. Spring 2001

Preface to the Third Edition

The publication of this first colour edition of the Pallas Athene paperback has allowed me to make a few essential up-dates to the 1996 text, and to include an idiosyncratic listing of places to eat and stay. Cristina Fuentes has helped to keep me abreast of recent changes, and to maintain my enthusiasm for the city, as have Kuki Gonzalez de Caldas, her partner Jesús, and their circle of friends at De Pura Cepa. This book is dedicated, as it always has been, to Chata, Pepe, Miguel and Javier.

M. J. Autumn 2003

Introduction

Certain cities such as Venice, Prague or Paris are unfailingly and tiresomely praised. Madrid is not one of these places, and a love for it cannot so easily be explained or acquired. There are few other cities that excite me to the same extent as Madrid, but I have often found myself in the company of first-time visitors who fail to see beyond the grime, traffic and dearth of famous monuments. Hemingway, writing of Madrid in 1932, did not believe that 'anyone likes it much when he first goes there'. Yet he himself became one of the city's greatest enthusiasts, finding it the best of all Spanish cities to live in, and becoming such an ubiquitous presence in its bars and restaurants that one establishment off the Puerta del Sol still makes the lone claim that 'Hemingway never came here'.

'Madrid was until recently the European capital least visited by foreigners,' wrote Fernández de los Rios in his *Guide to Madrid* of 1876, one of the first and most detailed guidebooks ever written about the city. Though Madrid enjoys today an increasing popularity as a tourist destination, the great majority of its visitors see little more than the Prado Museum or the Royal Palace and spend the rest of their time escaping to the surrounding towns and villages. Madrid as a whole remains a remarkably neglected and baffling city, and as yet there are few books other than in Spanish that will guide you beyond the main and obvious attractions, or try to define the appeal of a place which was described early this century by its outstanding native writer Gómez de la Serna as 'the most difficult capital in the world to understand'.

Not even those who love Madrid over all other cities would call it a conventionally beautiful place. Hardly anything has survived from its medieval and renaissance periods, while its 17th- and 18th-century monuments lack on the whole the exuberance of those of other Spanish cities such as Seville and Santiago de Compostela. Its old centre is composed largely of late 19th- and early 20th-century buildings, but few of these are in the fantastical Art Nouveau style which makes the architecture of turn-of-the-century Barcelona so popular. Furthermore the people of Madrid have shown almost to the present day an irreverence towards the architecture of the past, and have had little hesitation in pulling down old buildings to make way for the new. By 1895 one English traveller, C. Bogue Luffmann, was writing that Madrid was 'one of the most modern-looking cities' that he had ever seen, and it is precisely this feature of Madrid that has disappointed so many of its visitors, who have come to Spain with a romantic vision of a country steeped in the past.

Richard Ford, whose *Handbook to Spain* of 1845 did so much to influence foreign attitudes towards this country, disliked Madrid for lacking those qualities that he considered to be typically Spanish, such as Moorish monuments, jasmine-scented patios, and colourful folkloric traditions. To Hemingway, however, Madrid was 'the most Spanish of all cities', and this is certainly true in terms of its population, which comprises few families of pure Madrilenian origin, but features instead people from every corner of Spain. What is more, in contrast to the traditionally more cosmopolitan Barcelona, Madrid remains one of the most idiosyncratic of Europe's capitals, distinguished by a quite exceptional vitality. George Borrow, the eccentric author of *The Bible in Spain* (1843), was virtually alone among the travellers of the Romantic generation truly to appreciate Madrid. He claimed to have visited 'most of the principal capitals of the world', but found that Madrid fascinated him more than any of these places, above all for its human interest: 'I will not dwell upon its streets, its edifices, its public squares, its fountains, though some of these are remarkable enough... But the population! Within a mud wall, scarcely one league and a half in circuit, are contained two hundred thousand human beings, certainly forming the most extraordinary vital mass to be found in the entire world; and be it always remembered that this mass is strictly Spanish!'

In terms of its gossip and the ease with which friends and acquaintances meet up in its centre, Madrid has retained some of the endearing qualities of a small town. However, in its vitality, and in the scale of its streets and architecture, Madrid gives a greater impression of being a city than do many other cities that are much larger in size, such as London. Madrid, like New York, will appeal above all to those who thrive on the excitement of a large metropolis, and begin to feel uncomfortable when exposed too long to the peace of the countryside. In the itineraries that make up the bulk of this book, I have resisted the temptation to take the reader further afield than the former hunting grounds of

El Pardo. I have omitted the impressive peaks of the nearby Sierra de Guadarrama, and such beautiful surrounding towns and villages as Toledo, Segovia, and Chinchón, all of which are worlds in their own right, demanding separate treatment. Though the Madrilenians have developed today a taste for country excursions, this was not always the case, and Antonio Díaz-Cañabate – a passionate recorder of Madrid life in the early years of this century, seen at his most urbane on p. 282 – amusingly described an extreme Madrilenian attitude of old which considered the countryside to be not only oppressive but also positively dangerous. According to Díaz-Cañabate, there were even those whose discomfort in the face of Nature was such that they went only occasionally to the city park of El Retiro, the large pond of which inspired immediate fears of rheumatism.

I hope that the present book will convince the reader of how much there is to see and do without even leaving the boundaries of the city, and I am sure that many of the places I have included will be unknown even to many Madrilenians.

While the Prado alone might justify a visit to Madrid, there are numerous other excellent but often little-visited art collections that reinforce the city's reputation as one of the great art centres of Europe. Even the architecture of the city, though easily dismissed on a first impression, offers countless surprises, such as perfectly preserved 17th-century interiors hidden behind austere brick walls, or massive 19th-century buildings enlivened by a wealth of bizarre and colourful detailing. A pleasure very special to Madrid is provided by the remarkable number of old shops, cafés, bars and restaurants that have maintained over the years their traditional appearance, even down to the ceramic advertisements on the exterior, and their often surrealistic window-displays. Several of these places have the additional interest of having been the scene of literary gatherings or *tertulias*. One of the most celebrated of these tertulias is shown opposite in a famous painting by the Madrid artist Solana, who portrays the charismatic writer Ramón Gómez de la Serna addressing a group of his disciples at the Café El Pombo. In fact, Madrid is a city particularly rich in literary associations, and a tour of the place can form a wonderful introduction to Spanish literature, itself a subject that has been unfairly neglected by foreigners.

To all these specific attractions – and to others of a more hedonistic kind to be outlined at the end of this introduction – must be added an elusive element of magic which poets have vaguely attributed to something in Madrid's air, an air which owes its special properties to the city's situation in the middle of the vast Castilian plateau. The climate of Madrid is known for its great extremes, and also for its deceptively gentle winds that creep in unexpectedly from the Sierra, causing sudden drops in temperature even on the sunniest day; these winds, in the words of a much-repeated proverb, 'will not extinguish a candle, but will put out a man's life'. The penetrating air of the Sierra has also the effect of clearing away the hovering pollution and creating intensely blue skies that Salvador Dalí compared to those by the pioneering 15th-century landscape painter, Joachim Patinir.

Nina Epton, a prolific writer who had been

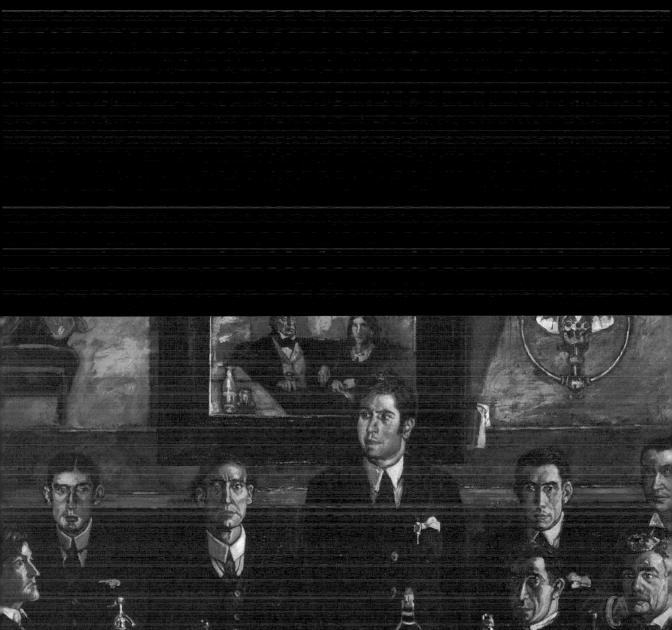

brought up in Madrid in the 1920's, was forced to look to the skies to find an explanation for a phenomenon which she observed among her fellow passengers every time she approached Madrid on the train from Paris:

> Everybody in the compartment stood up and shouted: 'Madrid!'... 'Madrid!', Mother echoed with tears in her eyes. People reacted as if there had been a free distribution of champagne. The sight of Madrid in the distance revived the drooping, unruffled the bad-tempered, bestowed the gift of tongues upon the inarticulate. Everybody waved, laughed, cried and shouted.

Sadly, I have yet to experience such a scene myself, but I can nonetheless vouch for the excitement of arriving at Madrid by train from the north. After crossing the frighteningly monotonous expanses of northern Castile, the train makes its way over the gaunt and often snow-capped granite peaks of the Sierra de Guadarrama. On the southern slopes of the range, near the Palace and Monastery of the Escorial, you are suddenly offered an extensive view over a flat and scraggy landscape of boulders and shrubland, above which hover in the far distance the whitened profiles of apartment blocks. Arriving at Madrid at the height of summer, the city can seem as if it were built right in the middle of a desert, and this impression was at one time strengthened by its modern railway station of Chamartín being situated in a virtual wasteland beyond the city's northern boundary. My favourite point of arrival is the Estación del Norte, the quietest of Madrid's main stations, and a place used mainly by trains coming from Ávila and Salamanca. Lying on the northeastern side of town, the station obliquely faces the most distinctive element in the Madrid skyline – a long and dramatic cliff supporting the massive bulk of Madrid's Royal Palace. It is there, on that cliff-top site projecting high above the modest river of the Manzanares, that the disputed origins of Madrid are to be sought. (The painting opposite shows the view in about 1900, with the Segovia Bridge in the foreground.)

When the relatively insignificant township of Madrid was transformed from the late 16th century onwards into a major city and the capital of a kingdom, it was perhaps inevitable that historians should try to dignify its history through the claiming of ancient, and mythical roots. Thus Madrid became a city of legendary Roman origins, founded by Prince Ocno-Bianor, and named after his mother, the prophetess Manto, a daughter of Hercules. Known as *Mantua Carpetana* to distinguish it from the Mantua in Italy, Madrid was to be referred to by this bogus Latin name up to the 19th century.

The actual, and more prosaic origins of Madrid appear to have been in the small Arab settlement of *Margherit*, which was built high above the Manzanares in *c.* 856 to guard the important line of communications between Toledo and the kingdom of Aragón. This defensive outpost fell to the Christians shortly after they had captured Toledo in 1085, and lived on subsequently as an agricultural and crafts centre with a population made up of Christians, Jews and the Christianized Moors known as *mudéjars*. During the brief ooccupation of Madrid by the Moors, the arid terrain around the city had apparently been transformed into fertile countryside covered with vines, orchards and kitchen-gardens. Under the Christians, however, the Moors' brilliant irrigation schemes came eventually to be neglected, and by the 17th century the surroundings of Madrid had been encircled by what one 19th-century traveller was to describe as a 'hideous, grassless, treeless, colourless, calcined desert'.

The one feature of the countryside which was to remain unchanged over the centuries – and survives to this day, albeit in a greatly reduced form – was the forest of El Pardo on the north-western outskirts of the city. From Moorish times onwards, this forest enjoyed considerable renown as a hunting-ground, and was indeed the main attraction of Madrid for the Spanish kings who occasionally took up residence here. Philip II was a passionate huntsman, and the presence of a nearby hunting-ground might have been a factor in his eccentric decision of 1561 to establish Madrid as the permanent seat of the hitherto itinerant Spanish court. (The picture opposite shows one of the little hunting lodges built at this period, together with its formal gardens, forested areas, and wilderness beyond.) There were several other reasons apart from hunting for honouring Madrid in this way, including the fact that the city was not ruled by a powerful and potentially independent-minded Archbishop as was Spain's ecclesiastical capital, Toledo; neither had the citizens of Madrid ever toyed with heresy, as had those of Valladolid, the Castilian city most favoured by Philip's great-grandparents, Ferdinand and Isabella. But, above all, Madrid had the advantage of being at the very centre of Spain, something which greatly appealed to Philip II's autocratic spirit and led him to overlook Madrid's main drawback as a capital city, namely its lack of a navigable river. This unfortunate oversight was to have disastrous consequences for Spain's economy in the 17th century.

Madrid's population rapidly increased after 1561, but much of the new urban development was unplanned and architecturally modest. The majority of the new houses were white-washed brick and adobe structures, such as you still find today in many of the more backward Castilian communities; they were rarely built higher than one floor, for the owners of taller houses were forced by law to accommodate members of the court. Philip II gave Madrid scarcely a single monument of note, his principal commission here being the Segovia Bridge, which was erected in 1583 as the first stone bridge to span what Cervantes called 'a rivulet with the reputation of a river', the Manzanares. The attention of the monarch was otherwise engaged, for only two years after choosing Madrid as the capital of Spain, he began to neglect the city almost entirely in favour of the nearby monastery and palace of El Escorial, the construction of which became the overriding obsession of his later years. We see it opposite, crystal hard in an anonymous 17th-century view, with the inaccurately placed towers and domes of Madrid shimmering white in a misty background.

Commissioned in 1563 from Juan Bautista de Toledo, the Escorial was completed in 1584 by the architect of the Segovia Bridge, Juan de Herrera, under whom the place became the supreme

expression of Philip II's uncompromising architectural tastes. A visit to the Escorial is the usual complement to any tour of Madrid, and is perhaps essential for anyone who wishes to understand the architectural development of the Hapsburg city. The prospect of coming here is also a potentially daunting one, and we might well feel certain misgivings when first confronted with this granite monster of a building, with its unadorned granite surfaces and megalomaniac scale. Guided tours – which in the 19th century lasted up to five hours – are fortunately no longer obligatory, and the clear and modern sign-posting has lessened the chances of our being disorientated by the monotonous regularity of the ground-plan, with its two vast and near identical cloisters. The most popular and intimate part of the Escorial are the Hapsburg Apartments, where melodramatic notions about the fanatical Philip II are usually fuelled by the sight of the very bed from which the gouty, sore-ridden and rotting monarch could look directly down to the high altar of the monastery church. As for the church itself, this provides a tour of the Escorial with its oppressive highpoint, especially on a dark day, when the scant detailing of this domed and barrel-vaulted structure is largely lost to the enveloping gloom. The Gothic fantasist William Beckford came here on one such day, and was no sooner past the 'cavern-like' porches of the front façade than he was seized by a premonition of entering 'a subterranean temple set apart for the service of some mysterious and terrible religion'. Inside he was immediately overcome by a 'sensation of dread and dreariness', particularly on finding that his sole company here was Pompeo Leoni's gilded but hauntingly life-like representations of the kneeling families of Philip II and Charles V.

No matter how awed or impressed visitors have been by the Escorial, many would have sympathized with H. V. Morton when he and his group, on leaving the building, had 'hastened with pleasure into a first-class hotel and ordered sherry and dry martinis'. The French 19th-century writer Théophile Gautier even went as far as to suggest that anyone who had ever spent a day in the Escorial would always be able to console themselves with the thought of no longer being there; for him the place was 'the deadliest and most wearisome edifice that a morose and suspicious tyrant could ever conceive for the mortification of his fellow-creatures'. The Escorial is certainly a building of unprecedented austerity, and it also brought to an end a period in Spanish architecture that had been characterized by joyous exuberance and ornamentation. A recent travel-writer, Archibald Lyall, wondered fancifully if the transition between the two styles could in any way be 'connected with the introduction of syphilis to Europe'; others, more sensibly, have pointed out the links between the so-called 'Herreran style' and totalitarianism, the Spain of the Hapsburgs being often described as the first totalitarian state in Europe. The style was at any rate to have an enormous impact on the look of Madrid, as the city finally entered, at the beginning of the 17th century, the first important period in its architectural history.

Philip II was succeeeded in 1598 by Philip III, whose first minister, the Duke of Lerma, was able to persuade him at the beginning of his reign, to transfer the capital to Valladolid. Madrid was once more and definitively the capital in 1606, and by 1617 had managed in only twenty years to double the size of its population, which was now as high as 150,000. The boom was to continue under Philip III's own successor, Philip IV, during whose rule the city came to supersede Seville in size and become the fifth largest in Europe. During these years of dramatic expansion, Madrid acquired several of its most salient later features, the Plaza Mayor, for instance, becoming transformed after 1610 into a grand and impressive showpiece, and the nearby Puerta del Sol emerging as the bustling, social heart of the city. Curiously, for a European city in an early and critical stage in its development, all the new building activity did not include the construction of a cathedral. Madrid was to remain until 1886 in the anomalous position of belonging to the diocese of Toledo, for which reason the place was referred to in the past not as a city but as a *villa*, or fortified town: work on Madrid's own cathedral was not begun until the end of the 19th century, and was only completed in 1994.

Religious architecture otherwise flourished in

27

Madrid in the early 17th century and accounted for most of the important new building work. Churches, religious hospitals, and, above all, convents, took up much of the city centre, and had proliferated to such an extent that by 1629 one chronicler, Jerónimo de la Quintana, recorded as many as seventy-three such institutions. As for secular architecture, the most ambitious and controversial new building was unquestionably the Royal Palace of the Buen Retiro. This was the brain-child of Philip IV's all-powerful minister, the Count-Duke of Olivares, who was determined that the Madrid court should be the focal point of a brilliant cultural life. The construction of the palace, on the eastern outskirts of Madrid, was to establish the surrounding area as the city's elegant and verdant playground, complete with an animated public promenade or *paseo* known as the Prado. Madrid's adobe defensive walls, which had been extended at the begining of the century as far east as the Puerta del Sol, now had to be taken further east to include the Buen Retiro. But from about 1660 onwards, they were to remain unchanged, and up to as late as the mid-19th century, the city was not to spread beyond them.

The first century of Madrid's existence as capital of Spain coincided with what is generally known as the Golden Age of Spanish culture. To begin with, it was Seville rather than Madrid that was the undisputed cultural capital of the country, but this situation began to change in the course of the 17th century, particularly in the fields of literature and painting. The first major novel in European literature, Cervantes' *Don Quixote*, was published in Madrid after 1605, while the recently founded public theatres of La Cruz and El Príncipe put on plays by such outstanding talents as Lope de Vega, Tirso de Molina and Calderón de la Barca. Naturally the court played a vital role in this literary life, commissioning plays for its theatres at the Buen Retiro and the nearby summer palace at Aranjuez, sponsoring respectively the greatest poet and satirist of this generation, Luis de Góngora and Francisco de Quevedo. Under Philip IV the court also became a major centre of painting, thanks principally to having attracted in 1623 a young prodigy from Seville, Diego Velázquez, whose presence here for nearly forty years provided the main impetus to a local school of painting which came to supersede that of Seville. It is symptomatic of the changing fortunes of Seville and Madrid that Velázquez's former colleague from Seville, Francisco de Zurbarán, was forced to move to Madrid in 1658 in search of commissions. Velázquez himself, as we see here in a detail from *Las Meninas,* achieved such prestige in this city that he was able to include his own portrait alongside that of royalty. A broad cross-section of the Madrid of his day can be seen overleaf in the foreground of his painting depicting the royal hunting ground of El Pardo, *La Tela Real.*

The architects working in 17th-century Madrid are much less well known than its painters or writers. The dominant figure was Herrera's pupil, Juan Gómez de Mora, who had a hand in just about all the principal civic, royal and religious commissions of the early 17th century, including the Buen Retiro, the magnificent Convent of the Encarnación, the Plaza Mayor, the Cárcel de

Corte and the Casa de la Villa. While never creating an architecture of such extreme austerity as his master's, he emulated the latter's ornamental restraint, love of rigidly geometric compositions, and characteristic use of high-pitched slate roofs and corner turrets. Herrera's legacy, combined with the sophisticated influence of the Court, were to affect the whole course of Madrid's architectural development. They held in check some of the wilder fantasies of the baroque, and gave to most of the buildings of this period a character far more sober than that to be found elsewhere in Spain. This is particularly evident in the city's churches, which are strikingly similar in their appearance, nearly all being barrel-vaulted, single-naved structures, with shallow transepts, and interiors relieved of their architectural austerity largely by long rows of elaborate consoles supporting richly-modelled cornices. Where they differ markedly from the church of El Escorial and other Spanish buildings of the late 16th century is in the cheapness of the materials used, brick and plaster being preferred to granite and marble. This feature, common

not only to the city's churches, but also to most of its other buildings of this period, highlights one of the main contradictions of Hapsburg Madrid. Though a rapidly growing city, so anxious to impress, Madrid seems for much of the century to have been pathetically short of funds. Regular mule trains journeying to Madrid from the Andalucían ports brought to this city much of the fabulous wealth coming in from America, but somehow this was dissipated through gross mismanagement, and constant foreign and internal disputes, so that even the royal coffers were seriously depleted.

'Madrid is still as your lordship left it, Prado, coaches, women, dust, executions, comedies, a lot of fruit – and very little money.' These words of Lope de Vega to his patron the Duke of Sessa admirably convey the vitality, confusion, brilliance and squalor of a Madrid that was perhaps not so dissimilar to the city of today. Even at this relatively early stage of its history, Madrid had all the positive and negative qualities of a large city, but to an exaggerated degree. One of the aspects most commented on by travellers of this time was its dirt, which, even by the standards of a 17th-century city, was apparently exceptional, with its inhabitants enjoying much notoriety for their habit of throwing all their rubbish out into the streets. The air of Madrid was already becoming polluted by the late 17th century, but, in dramatic contrast to the attitudes of today, there were many people who believed that such contamination of the environment was necessary to counteract what was thought to be the excessive and dangerous purity of the Madrid air in its natural state. So widespread was this belief that a local doctor, Doctor Juanini, felt compelled in 1689 to write a book putting forward the controversial suggestion that pollution itself might be detrimental to the health.

Madrid was clearly in need of renovation and embellishment by the time that the last of the Spanish Hapsburgs, Charles II, died in 1701. The advent of the Bourbons to the Spanish throne following a fourteen-year-long war of succession was fortuitously timed, leading as it did to a series of major reforms in Madrid that were to bring the place in line with some of the most advanced cities in Europe. The Bourbons were eventually to introduce here the latest French and Italian fashions, but the first of their Spanish kings, the Versailles-educated Philip V, made no attempt at first to impose his own tastes on local traditions, and gave the brilliant governor of Madrid at this time, the Marquis de Vadillo, a virtually free hand in the latter's ambitious plans for urban renewal. The Marquis was fortunately assisted in these plans by one of the most individual and versatile architects ever to have worked in Madrid, Pedro de Ribera.

Ribera's extraordinary achievement must be seen against his provincial training as an architect, and the meaness of the funds at his disposal, Madrid still being in a state of near-bankruptcy. His early career was spent almost entirely working for the municipality of Madrid, in which capacity he helped solve the difficult problem of access to the city by constructing the Toledo Bridge, a structure that combines functionalism, grandeur and exuberant decorative flourishes, as can be sensed in the 1950's photograph on p. 105, with gipsies beneath the arches. Among

Ribera's many other successes as a town-planner were the turning of the Paseo de la Virgen del Puerto into a handsome, garden-lined thoroughfare, the designing of several gates for the city, and the relaying of the municipal water supply so as to include a number of superbly ornate fountains. As an architect, Ribera was by far the most extreme representative of the baroque style in Madrid, and, to many of the 19th-century critics of this style, he was even to be considered as one of the worst of all Spanish offenders against good taste and classical decorum. However, the baroque elements in his buildings were often limited to his portals, the rest of the structures being left remarkably severe. Thus his Hospice of San Fernando (now the Museo Municipal), his culminating Madrid achievement, has one of the most gloriously elaborate of all Spanish portals (see overleaf) while the church attached to this building is fully in the austere tradition of Herrera and Gómez de Mora.

In later life Ribera was to be active largely as a designer of palaces for the aristocracy, but he was to live to see his work go out of fashion, and be ignored by the Bourbon monarchy. Philip V, under the influence of his second wife Isabel Farnese, recently arrived from Italy, began to tire of the Spanish baroque style and felt that local tastes needed to be tempered by the example of contemporary Italian architecture. The perfect opportunity to put these ideas into practice came after the Christmas Eve of 1734, when a disastrous fire swept through the *alcázar* (royal palace, seen in the background of the illustration on page 211), thus destroying the town's main symbol of Hapsburg dominance in Madrid. In his desire to create a new palace worthy of the reforming and cosmopolitan spirit of the Bourbon monarchy, Philip V called in from Italy the most renowned exponent of the late baroque, the aged Sicilian architect Filippo Juvarra. Juvarra died shortly after his arrival in Madrid, falling victim to the icy winds of the Guadarrama; but he was succeeded in his task of rebuilding the Royal Palace by his Piedmontese follower, Giovanni Battista Sacchetti. The vast Royal Palace, built on a scale virtually unrivalled in

18th-century Europe, took nearly thirty years to complete, and was to involve the participation of the two leading foreign painters of the day, the German A. R. Mengs, and the last great exponent of the Italian tradition of large-scale decorative painting, G. B. Tiepolo. The palace initiated a period in Madrid's architectural history which was to be dominated by foreign tastes. The French architect François Carlier received the most important commission of the reign of Philip V's successor, Ferdinand VI, while the Italian Francesco Sabatini was to be the favourite architect of the subsequent Bourbon ruler, Charles III. Only two Spanish architects were to break this foreign hegemony, Ventura Rodríguez, and Juan de Villanueva, the latter being the creator of that neoclassical masterpiece, the Prado Museum.

The Prado Museum was one of the many legacies to Madrid of Charles III, the greatest of Spain's Bourbon rulers, and a man who did even more than Philip V to change the face of this city. The construction of the museum, which was intended initially to house a collection of natural history items, was one of a number of Charles'

schemes intended for the instruction and enjoyment of the Madrilenians. Botanical gardens were beautifully laid out alongside it, and the neighbouring park of El Retiro was opened as one of the earliest public parks in Europe, complete with a neoclassical Observatory. The Promenade in front of the Prado Museum was entirely renovated and adorned with alleys of trees and three superlative fountains, one of which, representing the goddess Cybele, was to become the popular symbol of Madrid (there is a picture of her on page 187). Another of the fountains, that of Neptune, is shown overleaf against a background comprising the Prado Museum and the monastery church of San Jerónimo.

In addition Charles saw that the city was systematically paved, introduced regulations for the collecting of rubbish, initiated Madrid's first sewage system, and became a figure of the Enlightenment even in the literal sense by providing the city with its first street lights. These helped in turn to reduce the city's notorious crime-rate, as did the bringing in at the end of the 18th century of nightwatchmen or *serenos*, who,

with their dangling keys, were a regular feature of Madridlenian night-life right up to the 1950's.

The least popular of the reforms attempted in Charles' reign was also intended to curb the crime rate. This was a law brought in briefly in 1766 by Charles' unpopular Italian minister, the Marquis of Squillace, who, on the grounds that the streets were becoming cleaner, banned the use by men of ground-length capes, and appointed tailors to stand in doorways to cut off the extra cloth of those who defied this decree. These capes supposedly allowed robbers easily to conceal themselves, but they were also symbols of male pride and a typically Spanish fashion. The banning of them not only sparked off a revolt which led to the sacking of Squillace, but also highlighted the general and growing resentment of what was thought of as Bourbon contamination of the traditional Spanish way of life through the imposition of foreign, and specifically of French ways. This resentment led to several recorded attacks on those wearing French clothes and was to provoke a further outcry when a later minister of Charles III proposed the introduction of shoe-cleaners in the streets, an idea which was popularly thought to derive from the French pilgrims on the way to Santiago de Compostela.

A wonderful picture of everyday life in 18th-century Madrid is provided by the one-act plays or *sainetes* of Ramón de la Cruz, who also played a pioneering rôle in the history of the musical genre known as *zarzuela*, which combines song, dance and dialogue. In his *Reapers of Vallecas* of 1768, Ramón de la Cruz created the true modern zarzuela by breaking away from the classical themes and Italian music of earlier zarzuelas, and depicting instead everyday scenes to the accompaniment of popular Spanish airs composed by Antonio Rodríguez de Hita. This new type of zarzuela acted as a powerful rival to the Italian opera in Spain, and came to represent what is still one of Madrid's most characteristic and best-loved forms of entertainment.

The world of Madrid's low life, which Ramón de la Cruz so wittily portrayed, found its most famous chronicler in an artist of Aragonese birth, Francisco de Goya. The greatest Spanish painter of the late 18th and early 19th centuries, Goya began his career in Madrid executing cartoons for the Royal Tapestry Factory, which had been founded by Philip V, and is still functioning today, with virtually unchanged working conditions. In these cartoons – one of them is shown here –, as in many of his later works, Goya found inspiration in popular customs and entertainments. A favourite was the annual *romería* or festive pilgrimage to the Hermitage of San Isidro, which we see in the plate on pages 12-13 and the details. Goya also immortalized the working-class dandies known originally as *majos*, a word which probably has its origins in May Day festivities, more specifically with the beautiful costumed girl chosen as the May Day queen. Dressed flamboyantly, sometimes in imitation of the ladies of fashion, the *maja* had a reputation both for brazenness and volubility, her readiness to take up a quarrel being indicated by the sheathed poniard which she carried in the garter of her left stocking. (We see overleaf the typical Maja costume in a fancy-dress version worn by the Marquesa de Llano.) The maja's equally excitable male equivalent, the *majo*, shared the

maja's contempt of the French, and proudly wore the Spanish cape instead of the French full-skirted coat, the long hairnet instead of the French wig and the *chambergo*, or large soft-brimmed hat, instead of the three-cornered hat. Madrid may not have boasted the colourful folklore traditions of other Spanish cities and regions, but it had its majos, who, as portrayed by Goya, became essential components of the romantic tourist image of the city. Fernández de los Ríos, in his *Guide to Madrid* of 1879, observed how even in his day, there were foreigners whose preconceptions of the city were based to a large extent on popular types and forms of behaviour that had survived after 1800 only in the genre paintings of Goya. The colourful and essentially pleasure-seeking Madrid of Goya's tapestry cartoons gave way in the artist's later life to a darker world, closely inspired by the major political upheavals that Spain experienced from the early 19th century onwards. Charles III's son and successor, Charles IV, was a weak and unintelligent man, who let his country be run by his lecherous and devious minister Manuel de Godoy, whose rise was not unconnected with his having enjoyed the favours of Queen María Luisa. Godoy, shown here by Goya in an almost contemptuous posture, failed to prevent the execution of Louis XVI, and compromised with the French revolutionaries to such an extent that he eventually became actively involved in Napoleonic schemes. Such was his unpopularity that in 1808 a mob stormed his house in Aranjuez, an event which was followed immediately by the flight of the Spanish monarchy to France and the occupation of Madrid by French troops led by Marshal Murat. The arrival of the French posed an enormous dilemma to Spanish liberals, who were torn between admiration for the social ideals of revolutionary France and patriotic resentment of the invader. The popular antagonism to the invasion manifested itself most famously in an uprising which broke out on 2 May 1808 in the Madrid district of Las Maravillas. The date was to be permanently enshrined in the heroic mythology of Madrid, and the subsequent massacre of the Spanish rebels by the French on the 3rd was the subject of a painting by Goya (detail overleaf)

En la ermita de Baco arrodillado
Jose-pillo se muestra fervoroso,
Y con el eco dulce y armonioso
Se queda cada vez mas elevado:
Triste se mira por que no ha logrado
Que su garganta pruebe el generoso
Agradable licor, y humildemente
Suplica, qual veras en la siguiente.

" ¡Oh Madre del licor, mi protectora!
" No desprecies la suplica, ni el ruego
" De este tu fiel devoto, que te adora
" Y que por ti fallece de amor ciego:
" Ya ves, Madre amorosa que no llego
" Con el labio al licor que me enamora;
" Cubridme sin tardanza la cabeza
" De Malaga, Xerez, Tinto y Cerbeza.

El amor a la botella. Es de tu Norte la estrella.

which must surely be one of the most harrowing in western art.

Napoleon's brother, Joseph Bonaparte, was placed in charge of Spain, and took up residence in the Royal Palace, where, according to an unlikely remark by Napoleon, he was thought by the latter to be 'better lodged' than he himself was at the Louvre. Joseph was only to be in power until 1813, but during the six years of his rule was significantly to alter the look of Madrid and to acquire two nicknames. One of these was *Pepe Botellas* (roughly equivalent to 'Joe Bottles' – see opposite), a reference not to any drinking habits but to his having freed alcohol from crippling taxes. The more significant of his reputations was as *El rey de plazuelas* or 'king of the squares'. Beginning with his demolition of the jumble of buildings in front of the Royal Palace so as to form the Plaza de Oriente, Joseph developed an apparent obsession with creating town squares, and ample opportunity for doing so was provided by his suppression of Spain's convents and monasteries. Many of Madrid's squares of today, such as the Plaza de Santa Ana, were created as a result of the demolition of the religious institutions that had once congested the city centre.

The Bourbon monarchy was restored to Spain in the form of Charles IV's son, Ferdinand VII, a man generally described as odious by his contemporaries. He had agreed to abide by the famous 1812 constitution drafted by the exiled liberals in Cádiz, but soon repudiated this, and set about introducing the most rigid censorship. In terms of architecture and the urban development, his long rule was a period of stagnation in Madrid. The few monuments associated with him in Madrid are largely unmemorable, and it is instructive to compare the richly modelled Alcalá Gate, which had been built to commemorate the advent to the throne of his grandfather Charles III, with Ferdinand's dreary and protracted reconstruction of the Toledo Gate, through which he had entered the city on his return to Spain in 1814. The only commemorative monument of genuine distinction was the one built on the Paseo del Prado by Villanueva's pupil Isidro González Velázquez to honour the victims of May 2nd, but even this took over eighteen years to complete. The talents of González Velázquez, like those of all the other architects of this generation, were largely squandered on the designing of minor decorative works or of grand projects that were never to be realized.

The repressiveness of Ferdinand's regime had at least the beneficial effect, however, of stimulating Madrid's intellectual life, which flourished as a way both of sustaining the spirit under these adverse conditions and of maintaining the underlying political opposition. The year 1820 saw, significantly, the foundation of what was to become one of the great intellectual institutions of Spain, the Ateneo, a scientific, literary and artistic society which was also to enjoy a reputation right up to the Franco era as a centre of liberal politics. Furthermore, political censorship, combined with an atmosphere of growing revolutionary tension, has always bred the right conditions in which café society can thrive, and it was in these hard years of Ferdinand's rule that Madrid was gradually turned into a city of cafés rivalled only by Paris and Vienna.

The origins of Madrid's cafés were in the botellerías, shops mainly specializing in wines but that also sold hot chocolate, sweets and soft drinks. The Spanish love of drinking chocolate, which had existed since the discovery of the New World, came to be replaced at the beginning of the 19th century by a taste for coffee. The botellerías largely died out at this time, and their premises were frequently taken over by cafés, the greatest concentration of which were in and around the Puerta del Sol. Women who considered themselves true ladies had never actually entered the botellerías, but had insisted on being served while seated in their carriages outside. Similarly, women of a certain class were never to be seen in the cafés, which until as late as the 1920's preserved the character of male clubs. Each of these cafés attracted its particular circle of people, who were brought together by a common profession, interest, political standpoint, or region of origin; some of the more intellectual of these groups held regular discussions or *tertulias*, a tradition which goes back to the humanist gatherings in 16th-century Seville and was to be a major force in the history of Spanish culture and ideas.

The leading political café during the reign of Ferdinand VII was the Fontana de Oro, which was situated off the Carrera de San Jerónimo, and became the seat of a patriotic society named *Los Amigos del Orden*. Meanwhile, off the nearby Plaza de Santa Ana, a café of dark and unprepossessing appearance called the Café del Príncipe attracted such a glittering group of artists, writers and architects that it became commonly known as *El Parnasillo* or 'The Little Parnassus'. The history of Spanish Romanticism can almost be told through the gatherings at El Parnasillo, which drew into its basement room such luminaries of this movement as the landscapist Pérez de Villaamil, the poet José de Espronceda (left above), and the playwrights Juan Eugenio Hartzenbusch (right) and José Zorrilla (centre), the latter being the author of the Don Juan story that is still the most performed in Spain today. The key figure in this group was

MESONERO ROMANOS

CODERCH

Mariano José de Larra, an esssayist and satirist of caustic humour, whose much publicized suicide in 1837, at the age of twenty-eight, was one of the key moments in the history of Romantic Madrid.

The Parnasillo, like the Fontana de Oro, has long ceased to exist, but the place lives on in a long and vividly detailed description by a friend of Larra's of completely opposed temperament, Ramón de Mesonero Romanos. A bespectacled man of sober and portly appearance, Mesonero Romanos spent much of his life in a meticulously ordered municipal office which has been preserved to this day (see page 361). Though lacking the charisma of a Larra, the importance of this unassuming man in Madrid's history cannot be overestimated, for he was the first of the true *Madrilenistas*, and devoted his entire literary output to recording obsessively every aspect of his native city. With characteristic modesty, he defined his literary approach as 'writing for the general public in a plain style without affectation or carelessness, usually describing, rarely arguing, never causing tears, almost always causing laughter... and, to sum up, attempting... to become a true observer'.

In 1861, almost thirty years after publishing his painstakingly researched *Manual of Madrid*, Mesonero Romanos brought out a work entitled *Old Madrid*, in which the phlegmatic and objective style of the earlier book has become overlaid with a certain nostalgia, a nostalgia which was to intensify in his marvellous autobiography of 1881 entitled *Memories of a Seventy-Year Old, Born and Bred in Madrid*. Not since the first half of the 17th century had Madrid expanded in so rapid a fashion as in those years between 1830 and 1868, and in the process much of the character and many of the monuments that Mesonero Romanos had so admired had been lost. The climate of change had set in with the death of Ferdinand VII in 1833, but had become especially pronounced during the reign of his daughter Isabel II, who finally acceded to the throne in 1847 following the first of the Carlist Wars and a long period in which her mother, María Cristina, had acted as regentess. The population of Madrid during Ferdinand's reign was scarcely bigger than in the middle of the 17th century, and had been happily contained within the old adobe defensive walls. But by the middle of the century, Madrid was bursting at its seams, and in 1860 permission was finally given to pull down the walls and carry out a plan of expansion drawn up by the engineer Carlos María de Castro to accommodate a growing population which by the end of the century was to reach the half million mark.

Castro's plan, taking the form of a regular grid of streets in keeping with the latest theories of town-planning, earmarked as the main zone of expansion a large area to the northeast of the old walls. The northern continuation of the Paseo del Prado, the Paseo de Recoletos, was extended northwards to form the grand avenue known at first as the Paseo de las Delicias de Isabel II and now simply as the Castellana. To the east of this a wealthy middle-class district was built up which bears today the name of the banker and railway entrepreneur responsible for much of the property speculation here, the Marquis of Salamanca (see page 256). In a poem of 1876 Mesonero

Romanos sarcastically refers to Madrid as

> Tired of being always a *villa,*
> Now aspires to be a City;
> Drawn like a magnet
> To a powerful banker,
> It flees from itself
> Through its eastern border.

And this city which for the ageing Mesonero Romanos was so rapidly losing its human scale, was also one rapidly undergoing a technological transformation. Gas lighting had been introduced here in 1832, followed in the 1850's by a radically improved water supply drawing water from the Sierra de Guadarrama. The city's first public urinal was set up in the recently rebuilt Puerta del Sol in 1863, and eight years later public transport came to Madrid in the form of a mule-drawn tram. The street lights were electrified in 1875, as were the trams in 1879.

This changing Madrid of the late 19th century was fortunate enough to have a chronicler who, unlike Mesonero Romanos, transcended the rôle of mere *costumbrista* (an observer of customs and manners) and penetrated the minds of the city's inhabitants. This man, Pérez Benito Galdós, was born in the Canary Islands in 1843, but after settling in Madrid as a law student in 1862, developed such an immmediate and consuming obsession with this city that his whole life up to then ceased to hold any importance for him. In old age he was to recall how in his first years in Madrid he would escape whenever possible from the University and spend much of his days 'gliding like a gondola through the streets, squares and alleys (of Madrid), delighting in observing the bustling life of this huge and multi-faceted city'. By night he frequented the cafés and devotedly attended all of the city's theatres, for in his burgeoning literary ambitions to be a writer he aspired at first to drama. He was to find his true vocation only in 1870, with the publication of his first novel, *La Fontana de Oro*, a work of historical fiction set around the famous political café of that name. As a novelist, Pérez Galdós enjoys today the reputation of being the greatest Spanish writer after Cervantes, and, though still shockingly neglected outside Spain, deserves to be among the giants of European Realist literature of the late 19th century. We see him here, towards the end of his life, flanked by two boulevardier playwright brothers, the Alvarez Quinteros.

Galdós' vast output as a novelist is divided between works chronicling key moments in Spain's recent political history – his so-called *Episodios Nacionales* – and novels of contemporary life, which constitute his greatest achievement. Despite being a passionate traveller with a knowledge of most countries in western Europe, Galdós' interests as a writer on the modern world were concentrated almost exclusively on Madrid, which he portrayed with an intimacy which has never been equalled. A timid man who gave little away about his own personal life, he mercilessly exposed the private thoughts of others, and showed a remarkable understanding of schizophrenia and other pathological states. His broad-mindedness and fascination with people led to his becoming acquainted with an exceptionally wide range of Madrid society, while his

life-long status as a bachelor and belief in free love (but not in promiscuity) gave him access to a variety of close female friendships which was denied to many other men of his time.

Galdós' talents as a novelist and as an observer of Madrid life are shown at their greatest in his epic novel *Fortunata and Jacinta* (1886-7), which deals with a spoilt young man from a wealthy middle-class family, and the love for him of two women of opposite social backgrounds, one his mistress, the other his wife. The telling of this tale involves an enormous and motley cast of characters, and much of Galdós' skill and originality as a novelist derives from his constant changes of narrative perspective, so that events are always seen through different eyes, acquiring a particularly grotesque dimension as the reader is taken into the disintegrating mind of the pathetic and deluded man whom the mistress Fortunata, down on her luck, is forced by circumstances to marry. The main part of the action takes place around the Plaza Mayor, but as the novel unfolds, a truly panoramic picture of Madrid emerges, with its developing wealthy suburbs to the north, and the scorched slumland to the south. For the traveller to Madrid, part of the fascination of reading Galdós is that the city which he so vividly described is still one which is immediately recognizable today, even down to some of its smallest details.

Much of the present-day appearance of Madrid is the legacy of those years between Galdós' first arrival in the city and the outbreak of the Civil War in 1936. This period began, as it was to end, in political turmoil, and Galdós was an enthusiastic witness of the Liberal uprising of 1868 – which resulted in the abdication and flight of Isabel II – and of the subsequent and short-lived First Republic. The restoration of the Bourbon monarchy in 1875 in the form of Isabel's son Alfonso XII, dismayed Galdós and other liberals, but it heralded years of relative tranquility. Architecturally the reign of Alfonso XII was characterized in Madrid by a pompous eclecticism which differed from that of other European capitals in comprising a wealth of neo-mudéjar monuments and only a few neo-gothic ones, the Madrilenians having an apparent aversion to the gothic style. Most of what was put up, though often highly entertaining and splendidly elaborate, lacks architectural genius, but, in compensation, there can be few other places in Europe where even the most modest buildings are enlivened by brilliant ceramic decorations on their exteriors. Madrid's ceramic tradition is not of long standing, but from the 1870's up to the end of the 1920's it flourished as an adjunct of architecture, thanks largely to the vision of the architect Ricardo Velázquez Bosco, a man of orientalist leanings who had begun his career restoring the Mosque of Córdoba. The ceramics that came to decorate almost all of González Velázquez's buildings were produced in the recently founded Madrid factories of 'La Cerámica Madrileña' and 'La Moncloa', the latter benefiting from the services of one of the greatest ceramicists of the age, Daniel Zuloaga.

Many of the most radical changes to the Madrid skyline were carried out during the reign of Alfonso's successor, Alfonso XIII, which had got off to a suitably explosive start with a bomb attack on the occasion of his wedding in 1906 to

Victoria Eugenia de Battenberg. The principal urban reform during this period was the construction after 1911 of the Gran Vía, which cut a great swathe through the old centre of Madrid and initiated the upwards growth of the city. (The Gran Via as it appeared in the 1970's is seen opposite, in a celebrated painting by Madrid's best-known contemporary painter, Antonio López. It is a grey, empty dawn and the scene is unsettling for its total absence of traffic.

The first of the many American-style skyscrapers was built on the Gran Vía to house Bell Telephone, an American company that was later to be nationalized. Alfonso said on the inauguration of this building that Spain had truly entered the 20th century, and that the old adage that 'Africa begins at the Pyrenees' was no longer applicable. The building, for all its modernity, has none the less unmistakable borrowings from the Spanish baroque, as have the works of the most renowned Madrid architect of these years, Antonio Palacios. The latter's masterpiece is the vast and overwhelmingly sumptuous Post Office Building of 1904, prominently situated at the northern end of the Paseo del Prado, and so dominating and cathedral-like that it amply justifies its sarcastic nickname of 'Our Lady of Communications'.

Spain, during the first thirty-six years of this century, was the scene of a cultural renaissance comparable to that of the Golden Age. This renaissance was centred principally on Madrid – and not on Barcelona, as many foreigners wrongfully assume – and had as its fathers the so-called Generation of 98, a group of writers and philosophers whose works express the need for a spiritual renewal of Spain in the wake of the country's disastrous loss in 1898 of Cuba, Puerto Rico and the Philippines. Miguel de Unamuno, one of the leaders of this movement, had a strong dislike of Madrid, once comparing it to a 'vast caravan of people with nomadic instincts', and adding that 'I shall resist going to it whenever I can'. However, the group's other associates, such as the essayist Azorín, the playwright Valle-Inclán, the novelist Pío Baroja and the poets Antonio and Manuel Machado, were intensely involved in the life of Madrid, and inevitably, therefore,

were impassioned habitués of its cafés.

The Madrid cafés experienced in these years leading up to the Civil War the busiest period in their history, and through them can be traced the emergence of the brilliant new generation of poets calling themselves the Generation of 27 (of whom the best known are the poets Rafael Alberti and García Lorca), as well as more ominous developments of the time, such as the growth of the Falange, the founder of which, Antonio Primera de Rivera, used to hold regular meetings in the Café Lion. Yet if one place in particular has to be singled out as the cultural centre of pre-Civil War Madrid , it would not be a café but instead the pioneering educational institution known as the Residencia de los Estudiantes. Almost every figure to have contributed to the heady cultural life of Madrid in these years was associated at some time with the so-called 'Resi', though today the place is popularly remembered above all for being the scene of the youthful friendship between García Lorca, the painter Salvador Dalí, and the film-director Luis Buñuel (seen together on page 267).

In surveying Madrid's cultural history during this period, mention must finally be made of Ramón Gómez de la Serna, whose life was inseparable from that of Madrid, and who indeed was the presiding figure of this period, holding court every Saturday night at the now vanished Café El Pombo, where we see him in this photograph. As a Madrilenista he is sometimes thought of as the second of the 'Ramones' (the first being of course Mesonero Romanos), but instead of minutely dissecting the city with cold facts as the latter had done, he did so with a tide of dazzling aphorism and witticisms that manage to make remarkable those features of Madrid that few others would consider worth noting, such as its rooftops, or balconies. Gómez de la Serna's capacity for wonder can be as bewildering to foreigners as his near untranslatable style. But of all the great losses that Madrid was to suffer as a result of the Civil War, it was above all that of Gómez de la Serna – banished to a disillusioned old age in Buenos Aires – which was to signify the closing of an era.

A most vivid account of what life was like in Madrid during the Civil War is given in the third part of Arturo Barea's powerful autobiographical trilogy, *The Forging of a Rebel* (1946). Those who visit Madrid can also have the evocative experience of descending into the bunker built in the neglected, outlying park of El Capricho. This was used by General Miaja as the headquarters of the Republican defence of Madrid, and it was here, in November 1939, that the Civil War saw its last ignominious moments, with dissension among the Republican ranks. Madrid had been left by then a devastated place, and even today you can still see the sad shell of at least one of the many churches that were gutted and pillaged by those whom priests and others continue to refer to as 'the Reds'.

A committee for the reconstruction of Madrid was established at the very end of the war, but the shortage of housing was so desperate that large blocks were to grow up higgledy-piggledy on the outskirts of the city before any official scheme could be implemented. A general plan for the development of the city, drawn up by Bigador, was finally issued in 1944, and entailed the considerable extension to the north of the Castellana, which was now renamed the Avenida Generalíssimo Franco. The civic architecture of these years immediately following the war was marked by a return to an austere Herrera-style classicism, one of the most impressive if chilling examples of which is the Air Ministry at Moncloa. In other respects, however, Madrid continued to develop the look of an American – and specifically South American – city, and by the early 1950's had acquired two of the highest skyscrapers in Europe. The Bloomsbury writer and Hispanist Gerald Brenan, visiting Madrid in 1949 after a thirteen-year absence, was amazed to find here more American cars than he had seen in any other European city. The irony though was that this same place – which thanks to new waves of immigration in the 1960's was to have a population of three million by 1970 – was to keep until very recently two centrally-placed stones marking the ancient sheep trail along which migratory sheperds crossed the harsh Castilian plateau.

One of the saddest and most significant changes to Madrid after the Civil War was the disappearance of most of its famous cafés, replaced either by the premises of large banks, or, more humiliating still, by American-style cafeterias. The ever sentimental Díaz-Cañabate, a chronicler of the literary cafés of old, rhetorically asked if a tertulia could ever be held in a cafeteria, and answered himself immediately with the words, 'A tertulia in a cafeteria! Don't even think of it!' However, despite the great reduction in the number of cafés, the literary café enjoyed in the post-war years a last but intense revival, nourished by repressive political conditions similar to those that had existed under Ferdinand VII. Gómez de la Serna might have gone, but new Madrilenistas had taken his place, most notably Cesar González-Ruano, whom the present-day writer Francisco Umbral remembered as the only person he had known actually to 'dress up as a writer'. The main venue for this new generation was the Café Gijón, which in its heyday in the 1940's and 50's swarmed with artists, writers and politicians, among whom was the novelist and future Nobel Prize-winner Camilo José Cela. A café life of this intellectual intensity did not outlive the Franco era, and though the great literary figures of old can still be seen in the Café Gijón, most of them would agree that the tertulia has finally had its day, killed off by a combination of political freedom and television.

The social revolution which Spain experienced in the wake of Franco's death in 1976 turned Madrid into what it had never been during the years of his rule – a city of fashion. The leaders of fashionable Madrid in the late 1970's and early 80's were those who allied themselves to the so-called *Movida* or Movement, a group of young artists, writers, designers and others, who used the elusive term *posmodernismo* to celebrate the tacky and ephemeral. Their reputations as cultural figures will probably prove as ephemeral as their interests, with the great exception of Pedro Almodóvar, right, whose witty films of Madrid life provide if nothing else a refreshing antidote to the earnestness of much earlier Spanish cinema. Almodóvar moved on, to be wooed by Hollywood and Madonna, and the Movement itself withered, but Madrid has survived as a city highly concerned with image, modernity

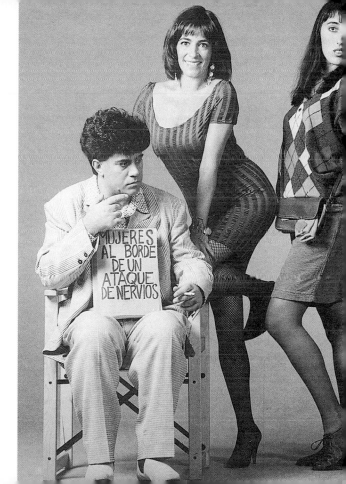

and design, as has been reflected in the exceptional stylishness and originality of recent architecture, and in the current vogue for creating cultural institutions, which have mushroomed in the last years in the same way that convents had done in previous centuries.

The Madrid of today promotes itself not only as a leader of cultural fashions, but also as a place where the visitor can whole-heartedly indulge a love of eating, drinking and night-life. The novelist Stendhal considered that the best way to understand a place was to see how its people enjoyed themselves, and there is certainly no question that one of the principal pleasures of Madrilenians is going out to restaurants and bars, on which they spend – according to a recent survey published in the newspaper *El Independiente* – more than five times as much money as they do on culture. It is appropriate that I should have left this subject to the end of this introductory chapter, for it is the one which perhaps best sums up both the charms and idiosyncrasies of Madrid.

Of all the attractions of Madrid, that of eating is the one most difficult to convey to foreigners, many of whom come to Spain with prejudices about Spanish food in general that date back to the time of Romantic travellers such as Richard Ford. The virtual phobia which Ford and others had for the use of garlic and olive oil in Spanish cooking has fortunately been superseded by a widespread recognition of the healthy properties of these ingredients, but even so there are those who critically assume that all Spanish food is 'greasy' and saturated with garlic to an unpleasant degree. What is more you will still come across certain guide-books that repeat Ford's comments that the Spaniards eat to live rather than live to eat. How untrue this last statement is of the Spaniards of today is evident even in Spanish attitudes towards 'Fast Food': Macdonalds and other hamburger chains have spread around Madrid, but they cater largely for foreigners, and have been counteracted recently by a Spanish chain calling itself the 'Museo de Jamón' ('The Museum of Ham'), where you can eat snacks of the finest hams and cheeses to the accompaniment of an equally wide range of wines.

Spanish food is one of exceptional regional

variety, and there are few better places to acquire a love for it than in Madrid, where you will find restaurants from every Spanish region, as well as from almost every former Spanish colony, such as Cuba. The traditional cuisine of Madrid itself is that of the region of La Mancha, and is a cuisine of great simplicity which was maintained in the modest inns and households of Madrid at a time when the Bourbons were introducing French tastes to the country. Its strengths are those deriving from the quality and freshness of the raw materials used. Lentil stew (*lentejas a la Manchega*) or soup made with bread and garlic (*sopa de ajo*) are popular starters, while characteristic main courses might comprise a thick fillet steak (*solomillo*) or a succulent breaded hake (*merluza rebosada*): the Spanish love of seafood is as strong here as it is in the country's coastal regions, as is apparent in the bewilderingly rich displays of fish and crustaceans to be found outside many of Madrid's restaurants. One of the most typical of Madrid dishes is tripe (*callos a la Madrileña*), which is stewed here with wine, black pudding, and spiced sausage. But the most famous of all local specialities is the meat and vegetable stew known as *cocido Madrileño*, which is a whole meal in itself and rarely eaten other than at lunchtime, the principal meal of the Spanish day. The broth of the *cocido* is served first, followed by the meats (usually chicken, salt pork, beef and spiced sausage), and lastly by the vegetables, which comprise cabbages, chickpeas and potatoes. Puddings, if eaten at all, are also simple ones, and though commercially-made *flan* (crème caramel) has become a depressingly ubiquitous feature of Spanish restaurants, the traditional Madrid sweets are custard creams (*natillas*) or the unappealingly named *leche frita* ('fried milk'), a custard-like mixture which has been fried in batter. To find this traditional Madrid fare you would do best to avoid the smarter and very expensive modern restaurants and go instead to the *mesones* (inns) or *tascas* (a humbler form of mesón), both of which function equally as eating and drinking establishments, and have intimate ceramic interiors often dating back to the last century. A grander survival from the same period is Lhardy, pictured overleaf with some of its

more distinguished bon-vivant customers, including the indefatigable connoisseurs Diaz-Cañabate and Julio Camba. The preference of most foreigners for eating earlier than Spaniards forces many to go to hotel restaurants or other such tourist establishments, but the unappetizing food served in these places will only confirm foreign prejudices about Spanish food.

Foreigners, if they are to get the most out of Madrid, have to a certain extent to adapt to the peculiarities of the Spanish life style, which, in relation to food, means having to enjoy sharing (it is common for Spaniards who go out to a restaurant to order as a starter a selection of dishes to share around). But above all it means having to respect as much as possible the Madrilenian time-table, which is more idiosyncratic than that of any other European capital, and – unlike that of Barcelona – has resisted all attempts at outside interference. The Madrilenians get to work as early as other Europeans, but between ten-thirty and eleven-thirty are usually out of the office having breakfast. *Tapas* (snacks) taken in bars from about one-thirty onwards provide the necessary sustenance to keep going until lunchtime, which tends to be after three o'clock, at the end of many a Spaniard's working day. Apart from the bars and restaurants, most of Madrid is closed until at least five o'clock, and there is something slightly absurd about those groups of foreigners who have lunched early and continue sightseeing when virtually nothing is open and the heat is at its worst. The late afternoon is traditionally the time for the stroll or *paseo*, and, in the summer months, this is the ideal moment to try that popular drink of Valencian origin, known as *horchata*, a cool and milky concoction made from tiger-nuts. Dinner is at ten, which is perhaps the aspect of the Spanish time-table that most infuriates foreign tourists, particularly those tired out by a day's sightseeing. 'And I,' wrote H.V. Morton in the appropriately named *A Stranger in Spain* (1954), 'who regard it as one of life's greatest pleasures to be in bed at ten, groaned inwardly.'

The Spaniards have not always kept such late hours, for Richard Ford makes no mention of this peculiarity, and Galdós, writing in 1867, said that Madrid was asleep by twelve o'clock. A few bohemians and literary types might serenade the statue of Cervantes by moonlight (overleaf), but the more general change seems to have set in by around 1900. Shortly afterwards Ramón Gómez de la Serna was reporting that the streets of Madrid were crowded with people until the early hours of the morning. Today the animation of a Madrid night can be almost unbearable, and there are many lovers of the nocturnal life style who make a point of never going out on Fridays or Saturdays, when the crush is at its worst. The choice of bars to go to after supper is as wide as the choice of districts, each one of which has its own particular night-time atmosphere. In the summer months the places to go to are the *terrazas* or open-air bars, the most animated of which were once those that lined the Paseo de Recoletos, a district which in 1990 was superseded in popularity by that of Rosas. The search for the latest fashionable bar and club is as much a preoccupation of Madrid society as it is among the inhabitants of any other city, but with the difference that the new smart venues are not just the domain of the young and fashion-conscious. For all the noticeable effects on the city's night life of the recent recession, Madrid is still a place where the streets are filled until the early hours with all types and all ages. Their nocturnal habits have earned the Madrilenians the nickname of *los gatos* ('the cats'), and the true nocturnalists will be prowling the streets until dawn, making as a possible last gesture a visit to a *churrería* for a necessary sustaining dose of doughnut fritters (*churros*) and hot chocolate. At least one such night is necessary to complete the full Madrid experience, but your mood the next day may not be conducive to carrying out one of the itineraries outlined in the following chapters.

The Hapsburg City

THE PUERTA DEL SOL *to* THE HERMITAGE OF SAN ISIDRO

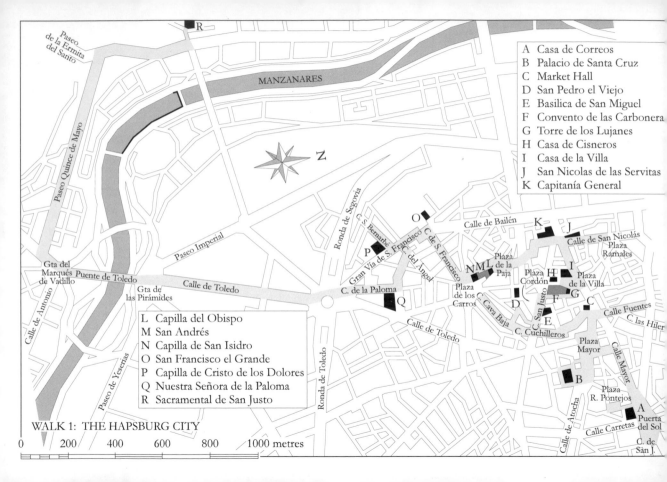

A Casa de Correos
B Palacio de Santa Cruz
C Market Hall
D San Pedro el Viejo
E Basilica de San Miguel
F Convento de las Carbonera
G Torre de los Lujanes
H Casa de Cisneros
I Casa de la Villa
J San Nicolas de las Servitas
K Capitanía General

L Capilla del Obispo
M San Andrés
N Capilla de San Isidro
O San Francisco el Grande
P Capilla de Cristo de los Dolores
Q Nuestra Señora de la Paloma
R Sacramental de San Justo

WALK 1: THE HAPSBURG CITY

0   200   400   600   800   1000 metres

MANZANARES

Paseo de la Ermita del Santo
Paseo Quince de Mayo
Gta del Marqués de Vadillo
Puente de Toledo
Gta de las Pirámides
Calle de Antonio
Paseo de Yeserías
Paseo Imperial
Ronda de Segovia
C. S. Bernabé
Gran Vía de S. Francisco
C. de S. Francisco
C. del Ángel
C. de la Paloma
Calle de Toledo
Ronda de Toledo
Calle de Toledo
Calle de Bailén
Plaza de la Paja
Plaza de los C. Carros
Cava Baja
C. Cuchilleros
C. San Justo
Plaza Cordón
Plaza de la Villa
Calle de San Nicolás
Plaza Ramales
Calle Fuentes
C. las Hiler
Plaza Mayor
Calle Mayor
Plaza R. Pontejos
Plaza R. Pontejos
Calle de Atocha
Calle Carretas
Puerta del Sol
C. de San J.

The Hapsburg City

THE PUERTA DEL SOL *to* THE HERMITAGE OF SAN ISIDRO

The novelist Peréz Galdós, discovering Madrid as a young man, was as much absorbed by the main architectural monuments of the city as he was by the cafés, the shops, the theatres and the humblest of its streets. In the routes that I have chosen to guide the reader around Madrid I have aimed above all to show a variety of attractions, so that 'the huge and multi-faceted city' which Galdós described comes fully to life. However, not wishing to lose the reader in the backstreets of Madrid's history and culture, I have ordered the chapters of the book in such a way that a roughly chronological portrait of the city will also unfold. Thus the first route, dealing with the area to the south-west of the Puerta del Sol, covers the few monuments that survive from medieval and renaissance Madrid, and has among its main attractions three outstanding squares that illustrate different moments in the city's development from the medieval period up to the late 17th century – the Plazas de La Paja, de La Villa, and Mayor. Much of what remains of the secular architecture of the 17th century is also featured here, including a number of inns that have maintained their hostelry traditions up to the present day.

I. The Puerta del Sol There are few more appropriate places to begin a tour of Madrid, or indeed of Spain, than the Plaza de la Puerta del Sol, which is the very hub of the city, on which converge no fewer than ten streets and from where the distances to all other Spanish towns are calculated. '*La Puerta del Sol!*', wrote Mesonero Romanos in 1861, 'What Madrilenian, or should we say what Spaniard, were he to be in one of the furthest corners of the kingdom, or in one of the most remote parts of the world, is not stirred by the mention of this name, and does not take pleasure in the thought of going one day to this celebrated place... this vital centre of Spain's monarchy, this emporium of its modern history, of its civilization, of its poetry.' The very name of this elliptical square – 'The Gate of the Sun' – seems befitting the splendour evoked in Mesonero Romanos' description, though in fact its origins are relatively prosaic, and are to be found in a medieval castle which was built at the time of the revolt of the Comuneros and apparently bore a decorative motif of a sun. Situated alongside what was once the eastern gate of the city, the castle was pulled down shortly after the suppression of the revolt in 1522. During the reign of Philip II, the gate itself disappeared as the city's walls were extended to the east, and the surrounding area took on the form of a square, which came to be lined by three important religious foundations – the Hospital del Buen Suceso (founded apparently at the time of a great plague), and the convents of Nuestra Señora de la Victoria, and San Felipe el Real. This is how we see it in the detail opposite from the first major cartographic survey of the city, Pedro Texeira's great map of 1656. The Buen Suceso is at LIX behind the fountain, las Victorias at VI and San Felipe at the western end, at IV. Not one of these institutions survives, but the last named, situated between what are now the streets of Correos and Esparteros, rose up above the square on the terrace visible in the map, which became such a popular meeting-place that it acquired the name of the *Mentidero* or 'Gossip Centre' of the city. All of Spain's Golden Age writers mention the Mentidero, which was the focal-point of a square already bursting with shops and market-stalls by the 17th century, and alive to the cries of hundreds of street vendors. In the early 18th century the architect Pedro Ribera provided the square with another popular attraction in the form of the fountain known as the Mariblanca, the waters of which served both as a convenient place in which

to duck the occasional drunkard, and as the main supply for the city's numerous water-sellers (as seen opposite), a trade usually undertaken by Galician and Andalucían immigrants.

The Mariblanca, together with the two convents, were removed in the course of the 19th-century renovations of the Puerta del Sol. The process of enlarging the square to double its previous size was initiated at the beginning of the century by Joseph Bonaparte, but it was not until 1858 that the rebuilding work was completed. The actual architecture of the square has changed remarkably little since then, the main difference being that the Hospital del Buen Suceso was replaced at the turn of the century with the imposing Hotel Paris. However, the character of the square as a meeting-place was lost irredeemably with the disappearance after 1939 of its market stalls, and, above all, its cafés. The numerous cafés that grew up in the course of the 19th century took over the rôle that had once been played by the Mentidero of San Felipe Real, and contributed more than any other factor to the square's extraordinary animation. This animation made a profound impression on many of the foreign visitors to Madrid in the 19th century, including an English doctor called Granville, who characterized the square in 1808 in terms of a 'perpetual revel'. George Borrow, with his fascination with people, was another of the square's enormous enthusiasts, though the greatest foreign tribute ever paid to it was made in 1870 by the gushing Italian novelist de Amicis, who found himself unable to leave the square, defining the place as a 'mingling of salon, promenade, theatre, academy, garden, a square of arms, and a market'. The exhilaration of the place is well conveyed in the print on page 75, of crowds disappearing to the races.

As well as being a playground, the Puerta del Sol was also the scene of most of the great disturbances to have troubled the capital from the late 18th century onwards, beginning with the rebellion in 1766 that deposed Charles III's unpopular minister Squillace. The square's 'baptism of blood' – to use the words of Mesonero Romanos – was received on 2 May 1808 when the troops of Napoleon's marshal,

Murat, aided by the infamous Egyptian cavalry known as the Mamelukes, viciously attacked a rioting crowd with their sabres, an event which was to be glamorously portrayed in a famous canvas by Goya (p. 242) as well as in the third novel of Galdós' *Episodios Nacionales*. Twenty-eight years later George Borrow witnessed here the failed 'Revolution of La Granja', while in 1865 the suppression of another uprising in the square was to give the young Galdós his first taste of political violence and lead him to run home and try and 'find relief in my dear books'. The writer and Republican Ramón Sender, describing anarchist disturbances in the square three years before the outbreak of the Civil War of 1936, compared the place 'to a bay of the sea, always in agitation'. Yet not only did the square reflect the political history of Madrid up to the Civil War, but also its technological transformation up to that time. It was here, in 1830, that gas lighting was used in Spain for the first time, and it was also here, in 1906, that the country's first arc lamps were put up, to celebrate Alfonso XIII's wedding. And when the city's tramlines were laid out after 1870, the square became the terminus of the new transport system, as was also to happen after 1919 with the inauguration of Madrid's underground railway. The most recent improvements to the Puerta del Sol were carried out after 1986 and included the laying out of a large pedestrian area, the erection of a statue of Charles III, and the repainting of the elegant mid 19th-century buildings on the square's curved, northern side. For all this face-lift, however, the place remains as Mesonero Romanos found it in one of his more sober moments, 'more renowned for its crowds and central position than for the beauty of its architecture'. The crowds today are probably as numerous as they were in the past, but the idlers and potential revolutionaries of old have given way to shoppers and office-workers rushing to the underground station. From being the social heart of Madrid, the square is now the Madrilenian equivalent of London's Oxford Circus, and the nostalgic traveller, mentally trying to recreate the brilliant café life of former days, might experience a particular feeling of poignancy on discovering what has happened to one of the most famous and long-lived of its cafés. The Universal was to be found as late as 1955 on the north-eastern corner of the square, at what is now No.14. Covered in a lavish decoration of gilded mirrors, the Café Universal was a famous liberal centre from the early 19th century onwards, and in the 1860's was a popular haunt of Peréz Galdós, who would meet many of his fellow islanders from the Canaries here. In 1955 it was converted into an American-style cafeteria with the name of Quick, and remains under the same management today, complete with a bland interior of formica and light polished wood. Ramón Goméz de la Serna – whose enthusiasm for the square in its pre-Civil War days had been so great that he had written a whole book devoted to it – made a sad return visit to Madrid in 1949. At the sight of the Cafeteria Quick he could only utter the words, *Sic Transit!*

Another monument testifying to the transience of earthly glory is the Hotel Paris, which was built in 1894 on the narrow eastern side of the square, in between the Calle de Alcalá and the Carrera

de San Jerónimo, where the Hospital del Buen Suceso had stood. At the time of its construction this was Madrid's most luxurious hotel, and as such was chosen in 1906 as the place to lodge the numerous dignitaries who had been invited to Madrid from all over the world to attend the ill-fated wedding of Alfonso XIII to Doña Victoria Eugenia de Battenberg. The stuccoed neo-baroque exterior of the hotel still retains much of its former grandeur, but the gloomy interior, tackily transformed in the 1950's, will appeal largely to those with a love of kitsch, and features such highpoints as a ceramic corgi dog patheti-cally tied by a chain to a table on the staircase landing.

Continuing this clockwise tour of the Puerta del Sol, we come, on its southeastern side, to one of the square's few shops to have survived the Civil War, the Librería de San Martín. Situated at No. 6, next to the Calle de Carretas, this small and crammed bookshop has specialized for many years in military books, and was itself the scene of a famous terrorist event when on 12 Novem-ber 1912, the radical liberal Prime Minister of Spain, José Canalejas, was assassinated while window-shopping. As we cross the Calle Carretas, we pass on our left, at what was once No. 4 of this street, the site of one of Madrid's most famous literary cafés, the Café Pombo. Its fame is due principally to Ramón Goméz de la Serna, who organized here in the 1920's the best attended of the city's literary tertulias. These were held every Saturday night in the café's basement, and became such a revered institution of Madrid that the basement came to be dubbed 'the Sacred Crypt of the Pombo'. A famous painting by Solana of the solemnities is reproduced on p. 19. Goméz de la Serna dedicated to the Pombo what must certainly be the longest book ever written on a café (which he clutches in the paint-ing), but a pithier description of the place is to be found in the spirited autobiography of the film-director Luis Buñuel, *My Last Breath* (1982): 'At the Café Pombo... we used to arrive, greet each other, and order a drink – usually coffee, and a lot of water – until a meandering conversation began about the latest literary publications or political upheavals. We lent one another books and foreign journals, and gossiped about our absent brothers. Sometimes an author would read one of his poems or articles aloud, and Ramón would offer his opinion, which was always respected and sometimes disputed.' The café did not survive Goméz de la Serna's exile to Argentina in 1936, and in 1963 Archibald Lyall wrote that 'to add insult to injury, the same building now houses a cafeteria called Tío Sam, decorated with pictures of Uncle Sam'. Later even this cafeteria was closed down, and in its stead a shop selling leather goods was opened. Today, the café's ignominious decline has gone one stage further, the walls of the sacred crypt having been cleared to make way for the extensive redevelopment of the whole area behind the former Casa de Correos.

This former Post Office, the most important building on the Puerta del Sol, occupies most of the southern side of the square, and was built for Charles III in the 1760's. Designed by the French architect Jacques Marquet, it served as the city's post office up to 1847, after which it became the seat of the Ministry of the Interior. In 1867 the pedimented frontispiece of this neoclassical brick structure was crowned with what is today the building's most popular feature, a clock tower which came to have the same symbolical and practical importance as London's Big Ben: it tells the time for the Spanish nation, and its chimes are daily heard on Spanish radio. The life story of the man who designed the clock's original mechanism, Ramón Losada, is itself of interest. A peasant from the Astorga region in north-western Castille, Losada fled to Madrid after having been beaten up by the owner of his flock. In Madrid he became involved in politics, and soon was persecuted for his beliefs by Ferdinand VII. Fortunately he was able to obtain a safe-conduct to France after having bribed Madrid's Mayor at this time, José Zorrilla, a man whom he had caught out having an affair. Losada went from France to London, where he married and made his way up from being an apprentice clocksmith to the owner of a highly successful clock factory. Though still illiterate at the time of his arrival in London, he soon achieved a reputation as an intellectual, and he

organized in his London shop a special tertulia for Spain's many distinguished literary and political exiles then resident in this city. Ironically, among these figures was José Zorrilla's son, the famous romantic poet also called José, who was to dedicate a poem to Losada. While in London Losada designed two clocks for Spain, one for his native village, and the other for the Puerta del Sol, the latter distinguished by a large metal sphere which is regularly lowered at the chiming of twelve.

A plaque to the victims of 2 May 1808 is placed on the façade of the Casa de Correos, while inside the main door is the stone slab marking Kilometric Zero, from where all the distances in Spain are measured. No longer the Ministry of the Interior, the building is now shared by the main offices of the local government of Madrid (the Comunidad) and the city's police head-quarters. A certain amount of ingenuity and bravado is needed to persuade your way past the armed police in the entrance hall, and visit the interior. The elegant neo-rococo Assembly Rooms on the main floor include a room which is named after Canalejas and leads out on to the balcony from which in 1931 the coming of Spain's Second Republic was proclaimed to the waiting crowds in the Puerta del Sol below. A less glamorous event in Spain's recent political history took place in the glazed courtyard belonging to the part of the building which is run by the police. This was an incident that still arouses strong feelings, and the friend with whom I was with lowered her voice as she indicated the window from where the Communist militant Grimau was supposedly thrown in 1963. Grimau did not die immediately and had to be finished off shortly afterwards by firing squad, an execution which was to lead to a large international outcry.

On the western side of the Casa de Correos the short Calle Correos heads south to the small and dignified square named after the Marquis of Pontejos, an urban reformer who died in 1840. This is a detour which should be undertaken by readers of Galdós, for it was around this square that he set much of the action of his greatest work, *Fortunata and Jacinta*. Juanito de Santa Cruz, the spoilt male protagonist of this novel, and the cause of the eponymous heroine's misfortunes, lived with his wife Fortunata in an immense first-floor appartment overlooking the square from the Calle Pontejos (the house, with its twelve balonies, can still be identified). The simple fountain in the middle of the square – erected in 1849 and graced with a bust of Pontejos – is mentioned in the novel, as is the jumble of narrow commercial streets that extend between here and the nearby Plaza Mayor. The best known of these streets is the Calle de Postas, so-called because the house at No. 32 was the site of Madrid's first Post Office, which dates back to the 16th century. The mother of Juanita de Santa Cruz, Barbarita Arnáiz, was born and brought up at a house on the corner of the Calles de Postas and San Cristobal, 'in one of those dreary rowhouses that look more like shoe boxes because of their miniature scale'. Her family was associated with the manufacture of manila shawls, a recent fashion of Oriental inspiration which was to give to her childhood memories a strong exotic flavour 'redolent of sandalwood and

Oriental fragrances'. Manila shawls can no longer be bought on this street, but a comparably exotic textile shop is to be found at No. 14, a musty institution from another era: it specializes in textiles used for religious garments, and is the place to come to for the repentant tourist in search of a hair shirt.

The principal street leading west from the Plaza de la Puerta del Sol is the Calle Mayor, a street of medieval origin which was widened for carriages in the 17th century, and became thereafter the main artery through the city. Favoured as a processional route for royalty and visiting dignitaries to Madrid, the Calle Mayor came also to attract from the 17th century onwards many of the city's important commercial enterprises and administrative institutions. Though rich in 17th-century associations, and with much of the character of the period, this dark and animated street is lined today mainly with buildings from the turn of the century. At the entrance to the street from the Puerta del Sol there once stood the Palacio de Oñate, in front of which the homosexual poet and courtier, the Count of Villamediana, was murdered with a cross-bow on the night of 21 August 1622. The pavement outside this building also served as a place where 17th-century painters exhibited their works, and it was here that the Sevillian artist Bartolomé Murillo attracted the attention of Charles II with a picture of the Immaculate Conception. The site of this palace is now occupied by a grand commercial building designed by Antonio Palacios in 1919, and featuring inside a lively elliptical patio glazed by colourful stained glass (the entrance to the building is at No. 4). At No. 3, on the opposite side of the street, a door next to a flamboyant turn-of-the-century structure by José López Sallaberry, marks the entrance to a building which houses one of Madrid's more traditional photographic studios, Bariego. The approach to these studios, up a dirty staircase with peeling paint and crumbling plaster, is distinctly seedy, and once inside we find ourselves in a world that seems scarcely to have changed since the 1920's, complete with old and dusty studio props and a white-bearded Mr. Bariego himself. Continuing west along the Calle Mayor, we pass, at the junction with the Calle Felipe III, another of the many relics of Madrid's commercial past, a jewellery shop adorned on the outside with amusing figurative reliefs of men at work. Before turning left here into the Plaza Mayor, those who enjoy assimilating esoteric information should direct a passing glance at the apartment block on the other side of the street, at No. 28. A long-time inhabitant of this block, until his death here in 1923, was Alfred Löwy, who had a distinguished career as a director of Spanish railways but is remembered today – if at all – as the uncle of Franz Kafka. This life-long bachelor, known always to Kafka as 'the uncle from Madrid', made frequent return visits to his native Prague, where he inspired in his young nephew a yearning to go to Madrid. The Spanish capital appeared to offer the future writer an exotic means of escaping from the claustrophobic influence of family life at home. Much to Kafka's disappointment, the uncle was not able to find a job for him in Madrid, but Löwy was nonetheless to play a significant rôle in his nephew's life through persuading him to work with an insur-ance company. The uncle lies today buried and forgotten in the ugly Madrid suburb of Carabanchel, but this story of Kafka and Madrid deserves – like that of Hitler and Liverpool – to be revived in the form of an imaginative novel.

II. The Plaza Mayor and the Plaza de la Villa The vast pedestrian square of the Plaza Mayor was by far the most formidable example of town-planning left by the Hapsburgs to Madrid, and rivals in its beauty the greatest squares of Europe. This bold and dramatic conception in fact had humble beginnings, for its predecessor was an irregular square surrounded by tiny, slum-like houses still outside the city gates. The architect of the Escorial, Juan de Herrera, was commissioned in the late 16th century to transform and dignify this chaotic space, but it was not until the time of Philip III that definitive plans for a new square were drawn up. The architect eventually chosen for the task was Herrera's pupil, Juan Gómez de Mora, who carried out the work with remarkable speed, beginning it in 1617 and completing it two years later. The end result (seen in the detail opposite from Texeira's map of 1656), could be described as an especially grand, tidy and homogenous version of the arcaded town centres traditional to Castile. A specific source of inspiration for so formal a work might have been the square which had been rebuilt in Valladolid by Philip II, but no other previous Spanish square had been conceived on such an ambitious scale. The surrounding buildings were able to house up to 3,000 people, while, on festive occasions, no fewer than 50,000 could be crammed inside the square itself. The architecture and scale of the Plaza Mayor were to be emulated in many later Spanish squares, but perhaps only that of Salamanca was to achieve a comparable grandeur. Something of how this grandeur felt in context can be sensed from the Plaza's appearance.

In its layout and overall austerity, and in such details as the slate spires and high-pitched roofs with dormer windows, the Plaza Mayor of today reflects Gómez de Mora's original conception, and in turn the architectural legacy of Herrera. However, owing to serious fires, the square has been the subject of several rebuilding campaigns, the last major one being that begun in 1795 by Juan de Villanueva. It was not until 1847 that the square was to receive – thanks to the initiative of Mesonero Romanos – one of its finest features, an equestrian bronze statue of Philip III, designed by the mannerist sculptor Pietro Tacca, and executed by his Italian pupil Giambologna. The most recent developments in the square's history have included the building of a large carpark underneath it, and a thorough restoration of its balconied houses to create what are now among the more fashionable addresses in central Madrid.

In common with the Puerta del Sol, the Plaza Mayor was once filled with shops and market stalls, and the names Panadería (Bakery) and Carnicería (Meat Market) are still given to its two most prominent buildings, on the northern and southern sides respectively. But it has also been regularly converted throughout history into a stage for grand and sometimes chilling spectacles, the action being watched by the king and other dignitaries from the balconies above the municipal bakery. The Plaza Mayor was officially

inaugurated in 1620 with festivities marking the canonization of St. Isidro, and since then the square has been used for such diverse events as public executions, trials by the Inquisition, jousting tournaments, coronations, bullfights and plays. The illustration opposite shows one such occasion, the entertainments hurriedly put together to celebrate the arrival of the Prince of Wales, the future Charles I, who had slipped into Madrid incognito with his favourite, Buckingham, under the ludicrous aliases of Tom and John Smith. Tense negotiations over Charles' suit to the sister of Philip IV foundered over the religious question, though Charles was said to have genuine feelings for the Infanta, gazing at her during festivities such as these and the procession seen on p. 290, 'as a cat does a mouse' in the words of Olivares. Ballets and theatrical performances are still put on in the Plaza Mayor during the summer months, but the last major festivities here were to celebrate the wedding of Isabel II in 1846. The square today is very different from what it used to be, and far more sedate; its commercial establishments have virtually all given way to expensive and unfriendly cafés catering almost exclusively for tourists, who – completely contrary to local habits – have a tendency to sit outside in the blinding sun. Few Madrilenians would ever think of coming to the square, other than to visit the stamp market held under its arcades every Sunday morning.

Another of the major civic monuments of Hapsburg Madrid, the former Cárcel de Corte or Court Prison, lies off the southeastern corner of the Plaza Mayor. Its main entrance, shown on page 87 (and, like many of the buildings mentioned in this walk, easily identifiable on the Texeira map), is on the small Plaza de La Provincia, which in its earlier days was animated by the noisy commercial life which overflowed from the larger, adjacent square. A prison had been built here by Philip II in 1563, and had had as one of its most distinguished inmates the dramatist Lope de Vega, accused in 1587 of writing scurrilous poems against the family of the actress with whom he had been conducting an illicit, adulterous affair. Stricter security regulations issued by Philip IV led to the old building being replaced after 1629 by the Cárcel de Corte, the new structure being intended both as a prison for persons of high rank (the window bars are gilt) as well as offices for justices of peace of the royal household. The view opposite is from Mesonero de Romanos' guide to Madrid of 1861. The main architect was Gómez de Mora, who created a symmetrical block in the style of the Escorial, but departed significantly from Herrera's austere influence in the richly modelled frontispiece and in the delicate carvings on the central staircase inside. Among the last people to be imprisoned here was the writer and adventurer George Borrow, who was arrested in 1838 for his evangelizing activities on behalf of the Bible Society. Prone to wild exaggeration and great flights of imagination, he was later to evoke the prison as if it were a dungeon of Piranesian proportions, 'so irregular and rambling' as to defy too close a description. To him the building did no 'credit to the capital of the Spain', and he seriously doubted if a place with such vile conditions had ever been intended as a prison in the first place. Typically for Borrow, however, he appears to have been far less concerned about his own well-being here than were his friends in England, and indeed he made use of his prison stay to study the dialect of thieves. Later in the 19th century the building was put to a variety of different municipal uses before finally becoming, in 1901, the seat of the Ministry of Foreign Affairs. The large annexe at the back dates from the Franco period and clearly indicates the way in which Fascist architects appropriated the principles of the Herrera school.

Leaving the Plaza Mayor by its northwestern corner we soon emerge at the junction of the Calle Mayor and the the Plaza de San Miguel, the latter dominated by a fanciful ironwork Market Hall dating from 1916, the only building of its kind still left in Madrid; the site was originally occupied by the church of San Miguel de los Octoes, one of the many religious institutions pulled down by Joseph Bonaparte. A short detour to the north of the square, crossing the Calle Mayor, can be made to see the former boarding house – at No. 3 Calle Fuentes – where Galdós stayed between 1862 and 1863, shortly after he had moved to Madrid from the Canary Islands. The

future novelist had a room on the second floor, which was reached in his time by way of a poorly lit staircase badly in need of a coat of paint. This elegantly classical building of the early 19th century, now a vivid ochre, is of great interest for being virtually the only one of Galdós' many Madrid dwellings to have survived.

South of the Plaza de San Miguel, the picturesque Cava San Miguel leads down, hugging the curved walls of the tall 17th-century houses that make up the western side of the Plaza Mayor. These houses all feature ground-floor cellars, as do those on the Cava San Miguel's continuation, the Calle de Cuchilleros, a street named after the knife makers who until comparatively recently had their shops here. Many of the cellars on the two streets have hostelry traditons of long standing, and at No. 17 Cuchilleros is to be found what the Guinness Book of Records calls the oldest restaurant in the world, the Casa Botín. Dating back to 1725, it even gets a mention in Galdós' *Fortunata and Jacinta*, as a plaque on the outside records. Inside is a series of intimate beamed dining rooms, where you can eat roast meats cooked in an old oak-fuelled oven. Hemingway described the place not simply as the oldest but also the best restaurant in the world, and this exaggerated assessment, combined with Botín's proximity to the Plaza Mayor, have ensured that the place is packed daily with tourists. A number of other famous old restaurants can be seen by continuing south from Botín, the first of which – at No. 11 Plaza de Puerta Cerrada – is Casa Paco, a small, ceramic-tiled establishment well known for its hams and steaks. Below the Plaza de La Puerta Cerrada runs the Calle de La Cava Baja, one of the Madrid streets that, for all its 19th-century buildings and recent changes, best conveys the domestic character of 16th- and 17th-century Madrid. Several traditional craftsmen still have their workshops here, but the fame of the street lies principally in its numerous mesones, or inns, of which the the most celebrated is the former Posada de San Pedro at No. 35. Known after 1921 as the Mesón del Segoviano, and now as Casa Lucio, this establishment was founded in 1740 and is the only Madrid inn to have preserved its traditional vestibule and quaintly irregular, balconied patio, above which the guests used to sleep. The place was until this century a staging post for diligences serving the provinces of Toledo, Segovia and Guadalajara, and it was not so long ago that a mule drawn cart from the Toledan town of Illescas – the *Ordinario de Illescas* – could be seen drawing up here every Friday, sometimes sharing the patio with the expensive cars of foreign visitors. The inn's restaurant has been popular both with tourists and writers, and in 1927 a famous literary banquet was put on here for the Burgos writer Francisco Gramon tagne, in whose honour such prominent members of the Generation of 98 as Azorín and Antonio Machado gave speeches.

Whereas the character of old Madrid is well evoked by the Calle de la Cava Baja, the actual look of the city before it was so drastically changed in the 19th century can be wonderfully appreciated in the small area of quiet squares and narrow ascending streets extending northwest of the Plaza de la Puerta Cerrada. Leaving the square on the Calle San Justo, we come almost immediately to one of the few churches in Madrid that purists would define as truly baroque, the Basílica de San Miguel. Most of Spain's so-called 'baroque' churches are 'baroque' only by virtue of their ornamentation, and are relatively simple structures, lacking the dynamic ground-plans characteristic of the works of the great Italian or Central European architects of the 17th and 18th centuries. San Miguel, in contrast, has an exciting concave façade and an interior of undulating bays and diagonally projecting piers. It comes as no surprise that the architect was an Italian, Santiago Bonavía, and one very much inspired by the great Piedmontese architect Guarino Guarini: the latter's influence is clearly apparent in Bonavía's combination of a baroque ground-plan with cross-vaulting and tall proportions of gothic derivation. The building was designed at the very end of the 17th century, but was heavily embellished in later years.

Immediately beyond the church of San Miguel the Calle San Justo widens into the tiny Plaza Cordón, which is bordered on its southern side by an 18th-century palace of Herreran simplicity. Adjacent to the northeastern corner of the square, at No. 2 Calle Sacramento, is an exquisitely carved Renaissance portal belonging to the Casa de Cisneros, the main entrance to which is on the Plaza de la Villa. The latter square can be reached from here by climbing north up the narrow Calle Cordón, but a more interesting route is to follow the alley called Puñonrostro, which begins its short ascent alongside the church of San Miguel, and passes next to the Convent of Las Carboneras. This Hieronomite convent, founded in 1607, has an exceedingly plain brick exterior, the austerity of which is relieved purely by the relief carving above the church portal. The interest of this institution, however, is less architectural than gastronomic, for this is one of the last remaining convents in Madrid to make and sell its own cakes and pastries. Ever since the time that St. Teresa of Ávila distributed sweetened egg yolks to the poor of her native Ávila, the making of sweets has been one of the great specialities of Spanish convents, and an important source of their income. Las Carboneras is a closed order convent, and buying from these nuns has its own exotic ritual, the negotiations being carried out behind a rotating drum on which both the goods and our money are placed. The traditional way of addressing a nun is with the words '*Ave Maria Purísima*', to which she will reply '*Sin pecado recibido*' (without inherited sin). This formality over, we then put in our request from a list of specialities pinned to the wall, one of the sweets on offer in this particular convent being a long, dry biscuit with the appropriate name of *Huesos de Fray Escoba* (Bones of Father Escoba).

After leaving the convent we only have to carry our bones a few more metres uphill before coming out at the magnificent Plaza de la Villa, noting just as we turn the final corner the mudéjar horseshoe arch of the Tower of Los Lujanes. The Plaza de la Villa, though backed on its northern side by the Calle Mayor, is a quiet and dignified square, which in 1980 was thankfully cleared of traffic, a car park, and a central landscaped reservation. In its stone-paved centre stands a statue, by the leading turn-of-the-century sculptor Mariano Benlliure, of Don Alvaro de Bazán, an admiral of Philip II who distinguished himself at the Battle of Lepanto. A suitably splendid backcloth to this great admiral is provided by the surrounding buildings, which make up Madrid's oldest architectural ensemble. The Tower and adjoining Palace of Los Lujanes, though heavily restored, date back to the early 15th century, and, together with the neighbouring palace at No. 3, are virtually the sole survivals of Madrid's civic architecture of this period. The Madrilenian nobility, led by the magistrate Vargas, defended themselves in the Lujanes Palace at the time of the Revolt of the Comuneros, and it is also said that the French king, Francis I, was imprisoned here after his defeat at the Battle of Pavia in 1525. The palace's boldly carved stone portal is particularly impressive, as is the large mudéjar arch through which we enter the smaller palace at No. 3. The latter has been turned into offices, but is well worth visiting for its fragments from the destroyed 15th-century hospital of La Latina, most notably a gothic balustrade and the finely carved plateresque tombs of Beatriz Galindo ('La Latina') and her husband, Francisco Mirez ('El Artillero'). The façade of the hospital is seen here in an oil

sketch by the turn-of-the-century Valencian painter Joaquín Sorolla (whose museum we will visit in Walk 7).

A palace slightly later in date and more sophisticated in appearance is the Casa de Cisneros, which takes up the southern side of the square, and is a typical example of the so-called plateresque, a term derived from the use by Spain's renaissance architects and sculptors of filigree detailing imitative of the work of *plateros* or silversmiths. The building dates back to 1537 but was almost entirely remodelled in the early years of the present century, when the 'plateresque' was taken up as the national Spanish style. A gallery now connects the palace with the adjacent Casa de la Villa or Town Hall, the largest and most important of the square's buildings. It is indicative of the absolutist spirit of Hapsburg Spain that the mayor of one the most rapidly growing capitals of Europe should be merely an employee of the Court, and that he and his city council should not have a building of their own until the construction of the Casa de la Villa in the middle of the 17th century. The initial plans were drawn up in 1640 by the now aged Gómez de Mora, but the building was not to be completed until the end of the 17th century, by which time the characteristic Herreran-style structure had acquired baroque portals and other fanciful details. In 1771 the façade overlooking the Plaza Mayor was modified by Juan de Villanueva so as to incorporate a balcony from which royal parties could watch the city's Corpus Christi processions. The building can be visited by guided tour every Monday afternoon, but this is not an experience that can be wholeheartedly recommended, especially as it entails listening to an interminable talk about the origins of Madrid's civic coat of arms. The interior has for the most part a drab municipal character of the early years of this century, and the original patio, damaged during the Civil War of 1936-39, has been glazed with stained glass. Most of the treasures that were once displayed here have now been removed to the city's Municipal Museum, including a late 16th-century *custodia*, and a famous allegorical work by Goya. For lovers of 19th century academic art there is at least the consolation of V. Palmaroli's huge canvas of 1871 depicting the *3rd of May*, the subject of Goya fame being interpreted here with hysterical women set against a dawn panorama of Madrid. But the best reason to visit the Casa de la Villa is to see the remarkable Sala de Actos, which, with its public gallery and facing benches, has been compared to a miniature version of the House of Commons. The sumptuously gilded and heavy decoration, however, is wholly Spanish, and features the main survival of the original interior – an illusionistic late baroque ceiling painting by Antonio Palomino.

On the northern side of the Plaza de la Villa, rising above the present Calle Mayor, once stood the 17th-century church which gave the square its original name of Plaza de Salvador. The church of San Salvador had fallen into ruin by the 19th century, and was pulled down in 1842, its memory being preserved today in a stone inscription attached to No. 70 of the Calle Mayor. A more recent plaque on the same building records that the tower of the church was used as the main setting for a highly popular novel of 1641 by the Andalucían-born satirist Vélez de Guevara: this work, *El Diablo Cojuelo* (The Lame Devil) deals with a student who releases a devil from an astrologer's phial, and through him is taken on a tour of Madrid and Andalucia. Just to the east of here, at No. 48 Calle Mayor, a modern building marks the house where the great dramatist Lope de Vega was born in 1562. His father had come to Madrid to move in with a Greek girl called Helen, but the wife whom he had abandoned in Valladolid soon caught up with him and managed to separate the pair. By great coincidence, Lope's main rival as Spain's leading dramatist of the Golden Age, Pedro Calderón de la Barca, died in 1681 on the opposite side of the street, in a house just to the west of the Plaza de la Villa, at No. 61. This house, though heavily restored and remodelled, retains much of its original appearance. Calderón spent the last years of his life here, during which time he served as a chaplain to the church of San Salvador. On the day following his death his body was carried from here by priests to the church, and buried temporarily in a chapel while awaiting transference to a splendid black marble mausoleum planned for the right transept. The mausoleum was completed shortly afterwards, but for some reason the body remained where it was, and was only moved when the church was finally destroyed. From that moment onwards the body was to make up for its previous inactivity by a series of constant transferrals from one part of Madrid to another, each one marked by a solemn procession. Opposite is a picture of the event in 1874, heading to a cemetery where Calderón stayed five years. The church where he was eventually reinterred in the Calle de San Bernardo, was gutted during the Civil War, and his mortal remains – like those of many other Golden Age writers – remain missing to this day. As Miguel de Unamuno once ruefully commented, the dead in Spain are never allowed to rest.

Continuing to head west along the Calle Mayor from Calderón's house, we pass to our right the Calle de San Nicolás, where we will find the charming small church of San Nicolás de las Servitas, the exterior of which is distinguished by a brick tower decorated with blind arcades of horse-shoe arches. The tower is thought by some to have been originally the minaret of a mosque, in which case it would be virtually the sole relic of Moorish Margherit; more probably a mudéjar work of the 12th century, it is in any case one of Madrid's oldest surviving structures. The light and cheerful interior of the building has been heavily altered over the centuries, but still retains mudéjar elements as well as a fine late 15th-century apse. On the other side of the Calle de San Nicolás to the church is a curious temporary-looking structure completely dwarfed by its surroundings. It is in fact a Basque club known as a Cloxto, the members of which take it in turns to cook for each other.

Near the westernmost end of the Calle Mayor, at No. 84, is a well known old tavern and restaurant called Casa Ciriaco, which was founded in 1917 by Ciriaco Muñoz. Among the many literary, artistic and other celebrities to have been regulars at this place were the bullfighter Juan Belmonte, the ubiquitous frequenter of tertulias Díaz-Cañabate, and the humorist and gastronome

Julio Camba (see page 282), in whose honour a regular monthly dinner is held in the modern dining room at the back. The attractively tiled bar displays numerous cuttings relating to the establishment's history, and there is also a plaque placed above the marble table where on 25 October 1943 the painter Ignacio Zuloaga enjoyed the last meal of his life.

The building in which Casa Ciriaco is housed carries further mortal associations, for it was from one of its second floor balconies that on 31 May 1906 one Mateo Morral threw a bomb at the nuptial processional carriage carrying Alfonso XIII and Victoria Eugenia de Battenberg. The moment was captured in a remarkable action photograph of the incident, reproduced opposite. The explosion killed several passers-by and even the horses of the royal carriage, but the young couple themselves escaped without injury. Morral had gone as far as to wrap the bomb in a floral bouquet, but this chivalrous detail did not save him from being executed a few days later. A bronze angel commemorating this assassination attempt and its victims is to be found on the opposite side of the street, in front of the late 17th-century church and convent of the Sacramento. From here we should descend down the Calle del Pretil de Los Consejos, noting to our right the impressively sober palace (now the Capitanía General) built between 1609-11 by Gómez de Mora to plans supplied by his father Francisco. Below the palace we have a good view of the bridge known as the Segovia Viaduct, which connects the hill of the Royal Palace with that of Las Vistillas. The deep hollow which the viaduct spans effectively divided Hapsburg Madrid in two, and the search for a way of joining the two areas was one that had long preoccupied the city's architects. The Italian architect Sacchetti proposed a solution to this problem in the early 18th century, and another one was to be put forward by Silvestre Pérez during the rule of Joseph Bonaparte. However, it was not until 1868 that a plan for a bridge was finally approved, the structure being inaugurated six years later with the procession carrying Calderón's remains from the church of San Francisco el Grande to the cemetery of San Nicolás that we saw on page

95. The original bridge – a metal structure based on a design of 1859 by Eugenio Barón – was replaced in the 1930's by the concrete functionalism of the present one, with its great parabolic arches. The Segovia Viaduct is much admired by some as an architectural and engineering achievement, but most Madrilenians tend to think of it simply as 'The Bridge of Suicides'. The last of Madrid's costumbristas, Emilio Carrere, popularized this nickname in a newspaper article which apparently gave rise to far more people throwing themselves off the viaduct than ever before. On this morbid note, it might be worth mentioning the ironic but hitherto unremarked fact that one of the most famous suicide victims in Spanish history, the Romantic poet Larra (p. 150), was born in 1809 in a house directly overlooking the site of the future viaduct. His birthplace, long since gone, is marked today by a plaque on the modern apartment building at No. 11 Calle del Pretil de Los Consejos.

III. The Plaza de la Paja and the Basilica de San Francisco   At the bottom of the street we find ourselves on the Calle de Segovia, which runs along the furrow between the two hills, and has several old taverns and ceramic shops. From the Plaza de la Cruz Verde we should head south on the gradually ascending Costa San Andrés, which – at the point where it widens into the Plaza de la Paja – passes immediately to the left the Calle de Príncipe Anglona. The latter street beautifully frames another of the rare survivals of mudéjar Madrid, a brick tower of 1354 attached to the church of San Pedro. The church itself, founded probably on the site of a mosque, was largely rebuilt in the 17th century, but has kept a renaissance west portal of 1525, and – on the south portal – the only royal coats of arms to have survived in Madrid from before the time of Ferdinand and Isabella.

The sloping and irregularly shaped Plaza de la Paja is one of the most enchanting but also least visited corners of old Madrid, and we might find it difficult to believe that, despite all the recent tidying-up and restoration, this was the largest and most important square of the medieval city. In contrast to the squalid predecessor of the Plaza Mayor it was an aristocratic square and lined on all sides with imposing palaces, one of which was to be known as the 'Palace of Isabel la Católica' for having lodged, on one occasion, the Castilian queen. Though all these palaces had been taken down by the end of the 19th century, the city's greatest renaissance jewel is still to be seen here, dominating the narrow, upper end of the square. The story of this monument, the so-called Bishop's Chapel (Capilla del Obispo), is connected with that of the most powerful family to have lived on the square, the Vargas. The Vargas palace occupied a site marked today by a 1920's building imitating the adjacent 16th-century façade which gives access to the Chapel. From the time of Iván de Vargas, in the 13th century, the family had in their possession the relics of Madrid's patron saint, St. Isidro, and it was to house these in a suitably dignified fashion that Don Francisco de Vargas – counsellor to the Catholic Kings as well as to the Emperor Charles V – commissioned the present chapel in 1520. It

was originally connected to the neighbouring parish church of San Andrés, but when a long dispute led in 1544 to the transferral of the relics to the church itself, Don Francisco's son, the Bishop of Plasencia, decided to convert the chapel into a family pantheon. The surrounding area was consequently rebuilt and firmly separated from the church, and it was thanks to this that the Chapel was able to survive the fire which gutted San Andrés in 1936.

Disgracefully and quite inexcusably, the Chapel has been closed to the public for many years, and special permission to go inside is required from the Archbishopric of Madrid, which has owned the monument since 1980. It is well worth persevering in your efforts to get in, however, for the dusty interior, reached through a ruinous cloister, forms a surprisingly unspoilt 16th-century survival, complete with flamboyant late gothic vaulting, as well as superlatively intricate furnishings that are amongst the finest expressions of the Spanish plateresque. Virtuoso relief carvings in wood of Old Testament subjects decorate the doors of the west portal, while on the south wall of the nave is the alabaster wall tomb of the Bishop of Plasencia, a work exquisitely adorned with renaissance detailing, and with a group of musical angels recalling those of Andrea della Robbia in the choir of Florence Cathedral. Finally, flanked by the tombs of Don Francisco and his wife, comes the High Altar, a dazzling structure in gilded wood rising in true Spanish fashion up to the ceiling. As with all the other works in the Chapel, the High Altar is by an unknown artist, but it is generally attributed today to Francisco Giralte, a pupil of Spain's sculptural genius of the renaissance, Alonso Berruguete. The abbot Antonio Ponz, the 18th-century author of an eighteen-volume account of Spain's artistic treasures, considered that this High Altar was 'one of the most elaborately worked pieces of sculpture that Spain possesses, and amongst the best produced in this country at the beginning of the 16th century'.

Leaving the Plaza de la Paja by its southern corner, we make our way round to the back of the complex containing the Bishop's Chapel. All that survives of the original church of San Andrés

is its bell-tower, but, rising up next to this, is a most eloquent domed structure which was added to the church in the mid-17th century to commemorate the recent canonization of St. Isidro. Gómez de Mora drew up the initial plans, but in the end the work was carried out by later architects, who conceived a sumptuously coloured and richly modelled interior, with a lower level of gilding and dark marble which was directly inspired by the early baroque Pantheon of the Kings in the Escorial. Terribly damaged by the same anarchist attack of 1936 which ruined for ever the adjoining church, the chapel has recently been excellently restored, and though missing its flamboyant baldacchino (the sketch for which is shown opposite), and surrounding altars by Coello, Rizi and others, still retains much of its original decorative splendour.

The Chapel of San Isidro looks out over an untidy series of interconnecting squares stretching in a southeasterly direction all the way to the Calle de Toledo. To the southwest meanwhile decends the broad Carrera de San Francisco, which will land us directly in front of the massive church of that name, the largest in Madrid, and the one which most forcefully dominates the city's skyline. The origins of the Basilica of San Francisco el Grande are in a Franciscan hermitage, founded, according to tradition, by St. Francis himself in the late 13th century. Originally it occupied a peaceful site outside Madrid, but later acted as a powerful magnet to the growing city. In exchange for their spiritual services, the monks extracted an annual tax both from the Court and from the citizens of Madrid, and in so doing soon acquired enormous wealth. A vast new monastery was begun in 1762 by the Franciscan lay-brother Francisco Cabezas, and completed in 1784 under the supervision of the royal architect Francesco Sabatini. Early the following century Joseph Bonaparte considered turning the church into a parliament building, but the place remained in the hands of the Franciscans until the confiscation by the State of monastic properties in 1836, after which the monastery buildings were taken over for use as army barracks. In 1869 the church was converted into a National Pantheon, and the much-moved

bones of Calderón, together with the bodies of such illustrious Spaniards as Garcilaso de la Vega, Quevedo, Ventura Rodríguez, and Juan de Villanueva, were brought here, only to be taken away several years later following protests from the churches where they had come from. In 1878, following the funeral obsequies that were held here for Queen Mercedes, the President of the Council of Ministers proposed that the church be made into a National Church where grand State ceremonies could be celebrated on solemn occasions. With this in mind, the whole church was extensively restored and redecorated and its huge dome covered with an ambitious cycle of paintings by Carlos Luis de Rivera.

Since 1926 San Francisco el Grande has belonged once again to the Franciscans, and the few visitors to this lugubrious place are obliged to follow a guided tour. The church, entered from an austerely classical portico, comprises an oppressively heavy rotunda surrounded by chapels, and so gloomy in its lighting that we might find ourselves tripping up over the stalls. An early painting by Goya of St. Bernardino of

Siena is to be found in one of the chapels, and is interesting for being virtually the only religious work by him in the colourful vein of his tapestry cartoons; the podgy-faced artist himself is depicted on the right-hand side of the canvas, clearly bored by St. Bernardino's sermon. Baroque choir stalls taken from the Segovian Monastery of El Parral line the walls of the presbytery, and set the tone for the cavernous sacristy and chapter house, which are filled with similarly elaborate stalls of earlier date, these ones originally from the Monastery of El Paular. Over-exposure to so much wood, combined with the mustiness and greyish-green colouring of these back rooms, begins to induce a certain feeling of nausea, and, by the time we are led around the suitably grand cloister, we may have difficulty in appreciating the many fine pictures to be seen here, in particular a late canvas by Zurbarán of St. Bonaventura. The immediate reaction on coming back to the entrance portico might be to rush out as quickly as possible into the open air, but we should walk through the side door to our left to visit the quite separate Chapel of Cristo de los Dolores. Built in the 1660's, this well preserved and very heterogenous building is a model of church architecture during the reign of Philip IV, its lavish furnishings and elaborate ornamentation being offset by its structural simplicity and sobriety.

The religious order responsible for the building of the Chapel of Cristo de los Dolores, the Tercerians, founded shortly afterwards a hospital and church just to the south of San Francisco el Grande, at the junction of the Calle San Bernabé and the Gran Vía San Francisco. Behind a most decrepit façade the hospital continues to function today, and is worth a short visit to see the grand staircase, where we will find two canvases by Velázquez's follower Carreño de Miranda as well as a religious work by van Dyck originally in the Escorial. Leaving the busy and unappealing Gran Vía de San Francisco, we should head east on the more homely Calle de Calatrava until we reach the Calle de la Paloma. Around the 15th of August these two streets become the scene of one of the liveliest of Madrid's local festivals, held in honour of the Virgin of La Paloma or The Dove. The story goes that a dove belonging to a local convent attached itself to a procession carrying a statue of the Virgin of Las Maravillas. Later a painting of the Virgin was discovered in the walls of the same convent, and it soon attracted such a widespread devotion that an oratory was built to house it in 1791. The fame of this Virgin spread well beyond the neighbourhood, and in the following century such distinguished people as María Luisa of Parma and Isabel II came to pay their respects to her. In the course of this century the population of the whole district was to grow enormously, and by 1896 plans were made to replace the oratory with the present, much larger church. The church, situated at the southern end of the Calle de La Paloma, was built by Lorenzo Alvarez Capra, and is a particularly light and cheerful example of the so-called neo-mudéjar style. Higher up on the street, at No. 5, is a candlemaker's shop, a delightful old establishment which was founded here in response to the popular devotion to the local Virgin.

IV. The Puente de Toledo and the Cemetery of San Isidro The Church of La Paloma stands on high ground, and from the open space beside it we can look down to the drearily neoclassical Puerta de Toledo, which was completed in 1817; the inscription honouring Ferdinand VII was desecrated at various times in the 19th century, but has recently been restored, for purely historical reasons. The gate, isolated by dense surrounding traffic, marks the southern boundary of old Madrid, and below it stretches the ugly modern development which makes up most of the southern half of the city. A tour on foot becomes undesirable from this point, but dedicated sight-seers might wish at least to see the Toledo Bridge, which can be reached by heading south down the broad southern end of the Calle de Toledo. This outstanding bridge, designed by Pedro de Ribera in 1719, is a nine-arched construction featuring approach ramps, turreted bridge-heads, and two delightfully elaborate roadside shrines housing statues of Santa María de la Cabeza and San Isidro (seen opposite in a photo-graph of the 1950's). At one time it must have made a most beautiful entrance into Madrid, but today the surroundings could scarcely be less appealing, with blackened apartment blocks, factories, and a great spaghetti junction. The urban landscape becomes even worse to the south of the river Manzanares, for this is traditionally the poor area of the city, and much of what has been put up here was completely unplanned. A sort of climax of desolation is reached in the enormous suburb of Carabanchel, but to those tourists hardy enough to make it as far as here, there is the consolation of the charming cemetery church of Santa María la Antigua, a neglected relic of the mudéjar past standing within earshot of the loudspeakers from Madrid's largest prison.

The most practicable and attractive excursion to be made from the Toledo Bridge is to the Hermitage of San Isidro, which lies a short distance to the west of the bridge, along the Paseo Quince de Mayo. This engagingly simple 18th-century structure occupies a quiet and shaded hill-top position with extensive views

down to the Manzanares and across to San
Francisco el Grande and the more distant Royal
Palace. Every year, on St. Isidro's day, a festive
pilgrimage or *romería* is made to the Hermitage,
the occasion vividly portrayed by Goya, an enormous bust of whom towers over the neighbouring
park. We have already seen his famous picture
of the picnic in the Pradera (pp. 12-13); we should
recognise the Royal Palace and San Francisco el
Grande in the background. Next to the
Hermitage can also be found the most pleasant
of southern Madrid's many cemeteries, this one
containing a superb Art Nouveau tomb at the end
of its overgrown central alley. Sculpted by
Agustín Querol to house the mortal remains of
one Doña Luisa Sancho Mata, this dynamic,
multi-figured work is at present in a most ruinous
condition, and, when I was last here I found
that the arm of a kneeling mourner had fallen off,
and was lying by the ground beside it. The
neglect of the San Isidro cemetery, however, is
as nothing in comparison to that of the adjoining Sacramental de San Justo, where many of
Spain's distinguished literary figures of the 19th

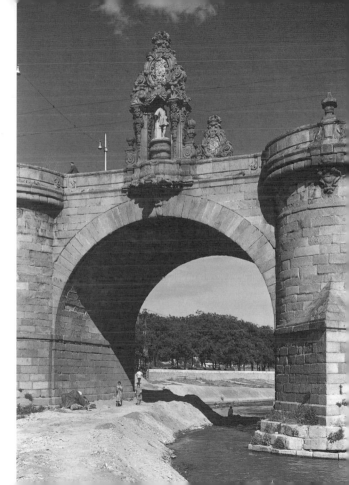

and 20th centuries lie buried, including Ramón Gómez de la Serna and most of the protagonists of the Romantic era such as Larra, Espronceda, Campoamor and Hartzenbusch (the poet Zorrilla's tomb is also here, but the body itself has been transferred to his native Valladolid). The young Luis Buñuel had a particular fondness for this cemetery, which was as run-down in his day as it is now, but he loved it for harbouring 'our great romantic poet Larra' and for having 'a hundred of the most beautiful cypress trees' that he had ever seen. Once, in the company of his literary friends, he paid the cemetery a midnight visit, and, in the haunting silence of this deserted place, was excited by stumbling across an open tomb. Underneath, lit up by a beam of moonlight was a coffin with its top ajar, from which protruded the dry, dirty hair of a woman. 'Nervous and excited, I called out, and the others immediately rushed down. That dead hair in the moonlight was one of the most striking images I've ever encountered.' Many years later he was to use this image in his film *The Phantom of Liberty*.

The Barrio de los Literatos

THE CARRERA DE SAN JERÓNIMO *to* EL AVAPIÉS

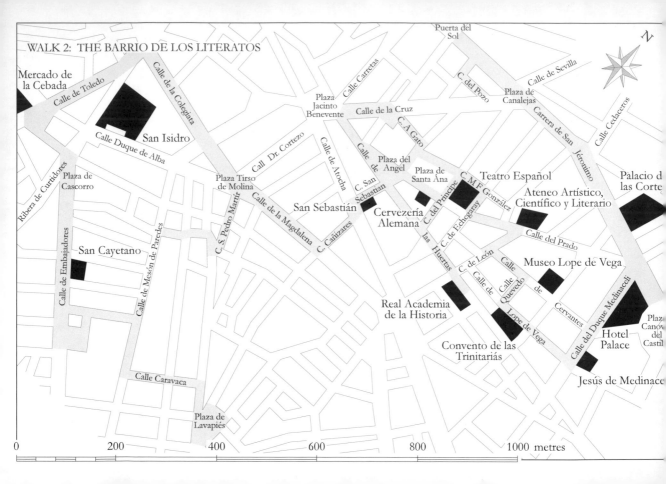

WALK 2: THE BARRIO DE LOS LITERATOS

Mercado de la Cebada

Calle de Toledo

Calle de la Colegiata

San Isidro

Calle Duque de Alba

Ribera de Curtidores

Plaza de Cascorro

Calle de Embajadores

San Cayetano

Calle de Mesón de Paredes

C. S. Pedro Mártir

Plaza Tirso de Molina

Call Dr. Cortezo

Calle de Atocha

Calle de la Magdalena

C. Cañizares

San Sebastián

C. San Sebastián

Calle Caravaca

Plaza de Lavapiés

Puerta del Sol

Calle Carretas

Plaza Jacinto Benevente

Calle de la Cruz

C. del Pozo

Calle de Sevilla

Plaza de Canalejas

Carrera de San Jerónimo

Calle Cedaceros

C. A Gato

Calle de

Plaza del Angel

Plaza de Santa Ana

Teatro Español

C. M F González

Palacio de las Cortes

Ateneo Artístico, Científico y Literario

Cervecería Alemana

C. del Príncipe

C. de Echegaray

Calle del Prado

Calle de las Huertas

C. de León

Calle de Quevedo

Calle de

Cervantes

Museo Lope de Vega

Calle del Duque de Medinaceli

Real Academia de la Historia

Lope de Vega

Convento de las Trinitariás

Hotel Palace

Plaz Canóv del Castil

Jesús de Medinace

0   200   400   600   800   1000 metres

N

The Barrio de los Literatos

THE CARRERA DE SAN JERÓNIMO *to* EL AVAPIÉS

As Madrid rapidly grew beyond its medieval walls after 1560, there rose up to the east of the Puerta del Sol a district where virtually all the leading writers of Spain's Golden Age were to live and work. This triangular-shaped district, bordered to the north by the Carrera de San Jerónimo and to the south by the Calle de Alcalá, is known to this day as that of *Los Literatos*, and sometimes even as *Las Musas* or *Parnasso*. Printers had their workshops here, and bookshops were later to proliferate, but the area's literary character was consolidated above all by its theatres, which in turn gave the place a reputation for being Bohemian, loose-living and pleasure-seeking. Already in 1635 the dramatist Castillo Solórzano was reporting that this was the Madrid district 'most frequented by the young and unattached, owing to the presence here of the city's two main theatres, as well as for being the home of many ladies of the profession'. Intensive rebuilding campaigns in the 19th and early 20th centuries were to rid the district almost entirely of its Golden Age monuments, but its literary character was maintained in later years by its theatres and wealth of literary cafés, and the place remains to this day the entertainment heart of Madrid. This district, richer in literary associations and night life than in architectural or artistic treasures, forms the main part of this chapter, but I have also wandered slightly to the south, into an area of Madrid which has given enormous inspiration to writers, owing to its celebrated flea-market, the coarse vitality of its street-life, and to its legendary world of majos.

I. The Carrera de San Jerónimo The Barrio de Los Literatos begins as soon as we leave the Puerta del Sol by its southeastern corner and enter the Carrera de San Jerónimo. The early growth of the district was initiated by this street, which has its origins in a carriageway built in 1538 to join the Puerta del Sol with the 15th-century Monastery of San Jerónimo, at that time the sole monument of note on the eastern outskirts of the city. The importance of the street increased enormously at the beginning of the 17th century, with the construction, alongside the monastery, of the royal palace of the Buen Retiro. The street, at one time bordered by modest artisan's houses, came now to be dominated by the palaces and convents we see on the detail from Texeira's map on page 116, and also became the scene of spectacular royal processions. Furthermore it served as the main route to the ever more popular recreational district of the Prado, to which all of fashionable Madrid would be drawn in their carriages for the evening paseo, in particular

from the late 18th century onwards. The 19th century was the lively heyday of the Carrera de San Jerónimo, but the character of the street was to change in the course of this century, what with the establishment here of the Spanish Parliament, the demolition of the convents, and the replacement of the aristocratic palaces with apartment blocks for the middle-classes. Today the street has been altered more than almost any other part of the Barrio de Los Literatos, having lost its residential function and nearly all of its cafés, and being lined instead with the headquarters of banks and other large companies.

At the beginning of the Carrera de San Jerónimo there once stood the late 16th-century Convent of las Victorias, the church of which was a popular meeting-place in 17th-century Madrid, and as such features in numerous plays of the Golden Age. We saw it on the right (No. VI) of the detail from Texeira on page 71, where it has a courtyard like the equally popular Mentidero. The pulling down of las Victorias in the late 1830's led to the construction behind the street of the Pasaje Matheu, a shopping arcade that was considered at the time to be one of the smartest in Europe; it survives today as a curious pedestrian precinct, lacking both its former roof and entrance arches. Nearby, at the junction of the Carrera de San Jerónimo with the Calle de las Victorias, a plaque records the site of the Fontana de Oro, the celebrated political café of the 1820's which gave Galdós the title and subject of his first novel. The opening chapter of this historical work imaginatively recreates what the Carrera de San Jerónimo must have been like in 1821, no less busy than it was in Galdós' time, but dark and narrow, and, as dusk falls, filling up with animated, argumentative groups who earlier in the day have lingered outside at the Puerta del Sol and are now making their way to the cafés, above all to the Fontana de Oro, 'the magnet for the city's ardent and clamorous youth, troubled by both impatience and inspiration, anxious to stir the passions of the people, and to hear the people's spontaneous applause'.

Of the places on the Carrera de San Jerónimo frequented by Galdós himself there remains today one solitary survival, but what a magnificent survival this is. The Lhardy restaurant and confectioners, situated at No. 8, almost next door to the site of the Fontana de Oro, has been running since 1839, and still retains a striking 19th-century interior behind the magnificent shopfront. Its founder was a Frenchman from near the Swiss border who styled himself Emilio Lhardy, and opened this establishment on the advice of his friend Prosper Mérimée, creator of another Spanish legend, Carmen. Functioning at first primarily as a confectioners, but with lunches and dinners prepared on request, it popularized in Madrid such French delicacies as *éclairs, millefeuilles* and *petits-choux*. The culinary repertory of Lhardy's increased in tandem with the place's growing reputation, and soon the establishment became the most fashionable gastronomic institution in Madrid, mentioned in all the books about the city, and visited by most of the foreigners who came here. Among them was Alexandre Dumas *père*, who for some reason was under the impression that the owner was Italian, a delusion which gave him an opportunity to voice his prejudices against all food cooked outside of France: 'In Italy, where one eats badly,' he wrote shortly after visiting Lhardy's in October 1846, 'the good restaurants are French; in Spain, where one does not eat at all, the good restaurants are Italian.' Dumas' was a lone dissenting voice, for right up to the present day the place has inspired paeans of praise from a list of distinguished patrons which includes almost every notable Spanish political and cultural figure of the last century and a half, and even the monarchy itself. The writer Azorín was not exaggerating too greatly when he wrote early this century that 'if the shop-window of Lhardy's were a film projector, the whole of modern Spanish history would be seen in it.'

The writer who can claim to have made the most references to Lhardy's in his works was Pérez Galdós, who was one of the place's most regular customers. Interestingly, the establishment of today is virtually unchanged in its decoration and furnishings from the one known to him, even down to the splendid silver used. At street level is the actual confectioner's, a tiny,

crowded room of mirrors and dark wood, where we can enjoy an aperitif of vermouth while standing at the counter. A custom peculiar to Lhardy's, and dating back to Galdós' time, is to help oneself to a cup of consommé served from a majestic silver samovar which forms the centre-piece of a glistening display of glasses, decanters and silverware at the back of the shop (see p. 64). Squeezed between this and the kitchen is a stair-case leading up to a series of small dining-rooms, one of which has walls adorned with Japanese inlay. The principal dining-room, overlooking the street, has diminutive wooden columns, dark panelling, and candelabra, and features several paintings by the founder's son, Agustín Lhardy, (opposite) a professionally trained landscapist who took over his father's business in 1887. The menu today still comprises a mixture of French and Madrilenian dishes, and this is perhaps the Madrid restaurant with the greatest tradition of tripe and cocido.

Gastronomic temptations are a major feature of the Barrio de los Literatos, and we will find immediately behind Lhardy's – at No. 8 Calle del

Pozo – one of Madrid's finest and oldest cake shops, the Antigua Pastelería del Pozo, which was founded by Julian Leal in 1830 and preserves a dignified, turn-of-the-century appearance. Continuing, if we still can, east down the Carrera de San Jerónimo, we soon cross a noisy round intersection, featuring, on its northwestern side, the oppressively grand Banco Hispano Americano of 1902-5. Beyond this the street widens as it begins its slow descent towards the Paseo del Prado. At the corner with the Calle Echegaray was once to be found the Cervezería Inglesa, a favourite haunt of late 19th-century writers, including the literary critic and novelist known as 'Clarín' (his real name was Leopoldo Alas), who referred to the place as 'The Spleen Club'. There are many surviving old bars to the south of here, but for the moment we should try to remain on the Carrera de San Jerónimo, allowing as the only further gastronomic stop a visit to Casa Mira at No. 30, another well-preserved turn-of-the-century institution, this one enjoying a reputation as Madrid's leading specialist in *turrones*, a soft, Spanish version of nougat. Just

beyond the shop, at the corner of the Calle de Ventura de la Vega, a marble plaque records the building where, on St. Isidro's day 1896, the films of the pioneering French cinéastes, the Lumière brothers, were projected in Spain for the first time. Admission was one peseta, and, by the end of the first month in which they were shown, it was reported that 'all of Madrid', from the royal family downwards, had been to see them.

On the opposite, northern side of the Carrera de San Jerónimo, an imposing baroque portal at No. 19 distinguishes the street's only surviving palace, a building by Pedro de Ribera which was heightened in the 1920's. In the middle of the quiet and very smart area extending east of here is the Teatro de la Zarzuela, a well-restored classical building of the 1850's specializing in light operas, most notably zarzuelas – that characteristically Madrilenian musical form, dating back to the 18th century. Adjacent to this, and with its main, pedimented façade overlooking the Carrera de San Jerónimo (in the foreground of the picture opposite, taken in 1845), is the Spanish parliament building or Cortes, which was begun three years before the photograph was taken, and twenty years after the Parliament's foundation by a group of radical patriots exiled in Cádiz. The interior of the building became known the world over when on 23 February 1981 Colonel Tejero of the Guardia Civil, in full view of television cameras, held the whole Parliament at gun-point, and threatened for a few tense hours Spain's newly found democracy. The architecture itself is not so exciting, though perhaps Théophile Gautier went too far in 1845 when he described this rigidly symmetrical, neoclassical building as being in such 'abominable taste' that he doubted whether any serious constitutions could possibly be drafted inside it.

Gautier was equally unenthusiastic about the bronze statue of Cervantes (page 66) which stands in the small garden directly in front of the main façade, though at least he was generous enough to acknowledge that the 'immortal author of Don Quixote' deserved some form of commemoration. The part of Madrid most closely associated with Cervantes and other Golden Age writers is

to be found a short walk to the south of here, and we should head towards it along the Calle del Duque de Medinaceli. As with the Carrera de San Jerónimo, this is a street which has been radically altered by turn-of-the-century development, the principal change being the demolition in 1910 of the baroque palace originally belonging to the Dukes of Lerma to make way for the suitably palatial Palace Hotel, a grand hotel in the style of those on the Côte d'Azur, complete with a sumptuous oval saloon covered in coloured glass. In ironic juxtaposition to this monument to materialistic decadence is the ugly modern church containing the miraculous image of Jesus of Medinaceli, one of Madrid's most venerated votive images, and one which attracts on the first Friday of every month a long queue of worshippers that spills over into the adjoining streets. The church it replaced formed part of an early 17th-century monastery which had been founded behind his palace by the Cardinal-Duke of Lerma for the Discalced ('Barefoot') Trinitarians. Greatly favoured by the many people of the area involved in the theatrical profession, this church (at XIX on the detail from Texeira opposite) had acquired considerable notoriety for its eleven o'clock Sunday Masses. These were regularly attended by the most famous actresses of the Golden Age, and came to be known as 'the Masses of the Marías' on account of the glamorous threesome of María Calderón, María Riquelme, and María de Córdoba, the last of these being the mistress of Lope de Vega whom the playwright dubbed Amarillis. Dressed in their most ostentatious finery, these actresses attracted far more attention than the religious functions, and helped fuel the wrath of the clergy, who were shocked by the way the church had been turned into a mixture of cat-walk and gossip parlour.

II. Golden Age Writers The literary and theatrical heart of Golden Age Madrid lies immediately to the west of the Jesus of Medinaceli, its entrance marked by the Taberna de Dolores, a lively bar serving excellent sandwiches and canapés, and decorated on the outside with attractive ceramic decoration of 1928. From here the Calle de Lope de Vega climbs up, one of a

grid of dark and narrow streets that can still be imagined in their Golden Age state despite having been almost entirely rebuilt in later periods. Luis Martín Santos, in his strange experimental novel, *A Time of Silence* (1962), referred to them as having 'preserved so well their provincial air like a cyst in the midst of a great city'. How these still-poky streets looked in the 17th century can be seen in the detail from Texeira (where the Calle Lope de Vega is called Calle de Cantarranas), dominated by the original monastery of the Trinitarian monks and its garden. Much of the upper part of the calle is taken by the austere brick walls of a sister institution, the Convent of the Discalced Trinitarians, which was founded in 1609 and rebuilt between 1668-73. Cervantes' daughter Isabel was a nun here, as was one of Lope de Vega's, who, under the name of Sor Marcela de San Félix, rose to become prioress of the convent, and the author of a codex of poetry which the place still possesses. But the literary renown of the convent is due largely to its being the burial-place in 1616 of Cervantes himself, an association which led the Spanish Academy to rescue the building from ruin in the mid-19th century. Every year, on the anniversary of Cervantes' death, the Academy holds a commemorative mass here both for him and the other great names of Spanish literature. However, as is the way with the famous dead in this country, the exact whereabouts of Cervantes' tomb are no longer known.

Directly across the street from the Convent begins the short Calle de Quevedo, at the entrance to which, on the right-hand side, is the site of a house associated not only with the 17th-century writer Francisco de Quevedo – who made his cruel and brilliant mark both in verse and prose – but also with the greatest poet of the Golden Age, Luis de Góngora. We are lucky enough to be able to see both these men in their maturity, in powerful portraits by Velázquez. Góngora is shown with the sober, stoic features befitting a native of Seneca's Córdoba, while Quevedo is portrayed behind a pair of heavy spectacles that accentuate the venomous smirk of a satirist whose view of life had been warped through physical deformity and a hatred of his mother. Their respective works represented the

two rival strands in 17th-century Spanish writing, the former's being associated with the exceedingly learned and artificial style known pejoratively by its detractors as *culteranismo*, the latter's with the at times equally impenetrable *conceptismo*, the complexity of which stems less from density of descriptive vocabulary or recourse to obscure classical allusions, than from the use of literary conceits, paradox, wit, ambiguity, and difficult images and metaphors. The rivalry between the two men, however, was not simply a professional one, but was fired by personal animosity of the most vicious kind. Góngora, who had managed to hold his own in an exchange of angry satirical verses with Lope de Vega, found himself defeated in his poetic outbursts against Quevedo, the greater and unrivalled master of vindictive. 'Be ashamed, go purple, Don Luis', is a characteristic title of one of Quevedo's sonnets directed against Góngora, and an aptly cruel one, for Góngora suffered from premature arteriosclerosis and was to die of apoplexy in 1627. No wonder that Góngora's time in Madrid was an unhappy one, and that he took refuge in pastoral verse, eventually retiring to a farm on the outskirts of Córdoba. Quevedo's triumph over Góngora, combined with the offhand manner with which the latter was treated generally while staying in Madrid, seem to have had lasting consequences for Góngora's future reputation here. Thus, when in 1848 the Madrid municipality decided to rename the street in the Barrio de Los Literatos where the two men lived, Quevedo was honoured and not Góngora, and, to compound this insult, the plaque marking the site here of the former's house makes no mention of the previous tenancy of Góngora. Góngora rented the house in 1619, writing afterwards to a friend that the place 'had the size of a finger and the price of silver.' In the winter of 1625, which was a particularly harsh one for Góngora, Quevedo bought the property, and had no hesitation in throwing his rival out into the street. Quevedo was to stay here until 1634.

Further up the Calle de Quevedo, at No. 5, is the birthplace of José Echegaray, a man who would be largely forgotten today were it not for the popular, bar-lined street named after him nearby. This versatile man, born in 1832, managed in his life to work as an engineer, become Minister of Finance and founder of the Bank of Spain, and to write melodramatic plays which earned him the Nobel Prize for Literature in 1904, thus making him the first of the two recipients of this prize from this small district of Madrid (the other was the playwright Jacinto Benavente). The obvious Spanish candidate for the prize in 1904 was Pérez Galdós, but in honouring the mediocre Echegaray instead, the Nobel Prize Committee in Stockholm displayed once again its uncanny knack for making the wrong choice.

At the top of the street, we enter the Calle Cervantes, and are plunged once again into the world of Golden Age literature. Almost directly in front of us, at No. 11, we find the Barrio's most eloquent survival of this era, the brick-fronted, two-storeyed house which Lope de Vega bought after deciding to settle permanently in Madrid in 1610. He lived here until his death in 1635, writing in the house the plays by which he is best remembered today such as *Peribáñez*, *Fuenteovejuna*, *El caballero de Olmedo* and *El castigo*

sin venganza. Known by Cervantes as 'the monster of Nature', Lope de Vega was always a prolific writer, but his work-rate increased enormously after moving in to this house, the apparent peace of which allowed him to work undisturbed from early in the morning until late at night. By 1613 Lope claimed to have written 230 plays, but by 1618 this number had risen to 800, and it was to rise to 1,500 by 1632. Even more remarkable was the way in which he managed to maintain both his work-rate and peace of mind while continuing to lead a personal life of a complexity few other writers could rival. After a series of scandalous affairs in his youth, and a first marriage which had ended with the death of his wife during childbirth, Lope had married again in 1598, but more for money than for love, according to his jealous rivals. At the same time he had kept an affair going with the actress Micaela de Luján, by whom he had five children, as opposed to only three by his second wife, Juana. The long-suffering Juana had come with him in 1610 to Madrid, but died here three years later, after which Lope brought into the house two of his illegitimate children by Micaela, Lope Félix, and the future prioress Marcela. In 1614, Lope prepared for ordination as a priest, though this did not in any way prevent him from having other furtive liaisons, the most passionate of which was with a married woman called Marta de Nevares Santoyo, by whom he had another illegitimate daughter, Antonia Clara. An increasing and perhaps inevitable element of tragedy entered Lope's life from this point onwards. Marta, who had come to live with Lope after the death of her husband, gradually went blind and died insane in 1632; the playwright's son, Lope Félix, drowned on a pearl-diving expedition to South America; and the seventeen-year old Antonia Clara was seduced by one Cristóbal Tenorio, an incident which caused the playwright enormous, and, some would say, deserved grief. Despite the many, well-publicized scandals of his life, Lope de Vega acquired in later years a saintly, mythical aura, and, on his forays into the street became one of the great sights of the city, gathering around him adoring crowds who kissed his hand and pleaded for his blessing. The print opposite shows him in his dashing youth.

Lope's house was in a ruinous condition by the 1960's, when it was turned into a museum to the writer, and lovingly restored to its original state. The delightful small garden which nourished Lope's verse was reconstructed, and the writer's rooms were furnished with items of his that had been kept over the centuries in the Convent of the Discalced Trinitarians. The decoration of the house is remarkably sparse and simple, for though Lope de Vega was the best paid of Spain's Golden Age dramatists, he was always very careful with his money, either out of a spirit of genuine meanness, or, more likely, because he had to pay dearly both for his complex personal life and for the upkeep of this relatively large building.

The Casa Museo Lope de Vega, after being closed for many years for further restoration, was finally re-opened in 1992: one of Madrid's greatest attractions, and a fascinating evocation of the Golden Age city, it is also a reminder of how much was lost by the destruction of the nearby house in which Cervantes spent the last years of his life. Formerly situated at the western end of the Calle Cervantes, at what is now No. 2, this had survived intact until as late as 1833, when it was pulled down despite the protests of Mesonero Romanos, who succeeded only in recording the site with the present plaque. Cervantes had moved from Valladolid to Madrid in 1606, following the Court, which supplied him with minor administrative posts. His Madrid years, as with those of Lope de Vega, were the most productive in his literary career, though they were also beset by financial problems and tainted by an unhappy marriage. In 1613 he published here his highly successful *Exemplary Novels*, and two years later brought out the second and greatest part of *Don Quixote*, after the success of the first part had encouraged a forger to write an unworthy continuation. (Cervantes was so popular that this second part was printed in the same year in Lisbon – the title page is shown overleaf – and the first part had been translated into English as early as 1612.) In the moving final pages the dying and repentant knight is finally cured of his fantastical delusions, and of

EL INGENIOSO
HIDALGO DON
QVIXOTEDELA
Mancha.

Compuesto por *Miguel de Ceruantes*
Saauedra.

EM LISBOA.

Impresso com lisença do Santo Officio por Iorge
Rodriguez. Anno de 1605.

his obsession with the courtly romances that Cervantes had so brilliantly parodied. It is therefore particularly ironic that the final year of Cervantes' own life was to be spent writing one such romance himself, *The Travails of Persiles and Sigismunda*, a work which appears to have been created in a spirit of pure escapism, the real world being now too hard for the ill, aged and near-destitute writer to bear. For many years he had suffered from a disease which could either have been diabetes or cirrhosis of the liver, and on Wednesday 20 April 1616, dictated, as the preface to his final work, what were to be the last of his words to have come down to us: 'My life is ending,' he addresses the reader, 'it will finish its course this Sunday at the latest; and I shall finish the race of life... Farewell, witticisms; farewell jests; farewell cheerful friends; for I am dying, and anxious to see you again soon, happy in the next life.'

The main entrance to Cervantes' house stood on the Calle del León, one block to the north of the former Mentidero de Representantes, a small square (now gone, but identifiable on Texeira) where all the people involved in Madrid's theatrical world of the 16th and 17th centuries would come to gossip and exchange opinions about the latest plays. The city's main theatres were to be found then, as they are now, just to the west of here, but before heading in this direction, we should walk north along the Calle del León towards Madrid's great literary and political institution of recent times, the Ateneo. The Ateneo Artístico, Científico y Literario, to use its full name, was founded in 1820 as a patriotic society devoted – like London's Royal Society – to the furtherment of the arts and sciences. The original institution was situated on the Calle de Montera, but, because of its Liberal politics was soon closed down by Ferdinand VII. On the initiative of Mesonero Romanos and other members of his intellectual circle, it was reopened in 1835 on the Calle del Prado, the street where most of the writers' cafés of the district were once concentrated. The present building, at No. 21, dates back to the 1880's and is far more impressive inside than its modest exterior suggests. Past the main entrance we ascend a grand flight of steps and enter a world darkened and impregnated with the smoke of over a century of Spanish intellectual life. Long rows of portraits of those who have contributed to this life run down the walls of a narrow gallery which disappears into the gloom, while, on the floor above, one of Spain's finest libraries spreads out from two fine turn-of-the-century halls into the surrounding, greying corridors. With luck we might persuade the porter to let us into the vast, oval Lecture Theatre, where, in a setting of faded splendour, so many of Spain's writers have made their literary début with a reading from their work.

III. The Plaza de Santa Ana West of the Ateneo we soon find ourselves drawn into the labyrinth of bars and restaurants that radiates from the Plaza de Santa Ana. The second street to our right as we walk up the Calle del Prado is the dark, narrow but nocturnally animated Calle de Echegaray, the name of which was given to a novel of 1950 by Marcial Suárez, who claimed in the preface to this that the numerous incidental characters featured in his episodic story were largely based on people he had met here. At No. 7 is one of the more popular of this street's bars, the Venencia, a cramped Andalucían establishment unchanged in its decor since the 1920's, with walls layered with grease and torn bullfight posters, and large oak barrels from which sherry is served, accompanied always by olives. A much smarter but less friendly bar, at the corner of the Calles Echegaray and Manuel Fernández y González, is the recently restored Los Grabieles, which is worth entering purely to see the superlative ceramic decorations inside, among which is an enormous reproduction of Velázquez's painting of The Topers. Walking west down the Calle Manuel Fernández y González we pass further ceramic scenes of the 1920's decorating both the exterior and interior of Viva Madrid, a bar which has now been taken over almost entirely by young tourists. Eventually we emerge at the southern end of the Calle del Príncipe, a street especially rich in literary associations, many of these being linked to its numerous, luxuriously appointed shops of the turn of the century. The famous wine shop of Pecastaing was frequented by both Hemingway and the Nobel Prize-winning dramatist Jacinto Benavente, while the elegant optician's shop known as Villasante was the scene early last century of literary tertulias presided over by the novelist Pío Baroja, seen opposite in his Basque beret. The now vanished café of El Gato Negro – where Benavente held court, and where the renowned Catalan painter Santiago Rusiñol could often be seen – was also on this street, and was an especially lively cultural haunt, deriving much of its popularity from its position next to the Teatro de la Comedia. Many of Benavente's plays were premièred at this theatre, a grand if rather decayed structure of the 1870's which was also where Pérez Galdós tried in later life to establish himself as a dramatist, enjoying in the process several popular triumphs but no lasting successes.

The name of the Calle del Príncipe is taken from the most important of Madrid's Golden Age theatres, the Corral del Príncipe, which was situated at the lower end of the street, on the site now occupied by the Teatro Español. Up to the late 16th century plays in Madrid had largely been performed in improvised, open-air settings in the yards or *corrales* of houses, the more distinguished spectators watching the action from the windows or balconies. The Corral del Príncipe, which was founded in 1583, was one of the first of the city's theatres specially built for the purpose, and, while emulating the layout of the original corrales, was probably roofed, and came in later years to acquire such attributes of a Court theatre as a proscenium arch, drop curtains and painted scenery. (It is visible, but not very distinctive, in the Texeira detail on page 116.) The passion for drama during this period was quite remarkable, and foreign visitors to Madrid were struck by the fact that plays were put on during the day-time, with people rushing in to reserve the best places as soon as the theatres opened their doors at twelve o'clock. A court official, aided by bailiffs, was responsible for maintaining order and deciding when the plays should begin, but chaos and long delays seemed to precede each performance, with fights invariably breaking out, caused either by impatient members of the audience, rivalries between

dramatists, people trying to get in without paying, or men being prevented from making their way to the actresses' dressing-rooms, which were strictly out of bounds. The spectators who were most feared by performers and playwrights alike were the so-called 'musketeers', a motley crowd made up largely of craftsmen and tradesmen, who stood in between the rows of seats at the front of the auditorium and the women's gallery at the back. Known also as 'the people's jury', they determined the success or failure of a particular production, and came to the theatre armed with rattles, whistles and bells. The author most pilloried by this jury was the hunch-backed, pigeon-chested and Mexican-born Ruiz de Alarcón, whose misanthropy and physical deformities earned him widespread hatred and ridicule, as well as some of the most brutal satires in 17th-century literature. Lope de Vega, a man much-loved by the Madrid public, employed friends of his among the musketeers to whistle every time one of Alarcón's plays was performed.

The Corral del Príncipe was demolished in the early 18th-century to make way for the more sedate Teatro del Príncipe, which saw performances of several of the charming one-act comedies or *sainetes* of Ramón de la Cruz, Spain's answer to Goldoni or Marivaux. In 1802 the building was replaced by the present Teatro Español, which, though remodelled inside after a recent fire, retains a neoclassical façade by Juan de Villanueva that features a large pediment and a giant order of pilasters. Many of the great classics of modern Spanish drama have had their premières here, including García Lorca's controversial study of a childless woman, *Yerma*, at the first performance of which, in 1934, right-wing hecklers taunted the author and principle actress with shouts of 'queer!' and 'lesbian!' The theatre had first come to prominence during the Romantic era, supporting that brilliant generation of writers who had been nurtured at the adjoining Café del Príncipe.

A reconstruction of this celebrated basement café, which had been known generally as 'El Parnasillo' or 'The Little Parnassus', can be found in the new building attached to the northern side of the theatre. Mesonero Romanos had described the place as dark and poky, without any fancy decoration or even comfort, its principal furnishings being a dozen pine tables painted a dark chocolate colour. Before being taken up by Madrid's Bohemia, the establishment was always half empty, patronised largely by a group of retired diplomats, who came here every night out of habit and inertia, apparently oblivious to the poorly-washed glasses and cups in which their coffee or chocolate was served, and even to the rats who fed off the clumps of grass growing between the cracks of the unwashed floor. According to Mesonero Romanos, it was precisely these 'negative conditions' that later made the café so appealing to young artists and intellectuals, all of whom came to feel far more at home here than they did at more luxurious establishments. But no-one perhaps would have predicted what an enormous impact the place would have on the cultural and intellectual development of Spain in the early 19th century. 'From here,' wrote Mesonero Romanos, 'from this miserable little room, the renaissance of our modern theatre was initiated; from here emerged the *Ateneo*; from here the briliant *Liceo Artístico*, the *Instituto* and various other literary societies; from here the renewal of the universities and the daily press; from here the parliamentary orators and fiery tribunes who brought about a complete transformation of our society.'

The Teatro Español faces the Plaza de Santa Ana, the verdant space created by Joseph Bonaparte's demolition of the Carmelite convent of Santa Ana. Despite its trees and 19th-century statue to Calderón de la Barca, it has about as much beauty as does London's Leicester Square, to which it can also be compared in being at the centre of Madrid's entertainment world. In the harsh light of day it is the visual equivalent of a hang-over, a confused medley of architectural styles, with the odd, painfully discordant note, and a general air of seediness. By night, however, the selective lighting, together with the ceaseless vitality of its nocturnal crowds, help you to forget the square's uglier aspects, particularly if you have had a few drinks yourself. The oldest and best known of its bars is the Cervezería Alemana, a beautifully preserved establishment founded in

1904 on the the southern side of the square. Its spacious main room, with its wooden tables and panelling, was popular with many Spanish writers in the early years of this century, including members of the Generation of 98 such as the dramatist Valle-Inclán. However, to the numerous foreigners who come here today, this is essentially Hemingway's bar, and indeed there is a story of two young American women who were trying to imagine what the place was like in Hemingway's day when, to their considerable surprise, they were approached by none other than the bearded old writer himself. The various paintings and photographs of bull-fights that line the bar's walls are an indication of what particularly attracted Hemingway to this place. It was a favourite haunt of bull-fighters, among whom were such luminaries of the art as Bienvenida, Manolete and Luis Miguel Dominguín (seen in the photograph on page 261). This is traditionally the bull-fighters' area of Madrid, and most of those who come to fight here continue to be put up at the Hotel Victoria, on the western side of the square. A plaque to Manolete has recently

been placed by the entrance to this tall and splendid hotel of the second decade of the last century, the architecture of which, with its rows of glazed balconies, seems more suited to a sea-side town in northern Spain than to the centre of Madrid.

At the northwestern corner of the square ceramic decorations of particular lushness cover the exterior of the Villa Rosa, now closed but once known for its flamenco shows or *tablaos*. From here we should head west down the tiny Calle de Alvarez Gato, where there is a bar displaying on the outside two distorting mirrors of concave and convex shape. They were mentioned by the fantastical Galician author Valle-Inclán (pictured opposite, minus the arm he lost in a ridiculous duel), who once wrote that 'absurdity is reality reflected in the mirrors of the alley of the Cat.' The bar itself, called Las Bravas, though ugly, is of interest in having been the birthplace of one of Spain's most popular bar-snacks of today, the so-called *patatas a las bravas*, a patented dish of cubed, deep-fried potatoes covered in a spicy tomato sauce. Should you wish to try out these potatoes at their source, I strongly recommend you not to observe the culinary proceedings too closely, for you might well be repelled by the sight of the dark-pink sauce oozing out from a metallic hose like a flow of lava. Diced pigs ears, or *orejas*, are also served here in this way, but this is an experience only for the very brave.

The 'alley of the Cat' will lead us out on to the Calle de la Cruz, at a point where once was situated the first of Madrid's permanent theatres, the Corral de la Cruz. Though it never enjoyed quite the same popularity as its main rival, the Corral del Príncipe, it was greatly favoured by Philip II, whose affair with one of its star-actresses, María Calderón (La Calderona), resulted in an illegitimate son, John of Austria. The attraction of this long and narrow street today lies mainly in its traditional shops, the most interesting of which is Seseña, at No. 23. Founded as a tailor's shop in 1902 by Santos Seseña Rojas, it was later transformed by his son Tomás into an establishment specializing exclusively in Spanish capes. Tomás was one of the great personalities of Madrid, and it was probably he who thought up the witty

promotional ruse of placing, one cold winter's day, a cape on the shoulders of the city's scantily-clad statue of the goddess Cybele. He earned for the shop the reputation of being the leading place in Spain for capes, but was a poor businessman owing to his habit of presenting these capes as gifts to his many famous friends. The interior of the shop is filled with photographs of caped celebrities, many of whose signatures and comments are inscribed in a series of bound books recording the names of all the customers. Among these names are such diverse personalities as Luis Buñuel, Andrés Segovia, Gary Cooper, Liberace, and Paloma Picasso, the last of these opining that capes 'make me feel so Spanish'. Spain, and Madrid in particular, is the last bastion in Europe of this age-old fashion, but these garments today are rarely worn in an everyday context, and are used instead mainly by those who wish to make a dramatic effect when going out to the opera or to some glittering social occasion. Perhaps the cape will enjoy a revival in popularity, for it is not just an elegant but also a practical fashion, and the shop manager of Seseña once gave me a demonstration of how it can be adapted to a variety of occasions, such as when standing in a crowded underground train.

South of the Calle de la Cruz is the Calle de Las Huertas, which runs east all the way down to the Paseo del Prado, forming an almost indigestible succession of bars and restaurants. A short architectural detour down the street could be made to see two fine buildings representing the stylistic extremes of the Spanish 18th century. The first of these, at No. 13, is a palace of 1734 by Pedro de Ribera, containing on its eastern façade an excellent example of his characteristically elaborate portals; meanwhile, further down the street, at No. 28, is Juan de Villanueva's impressively austere block of the Royal Academy of History, a brick and granite structure dating from the time of Charles III. We return to the western end of the street, where, on the Plaza del Angel, there is one of Madrid's leading jazz venues, the Café Central. Immediately to the south of here, on the short Calle de San Sebastián, a plaque marks the building which during Charles III's reign housed the Fonda de San Sebastián. This inn had been a great meeting-place for Spanish intellectuals of the Enlightenment such as Jovellanos (whose famously melancholic portrait by Goya is in the Prado) and Cadalso, and as such had given Madrid a foretaste of the literary cafés of the following century. As an appropriate farewell to the Barrio de Los Literatos, we should pay a brief and purely sentimental visit to the church of San Sebastián, on the opposite side of the street. The building itself, brutally restored after 1936, is grimly neoclassical, but the list of writers associated with the place is quite formidable, as a glance at the memorial plaques displayed in the south transept will testify. Lope de Vega, Ramón de la Cruz, Echegaray and Jacinto Benavente were among those who were baptized in the church, while Larra, Gustavo Bécquer, Zorilla, and Valle-Inclán were all married here. As for the deaths recorded in the parish register, these include Cervantes, Ruiz de Alarcón, Vélez de Guevara, and Espronceda, in addition to the architects José de Churriguera, Ventura Rodríguez and Juan de Villanueva. And this is where Lope de Vega was buried, though it goes without saying that his remains have since been lost, criminally mislaid – as Mesonero Romanos would have it – in the course of one of of those periodic changes of tomb to which Spain's dead have so often been subject.

IV. South to the Rastro Pérez Galdós wrote that the church of San Sebastián had two distinct faces, one of which looked up to the elegant, commercial district of the Plaza del Angel, the other down to the poorer quarters which lay below the Calle Cañizares. The descent south from the church is both a social and literal one, and some idea of the different and traditionally less sophisticated world into which we are now entering will be had the moment we cross the busy and ugly Calle de Atocha. The first part of *Don Quixote* was printed in 1605 at a building situated at No. 87, but a more telling indication of the street's status today is the presence at No. 24 of an establishment claiming to be the world's largest sex shop. The Calle Cañizares leads south to the Calle de la Magdalena, beyond which, at the beginning of the Calle Olivar, is a basement bar of extreme tackiness called Candela, which only begins to liven up in the early hours of the morning, when its largely gypsy clientèle burst suddenly into flamenco song and dance. Heading west along the Calle de La Magdalena we pass another outstanding portal by Pedro de Ribera (at No. 10) before emerging at the Plaza de Tirso de Molina, a noisy, triangular-shaped square marking the site of a Mercedarian monastery which was demolished after 1836. A statue of the minister who had confiscated this and other Church properties in that year, Juan Mendizábal, once adorned the square's unkempt, verdant centre, but it was replaced after the Civil War by the present monument to the former monastery's most distinguished son, Fray Gabriel Téllez, who is better known under his theatrical pseudonym of Tirso de Molina. Tirso de Molina entered the Mercedarian Order in 1600, when he was seventeen, and remained with it until his death in 1648, his activities as a playwright being combined with more worthy tasks such as writing up the official chronicle of his Order. A romantic and recent tradition believes Tirso to have been the illegitimate son of the Duke of Osuna, but his life seems to have been disappointingly free of scandal or gossip. The one major set-back in an otherwise smooth and successful career occured in 1625 when the Council of Castile admonished him for depicting vice too vividly on the stage, and threatened him with excommunication if he wrote secular plays again. As a playwright his output was very modest in comparison to that of Lope de Vega, since he was the author of a mere 400 works. Of these only *The Trickster of Seville* is widely known outside of Spain, not so much because of the play itself, but because of its protagonist, Don Juan Tenorio, whose cynical seductions were to inspire countless later writers and become an integral part of the Romantic image of this country.

One of the many dark, narrow streets running south of the Plaza de Tirso is the Calle de San Pedro Martír, where the young Pablo Picasso stayed at No. 5 in 1897 and 1898, this rather short-lived association with Madrid being marked on the house today with a ludicrous series of ceramic reproductions of some of his more famous works. Three blocks to the west of here, at No. 13 in the parallel Calle de Mesón de Paredes, is the delightful Taberna de Antonio Sánchez, another of Madrid's historic taverns, this one dating back to 1830. It owes its current name to a famous bullfighter, who bought the establishment in 1920, following his retirement. Sánchez was also a painter of some talent, and the dark-panelled walls of this cosy tavern – which has been virtually unchanged since his day – feature a number of his portraits of matadors, set alongside other bull-fighting souvenirs, including a large trophy of a bull's head. The artist who had taught Sánchez was Ignacio Zuloaga, an enormously successful painter who had been a close and influential friend of Picasso in the 1890's, but was later to become associated with the academic art of the Franco period. The back room of the tavern was where Zuloaga's last exhibition was held, and a plaque recording this has been placed above the marble table where the artist always used to sit, surrounded by his friends and admirers. A vivid picture of the tavern in Zuloaga's day can be had from reading Díaz-Cañabate's highly entertaining *Historia de una*

taberna, which can still be bought here. Among the aspects of tavern life that he described were the bread fritters or *torrijas* that were at one time common to most of the city's wine bars, and were supposedly the only sweet food that hardened drinkers could tolerate. Sánchez's wife was renowned for her fritters, and, in deference to her, this dying gastronomic tradition has been maintained in the present-day establishment, whose owner, incidentally, is another retired bull-fighter.

A short walk west of the Plaza de Tirso de Molina will take us to the large and depressing church of San Isidro, which served provisionally as Madrid's cathedral from 1886, when the city was finally given its own diocese. The building has its origins in a Jesuit College of the early 17th century, but was remodelled by Ventura Rodríguez in the late 18th century, following Charles III's expulsion of the Jesuits and the subsequent transference to this church of the relics of St. Isidro. The grey and grimy barrel-vaulted interior need not detain us long, and indeed the building's sole architectural distinction is its stately twin-towered façade, which was conceived so as to make an impression even when seen sideways from the once narrow street which it faces, the Calle de Toledo.

The façade of San Isidro is also the sole remaining monument of interest along the northern half of a street which the well-travelled Pérez Galdós considered to be one of the most beautiful in the world. When this part of the street was widened at the end of the 19th century, it lost the magnificent late 15th-century monastery of 'La Latina', which stood just to the south of San Isidro. Below this, on the Plaza de la Cebada, there was also an outstanding mid-19th-century market hall, but this pioneering ironwork structure was pulled down in the 1960's to make way for the present concrete building which houses Madrid's largest food market. Before becoming a market square, the Plaza de La Cebada had taken over from the Plaza Mayor as a place of public executions, and Larra could not pass here without thinking of the 'blood which has stained this square and will stain it again'. In Galdós' time the whole street was red, though not, as the novelist hastened to add, 'on account of the slaughter-house or of the blood from revolutionaries, but rather as a result of the painted signs of the eighty taverns which can be found here.' To Galdós the beauty of the Calle de Toledo lay essentially in its bustling life, which is also the main attraction of the streets lying to the east.

At the Plaza de Cascorro, which lies immediately below San Isidro, begins the celebrated Sunday flea-market of the Rastro, its stalls running all the way south down the sloping Calle de Curtidores and spilling over into the adjoining streets. All those who have written on Madrid since the last century have attempted to evoke the life and character of the Rastro, and Ramón Goméz de La Serna, with his characteristic effusiveness, felt obliged to dedicate a whole book to the market. Among the more successful descriptions was that of Arturo Barea, who came here frequently as a child in the years before the First World War, and remembered the whole district (which must then have looked just as it does opposite) pervaded by 'an acrid smell of rotting flesh' emanating from the tanners' workshops

that gave the Calle de Curtidores its name. On that street, Barea wrote, you could buy everything 'except what you set out to buy', and then proceeded at great length to list the diverse goods on sale, which ranged from 'river crayfish wriggling in dripping mud' to 'stuffed cats' and 'outworn files with iron dust choking their ridges'. In his day all of Madrid walked about the Rastro on Sunday mornings, and a visit to the market still remains a popular Sunday activity, in particular between the hours of twelve and two. Nonetheless it is already going the way of London's Portobello, and though there is still much life to be seen here, the bargains are fewer and the overall character much smarter.

V. El Avapiés Unless we are visiting this area on a Sunday, we should descend south from the Plaza de Cascorro, not on the Calle de Curtidores, but on the yet narrower and more attractive Calle de Embajadores. One of the finest of the city's baroque churches, San Cayetano, stands near the top of this street, its twin-towered brick façade distinguished by a wealth of its sculpture and ornamentation. José de Churriguera, whose family name is frequently invoked to describe the decorative excesses of the Spanish baroque, was involved in the design of this church, though the actual façade is more likely to have been the work of Pedro de Ribera, an architect who was more genuinely 'Churrigueresque' than Churriguera himself. Badly gutted during the Civil War, the relatively simple interior has now been almost entirely rebuilt. On the opposite side of the street, at No. 26, is a well-preserved old bar and wine shop, its interior lined with tiles, and its wooden frontage displaying a collection of bottles of venerable antiquity. Further down, at No. 31, we pass another engaging survival of the past in the form of a barber's shop with a ceramic decoration outside of a man having his hair cut. Craftsmen's shops, a lively food market, and cramped and decayed 19th-century buildings on the point of demolition, are among the features that we notice as we continue our descent. At the very bottom of the hill we might well mistake the large neoclassical building to our left for a palace, but in fact it was constructed in 1790 as a distillery. In 1809 it was converted into a tobacco factory, and it continues to function as such today, making it the oldest such factory still working in Europe. This building has a fascinating history, principally on account of its large female work force, which in the late 19th century made up almost a fifth of Madrid's working population. The so-called *cigarreras*, whose job was often proudly inherited over generations, enjoyed a reputation for their solidarity as a group, strength of character, relative freedom from the social constaints of the time, and their genius for organizing themselves. They were responsible for such social reforms as the instigation of special schools and crèches for their children, and it is even said that the pioneering Spanish trade unionist Pablo Iglesias formulated his plans for a worker's union after attending one of their strike meetings. Certainly the cigarreras contributed greatly to the renowned colour and vitality of this part of Madrid, and their flamboyant behaviour and refusal to be bullied around by the authorities were a cause of both admiration and scandal. A large veterinary college, attended mainly by men, once stood on the opposite side of the street, but it had to be removed to another district in consequence of the explosive combination of students and cigarreras.

The back of the tobacco factory overlooks the southern end of the long Calle de Mesón de Paredes, where we find, one block to the north, a large and dilapidated square featuring on one side the overgrown ruins of an 18th-century church and college destroyed during the Civil War. Facing the ruins is 'La Corrala', a tall and lone survival of a traditional Spanish tenement building of the early 19th century. Its balconies, supported by both wooden and metal pillars, would originally have looked out over a yard, but in their restored state of today, are now exposed to the square, together with their long and colourful lines of washing. A plaque now placed in front of the building records that it was in a crowded dwelling such as this, subjected to all the gossip of neighbours chatting to each other from the balconies, that Spain's popular singer of the turn of the century, 'La Revoltosa', was born and brought up. The Calle Sombrerete leads from here to the Plaza de Lavapiés, but we could take instead the parallel street to the north, the Calle de Caravaca, where, at No. 10, a wall with cheerful painted decorations marks the entance of a well-known pastry and liquor shop known as Los Madroños. The owner of this simple and modestly furnished establishment, Cruz Palomo, managed in 1941 to create a tasty liquor out of the insipid orange-red fruit from the *Arbutus* or Strawberry Tree, a tree which is normally grown purely for decorative purposes. He called this liquor 'the true liquor of Madrid', for the Arbutus is the tree that features in the city's coat of arms, together with a contented bear licking it as if it were a giant ice-cream cone. A quick visit to this shop will thus give us a taste of the real Madrid, and more than just a literal one if we are lucky enough to meet the aged Palomo himself, a legend of his barrio. Newspaper cuttings featuring interviews with him are pasted on the walls, and, according to one of these, he is someone who loves reading, but only 'books that recall the past'; he has no interest in the future.

Entering the Plaza de Lavapiés, we reach the heart of the district known traditionally as 'El Avapiés', a district which has preserved a very human scale, and which evokes so many memories of old Madrid that its name has been given to a publishing house which deals exclusively with the history of this city. The square itself, from which radiate tightly packed rows of 19th-century residential blocks, has little of specific interest to attract the vistor, but has always had sentimental associations for those who have come to Madrid in search of the colourful types who inhabit Goya's world. This was the main haunt of the low-class dandies known generally in Spain as *majos*, but who were more usually referred to in Madrid as *manolos*. The use of the word manolo in relation to these dandies is in itself very telling of the history of this square, for it derives from the habit of converted Jews of calling their eldest son Manuel. Until 1492 the Plaza de Lavapiés formed the nucleus of Madrid's Jewish ghetto, the synagogue of which was situated on the southern side of the square, on a site now occupied by the Teatro Olimpia.

The world of the so-called *manolería* belongs

today to an ever more distant past, and one that was always distorted by legend. In contrast a remarkably life-like and still recognizable picture of Lavapiés emerges from the pages of Arturo Barea's wonderful autobiographical trilogy, *The Forging of a Rebel* (1941-44). This great work, which appeared in English translation before it came out in Spanish, was written in exile in England, where Barea had to take refuge on account of his political affiliations during the Civil War. The knowledge that he would probably never return to Spain seems to have lent an added intensity to his vision of Madrid, in particular of Lavapiés, which was the domain of his childhood. Brought up in a garret by a poor widowed mother who supported her four children by washing clothes in the river Manzanares (see p. 21), Barea certainly had an early taste of life in the raw. He came to think of Madrid as a social ladder of which the highest rung was represented by the Royal Palace, 'with its gates open to plumed helmets and diamond-spangled *décolletés*'. Lavapiés, however, was by no means at the bottom of this ladder, for below it, near the Manzanares,

lay a semi-wasteland where gypsies lived surrounded by rubbish and 'evil-smelling trickles', an area 'where the city cast its ash and spume' and which was known by the ironic name of 'the New World'. To Barea, Lavapiés was a frontier district between poverty and wealth, populated both by those on the way down the social ladder and those on their way up: it was 'the pointer of the scales, the crucial point between existence and non-existence.' As a child he found himself constantly ascending and descending the hill which led between the Royal Palace down to the New World, and in so doing developed his acute social conscience of later years. Lavapiés, that delicate balance between these two extremes of Madrid society, was to be a formative influence of a most lasting kind:

There I learned all I know, the good and the bad, to pray to God and to curse Him, to hate and to love, to see life crude and bare as it is, and to feel an infinite longing to scale the next step upwards and to help all others to scale it.

WALK 3

The Royal Core

THE DESCALZAS REALES *to* THE ENCARNACIÓN

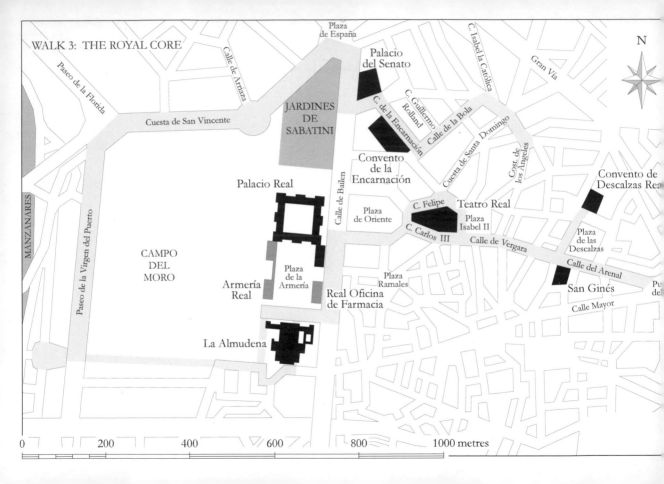

WALK 3: THE ROYAL CORE

N

Plaza de España

Palacio del Senato

C. Isabel la Católica

Gran Via

Paseo de la Florida

Calle de Arriaza

JARDINES DE SABATINI

C. Guillermo Rolland

C. de la Encarnación

Calle de la Bola

Cuesta de San Vincente

Convento de la Encarnación

Cuesta de Santa Domingo

Cost. de los Angeles

Convento de Descalzas Rea

Palacio Real

Calle de Bailen

Plaza de Oriente

C. Felipe

Teatro Real

Plaza Isabel II

Plaza de las Descalzas

MANZANARES

CAMPO DEL MORO

C. Carlos III

Calle de Vergara

Paseo de la Virgen del Puerto

Plaza de la Armería

Plaza Ramales

Calle del Arenal

Armería Real

Real Oficina de Farmacia

San Ginés

Pu de

La Almudena

Calle Mayor

0   200   400   600   800   1000 metres

WALK 3

The Royal Core

THE DESCALZAS REALES *to* THE ENCARNACIÓN

After having made the descent down to Lavapiés, it is perhaps only fair now to take the reader up to the highest rung of Arturo Barea's social ladder and enter the Royal Palace, where, 'from the marble galleries guarded by halberdiers' the young writer watched 'the pageant of the royalty, the princes and grandees of Spain'. To include the palace at this stage of the book is also to take the reader beyond the dirty, chaotically developed Madrid which had been left by the Hapsburgs, and witness the beginnings of the elegant transformation wrought by the first of the Bourbons. The Royal Palace is a world in its own right, and in the course of this chapter we will not stray far from its sight, concentrating on a small but exclusive area of Madrid that counts as its other main attractions two convents of royal foundation.

I. The Descalzas Reales Once again, and not for the last time, I propose that we begin our walk at the Puerta del Sol, more specifically at its northwestern corner, the start of a busy commercial avenue, the Calle del Arenal. This gently descending street marks the site of a fast-flowing stream which in the middle ages ran outside the city walls, and, in times of drought, dried up to form the area of sandy ground which was to give the future street its name. Already a lively thoroughfare in Hapsburg times, it acquired an added importance under the Bourbons, becoming in the course of the 19th century a direct link between the Puerta del Sol and the newly created Plaza de Oriente and Teatro Real.

The great bulk of the Teatro Real looms in the distance as soon as we enter the street, but, long before coming to it, we pass on our left the former Teatro Eslava, which was founded in 1872 as a lightweight, popular alternative to the aristocratic opera house at the other end of the Arenal. Specializing at first in light operas and zarzuelas, it experienced a change of artistic direction after 1916, when it became a home to the theatre company of Martínez Sierra. Martínez Sierra, who was both a playwright and director, managed in the course of three years to turn the Eslava into the most innovative theatre in Madrid, despite its small stage and inadequate equipment. In 1919, always on the lookout for new and exciting talent, Martínez Sierra commissioned for his theatre a work from the young García Lorca, a budding poet but as yet untried as a playwright. Lorca responded with a play on the unpromising theme of the amorous misfortunes of cockroaches, *The Butterfly's Evil Spell*, and this was premièred here on 22 March 1920. The result was a cat-calling, foot-stamping fiasco, and one member of the audience even brought the whole house down with laughter by suggesting loudly that one of the protagonists should be put down with Zotal, a well known brand of insecticide. Later in the decade Martínez Sierra's directorship of the Eslava came to an end following a real-life drama in the foyer of his theatre, when two of his authors got into a serious argument which culminated in one of them being shot dead. The Eslava is now a night club.

Just beyond the Eslava, past a tiny alley blocked by a well-known second-hand book-stall, is the porticoed main entrance to the church of San Ginés. Though dating back to shortly after the Christian conquest of Madrid, and as such one of the first churches to be founded in Madrid, this sober structure in stone and brick was entirely rebuilt in 1643 and restored the following century. Quevedo was baptized in the church, Lope de Vega was married here, and the celebrated polyphonist Tomás Luis de Victoria – who lived in the neighbouring street now named after him – was buried somewhere in the parish. All this information can be gleaned from a plaque underneath the portico, to the right of which – and completely separate from the main body of the church – is a chapel containing a fine painting by El Greco of the *Expulsion from the Temple*, another version of which is in London's National Gallery.

Further art treasures await us in the nearby Convent of the Descalzas Reales (Barefoot Royal Sisters), which can be reached from San Ginés by crossing the Arenal and walking north up the short Calle de San Martín. The convent's austere walls of brick and rubble-work conceal an interior of fabulous wealth and even a large orchard, incongruously situated within sight of the ugly modern department stores that make up the crowded shopping district just to the north of the Puerta del Sol. The building occupies the site of a medieval palace, which had belonged originally to the kings of Castile, but had later come into the hands of Alonso Gutiérrez, treasurer to the Emperor Charles V. Charles V's younger daughter, Joan of Austria, had been born in this palace, and it was she who later decided to have the building transformed into a convent for nuns of royal blood, entrusting the work in 1556 to the first architect of the Escorial, Juan Bautista de Toledo. The whole complex, which was thoroughly restored in the late 18th century by Diego de Villanueva, was magnificently endowed as a result of the numerous donations by the distinguished women who have resided here, among whom were the Infanta Isabel Clara Eugenia and her sister Marguerite of Austria. In recent times the Franciscan nuns who now occupy the convent turned part of the building into an evocative museum, which in 1988 received the Council of Europe award for best European Museum of the Year. The resulting publicity had the effect of making this hitherto little-visited place one of the main tourist attractions of the capital, but, having achieved this, the nuns then decided to claim back a section of the museum for their own purposes. The reduced museum of today has nonetheless a sufficient amount on show to satisfy most people, particularly those who do not relish obligatory guided tours, which are led here by the elegantly jacketed and officious-looking staff of the Patrimonio Nacional, the body responsible for the upkeep of Spain's royal monuments.

The tour of the Descalzas Reales begins with

a magnificent staircase hall, the walls and ceiling of which were decorated in the mid-17th century with illusionistic frescoes attributed to Claudio Coello and Ximenez Donoso, and featuring a delightful scene of Philip IV and his family staring down at the spectator from a fictive balcony. The staircase leads eventually to the upper cloister, around which are a series of small chapels founded by the royal nuns of the 17th and 18th centuries on being received into the order. Every detail of the sumptuous decoration of these baroque chapels will be outlined for us by our guide, but our lasting impression will probably be of the numerous sculpted images of the baby Jesus resting on a skull, an iconographic motif peculiar to Spanish art of this period and symbolizing the triumph of life over death. One of the chapels originally boasted a painting of the Annunciation by the Florentine artist Fra Angelico, but this was later removed to the Prado and replaced by a crude 19th-century version of the subject. It is not until we reach the former nuns' dormitory, which lies off the upper cloister, that we come to the most outstanding of the

convent's treasures – a series of Rubens tapestries presented by Isabel Clara Eugenia in 1627. Representing *The Triumph of the Eucharist*, and based on vivid oil sketches that can be seen today in the Prado, these are compositions of extraordinary energy framed by massive *salomonicas* or twisted columns comparable to those in Raphael's famous tapestry of *The Judgement of Solomon* in the Vatican. The remaining part of the convent includes the cell of Marguerite of Austria (complete with her sandals, crucifix and other belongings), and a charming nuns' choir decorated with quaintly unsophisticated wall paintings of scenes from the life of St. Francis. Numerous portraits (mainly school works) of members of the Hapsburg family give the guide an opportunity to bore us with involved genealogical accounts, and there is also an inordinate number of polychromed devotional images of the Virgin of Sorrows by 17th-century artists such as Pedro de Mena and Luisa Roldán. The overall atmosphere of the convent is in the end more interesting than the specific detail, and the religious images drift through our consciousness as if they were the distant sounds of polyphonic music. At the very end of the tour is a small picture gallery, filled mainly with dubious attributions, but with a curious Bosch-inspired *Ship of Fools*, and a fascinating 17th-century Flemish work depicting Marguerite of Austria travelling with members of her court from Prague to Madrid.

II. Opera Back on the Calle del Arenal, and continuing to head west, we soon come out on to the verdant square named after Isabel II, a statue of whom stands under the shadow of the pompous neoclassical bulk of the Teatro Real or Opera House. The latter, begun during the reign of Ferdinand VII by a pupil of Juan de Villanueva, was not opened until 1850, the inaugural production being of Donizetti's opera *La Favorita*. Subsequently the Teatro Real played an important role in popularizing Verdi's works in Madrid, introduced this city in the 1870's to the music of Wagner, and brought over here early this century Diaghilev, Nijinsky and Stravinsky. The building itself, finally renovated after some long years, is a singularly top-heavy structure when seen from the Plaza de Isabel II, but has a more elegant western façade, which was designed by Isidro González Velázquez to harmonize with the grand Plaza de Oriente.

If we choose to approach the latter square along the northern side of the Teatro Real, we will pass to our right, at No. 6 Calle de Felipe V, the Taberna del Alabardero, which was the first of one of several wine bars and restaurants founded by Fray Luis Lezama, a well-known Madrid personality of today who manages to combine the life of a priest with that of a highly successful entrepreneur. This particular establishment, originally a sculptor's studio, was converted by Lezama into a cosy imitation of a turn-of-the-century tavern, comprising numerous, authentic furnishings of this period, together with photographs of Lezama himself, and newspaper cuttings outlining his triumphs in America. On the southeastern side of the Plaza de Oriente is another of Lezama's successful ventures, the lavishly neo-baroque Café de Oriente, a popular afternoon retreat for the city's wealthier families.

If on the other hand we are walking to the Plaza de Oriente along the southern side of the

Teatro Real, we might wish slightly to lengthen our journey by turning off on to the Calle Vergara. This is strictly a detour for devotees of the Romantic writer Larra (left), for we pass almost immediately to our left the Calle de Santa Clara, on which stands – at No. 3 – the corner house where the twenty-eight-year-old essayist and poet put an end to his life on 13 February 1837. His satirical articles, written under the pseudonym of 'Figaro', reveal a mordant wit, misanthropy and linguistic brilliance worthy of Quevedo, all directed against the Spanish way of life which he had hoped to reform. Social and political disillusion might have underlain his much-publicised suicide, but the more obvious motive was connected with his unhappy personal life. In 1829, to use his own words, he had married 'young and badly', and had later entered a stormy relationship with one Dolores Montijo, who, in the company of a woman friend, had been to see him at his house on the day of his death. The reasons for her unexpected visit were to demand a final end to their scandalous affair and to be given back her letters to him. At eight-thirty that evening, shortly after Dolores had left, Larra shot himself with one of the guns that now occupy a special show case in Madrid's Romantic Museum. His body was taken to the neighbouring church of Santiago, and laid out briefly in the crypt, where a plaque has recently been placed to his memory. His shocked friends from El Parnasillo, including Mesonero Romanos – who had spoken to him on the morning of that fateful day – rushed in disbelief to the church, and saw the body before it was removed for burial in the cemetery of San Justo. The enormous sense of loss occasioned by Larra's early death was to be felt acutely by later Spanish writers, including the Generation of 98, who on 13 February 1901, strewed violets on his grave and read out a speech referring to him as 'the guiding light of today's youth'. An empty seat was always to be kept for Larra at the celebrated tertulias organized by Gómez de la Serna in the 'sacred crypt' of El Pombo.

III. The Royal Palace The landscaped Plaza de Oriente, under which a car park has now been built, was created so as to provide a full and dramatic view of the immensely long Royal Palace, which, up to the early 19th century, was obscured on its eastern side by a collection of medieval houses, one of which had belonged to the painter Velázquez. The demolition of the houses was undertaken by Joseph Bonaparte, but work on the actual square was only begun under Ferdinand VII, and not completed until 1842, the final plan featuring the Teatro Real as the apex of two diagonally placed residential blocks, which today contain smart shops and cafés patronized mainly by coachloads of tourists. Among the statues that decorate the square is a series of larger-than-life-size figures of kings, who appear, in their present weathered and marooned state, to be distinctly unhappy not to be occupying the commanding position which had been planned for them on the parapet of the Royal Palace. In contrast, a magnificent addition to the gardens is the bronze equestrian portrait of Philip IV (overleaf) which rears up at the very centre of the square as if trying to make a leap towards the Teatro Real. The Count-Duke of Olivares, as part of his ambitious promotional

activities on behalf of Philip IV, had commissioned the work in 1636 from the Florentine baroque artist, Pietro Tacca, who in 1616 had made the statue of Philip III now in the Plaza Mayor. To begin with Tacca planned a similar equestrian statue, but Olivares was not satisfied with the preparatory model, and insisted that the horse should be rearing this time rather than walking. (Olivares himself was fond of this royal pose, as we see opposite in his portrait by Velázquez, engraved by Goya.) The technical problems of such a composition in bronze were enormous, and it has even be said that Tacca was forced to call on Galileo to help him solve them. The monument, finally completed in 1639, has the distinction of being the first of a rearing horse ever to be realized in bronze. It was originally placed at the Retiro, where Texeira drew it with great spirit (see page 179) and proudly labelled it *Cavallo de Bronze*.

The time has finally come to gather all our strength and prepare for our assault on the Royal Palace itself, a daunting prospect. A mere glance at this inhumanly proportioned structure is exhausting enough, and we might find it difficult to believe that the plan which the Italian architect Juvarra had drawn up for it in 1735 was far larger in scale. To have carried it out would in fact have necessitated relocating the building, and Philip V refused to allow this, insisting that the new palace should rise phoenix-like above the ashes of the old one, which in turn had evolved out of the foundations of the original Moorish Alcázar. The cliff-top site was a difficult and restricted one, and even the more modest plan eventually carried out by Sacchetti – who replaced Juvarra after the latter's death in 1736 – involved the construction of massive basements on the northern and western sides of the building. The Royal Palace was completed in 1764, the first monarch to move in here being Charles III. In the following century the life within the palace inspired an outstanding novel by Pérez Galdós, *La de Bringas* (translated in English as *The Spendthrifts*) which deals with the months leading up to the flight of Isabel II and her court in 1868. Ideally this should be read by anyone coming here, for it manages to give a human

153

dimension to what would otherwise be a monstrous pile of statistics. Characteristically for Galdós, the novel focuses not on the protagonists of the Court but on its minor functionaries, specifically on the spendthrift wife of a miserly worthy, Bringas. This couple are among the various pathetic inhabitants who live forgotten in modest apartments on the palace's upper floor, people whose petty preoccupations form an ironic contrast to the splendour of the setting below. Even the dreary rooms where they live are named by their academically-minded son after the famous apartments below, the drawing room for instance being called the Ambassadors' Room and the matrimonial bedroom the Sala de Gasparini. The sharpness of Galdós' social satire, and his exposure of the hollowness and grotesque farce of Court life, becomes particularly acute in a description of a charitable banquet put on by Isabel II for a carefully chosen group of beggars. The terrified expressions of the beggars as they are magnaminiously served their food becomes a great spectacle to the bejewelled members of the Court, but this scene acquires an added awfulness through being described through the eyes of the Bringas' epileptic daughter, who deliriously observes the proceedings from a second floor balcony: 'In the courtyard below the halberdiers were going round and round with their coachmen and lackeys: it was like a great casserole in which many-coloured human limbs were turning round and round in the heat.'

The public entrance to the Royal Palace is alongside the southern gates of that vast forecourt known as the Plaza Armería, a bare, paved space which manages even to reduce the daily throngs of tourists to the size of scurrying ants. On a hot, sunny day the glare from all the surrounding stone can be quite merciless, forcing you to shield your eyes as you walk across the desert-like forecourt towards the palace's south and principal façade (opposite). Behind this lie the main state rooms of the palace, and it is a sobering thought that the windows to the central Throne Room – where the Italian artist G.-B. Tiepolo painted one of the largest frescoes in his career – occupy a proportionally small area of the enormous façade. The exterior, comprising a rusticated basement

supporting a giant order of columns and pilasters, impresses more through its repetition of architectural elements than through any specific detail, though we should note at main floor level two statues portraying Atahualpa of Peru and Montezuma of Mexico. They form part of that series of statues representing kings of Spain and Spanish possessions intended mainly for the parapet of the palace. Not only was this pair among the few works in this series actually placed on the building, but they were also two of the earliest sculptures of Americans to have been executed in Europe.

Though Spain's royal family no longer live at the palace, they use it frequently for official functions, and I have arrived here many times to find the building unexpectedly closed. Furthermore the palace is always being restored, and many of the rooms that were once open to the public might be taken over after their restoration for the exclusive use of the royal family. A more appealing recent development is that one is no longer obliged to follow a guided tour, but can wander around at one's own pace, directed solely by the occasional arrow. The layout of the palace is straightforward, Sacchetti having rejected the many courtyards that had been planned by Juvarra in favour of a single, central courtyard, the northern side of which is dominated by the royal chapel. From the moment we ascend the monumental main staircase in the southern wing, the overall impression of the interior is of a great sea of different coloured marbles, highlighted by gilding and a wealth of frescoes. The general style is late baroque with incipient neoclassical elements, but there is also the occasional foray into the rococo, as in the magnificent Salón de Gasparini, where all the available space is covered with chinoiserie stucco-work, Chinese porcelains, and lush oriental silks. The setting of the palace is almost too rich for one to be able to give too much attention to the many paintings on display here, though it must be said that the majority are minor or school works. The outstanding exception is a late 15th-century polyptych by Juan de Flandes, a Flemish artist who was brought to Spain by Isabel la Católica. This particular work comprises fifteen small and exquisitely painted panels of the life of Christ, some of which feature landscape backgrounds that combine minute detailing with atmospheric depth.

From the miniature vision of Juan de Flandes, it is a great step to the world of gods, angels and mythological heroes who fly around the palace's numerous and splendid ceiling frescoes. Among the main artists responsible for these were the German-born court painter A. R. Mengs, Goya's teacher Francisco Bayeu, and the Neapolitan Corrado Giaquinto, who painted the luminous, Correggio-inspired ceilings in the royal chapel. But the most renowned of the decorators at work here was Giambattista Tiepolo, who had arrived in Madrid in June 1762, after a tiring journey from his native Venice and an apparent reluctance to come here in the first place. The sixty-six-year old artist was accompanied by his two artist sons, Giandomenico and Lorenzo, but had left his wife and remaining family back in Italy. Early biographers of Tiepolo, in a desperate attempt to give some spice to a life which is almost entirely free of anecdote, have absurdly speculated that the artist had come to Spain with a gondolier's young and beautiful daughter. There is slightly more basis to the stories that Tiepolo's stay in Spain was beset by a ferocious rivalry with Mengs, though it is highly unlikely that the German painter had ever planned the attack recounted by legend, in which he lay in wait up a tree for his Venetian colleague with a group of henchmen. One of the tree's branches is said to have broken, throwing Mengs down a few feet in front of the nonplussed Tiepolo, who with characteristic munificence, reacted by having his injured rival immediately taken to hospital. The one certainty about Tiepolo's years in Spain is that they were not the spectacular conclusion to a glorious career that they might have been. The Throne Room ceiling, which he completed in 1764, portrays the grandiose theme of *The Triumph of the Spanish Monarchy*, but, for all its splendour and colour, lacks the painterly conviction of his earlier apotheoses, largely because of an increased reliance on studio hands, but also perhaps because the values that it represented were becoming increasingly difficult to sustain in

a world already touched by the Enlightenment. The artist undertook two further ceilings for the palace (in the Guardroom and so-called *Saleta*), and then, instead of returning home to Venice, asked Charles III if he and his family could stay on in the country; this was probably a reluctant acknowledgment that, in the changing social and artistic climate of the time, to work for the Spanish royal family was now the most he could hope for. He was subsequently commissioned to paint some canvases for the Royal Chapel at Aranjuez, but the finished works, some of the most emotional and moving of his career, did not apparently appeal to the church authorities, much to the consternation of the artist, who died suddenly in Madrid on 27 March 1770. His tomb in the church of San Martín was later demolished and the Aranjuez paintings dispersed, only two of them remaining in Spain (in the Prado). The sketch for one of them, reproduced here, portrays the subject of *St Francis receiving the stigmata* with both peculiar pathos and an emphasis on such simple homely details as the wickerwork mat on which the saint sits.

If we are still capable of standing on our feet after leaving the Royal Palace, we might wish to vist two other places on the Plaza Armería. One of these, on the eastern side of the forecourt, is the Pharmaceutical Museum, which incorporates the contents of a pharmacy founded by Philip II in 1594, as well as numerous elegant furnishings and furniture from the 18th and 19th centuries. Opposite this, suspended above the Casa de Campo, is the Royal Armoury, which is said to be the finest of its kind in the world. Collections of armour generally make for rather heavy viewing, and this particular one could well have benefited from the eccentric atmosphere of, say, Madrid's Army Museum. Nevertheless the sheer historical importance of the objects here – which range from El Cid's sword to Philip IV's coat of armour – amply makes up for the general dullness of the display. Of especial interest to art historians, and a valuable prelude to a visit to the Prado, is the coat of armour which was both worn by Charles V at the Battle of Mühlberg, and painted by Titian in his famous equestrian portait of the Emperor.

Immediately on leaving the Plaza de la Armería, we find ourselves facing the recently consecrated but unininspiring Cathedral of La Almudena, work on which was almost continuous between 1879 and 1994. The west façade, directly opposite the palace gates, is in a classical style in keeping with that of the palace, but the building had originally been intended as a neo-medieval monument. The first architect, the Marquis of Cubas, had managed by the time of his death to build the present neo-romanesque crypt, and also to start work above this on an east end with radiating chapels, based on that of Rheims Cathedral. The structure has now been completed by a dreary, pastel-coloured nave with gothic arches but neoclassical coldness and austerity.

From the back of the cathedral we can descend towards the Casa de Campo on the Cuesta de la Vega, passing to our left a large fragment of the city's 9th- to 10th-century walls, now surrounded by a small and pleasant park named after the Moorish founder of Madrid, Emir Mohammed I. At the bottom of the hill, on the other side of the modern Paseo Virgen del Puerto, we come to the quiet, shaded promenade laid out by Pedro de Ribera while working for the Marquis de Vadillo. Vadillo was later buried in the delightful hermitage which Ribera built in 1718 at the promenade's southern end, a brick structure of engaging simplicity crowned by an extraordinary tent-shaped roof. At the northern end of the Virgen del Puerto is the entrance to the Campo del Moro, which originally formed the gardens, but is now a wooded public park. Inside are superb views looking up towards the Royal Palace, and a modern museum containing a collection of old carriages, including a black 17th-century one which is known mysteriously as *Juana la Loca* (Joan the Mad) and is possibly Europe's oldest surviving funeral carriage. Of similarly macabre interest is the processional carriage in which Alfonso XIII received in 1906 his explosive floral tribute from Mateo Morral, which we saw on page 96.

We can climb back up towards the palace along the Cuesta de San Vicente, which skirts the northern side of the Campo del Moro, beginning its ascent alongside the Estación del Norte, a railway station with a turn-of-the-century grandeur that belies the very modest nature of the railway traffic which passes through the place today. Near the top of the street, we find steps to our right climbing up into attractive formal gardens that were laid out in the 1930's directly below the palace's northern façade. Due east of the gardens, on the other side of the street which heads south towards the Plaza de Oriente, is the narrow Plaza de la Marina Española, dominated by a monument to Cánovas del Castillo, Spain's political leader after the restoration of the monarchy in 1874. This grand and exceptionally pompous work, featuring allegories of History and Fame, was perhaps an inappropriate way of commemorating a man of notoriously unprepossessing appearance, who had a squint and a nervous tic, and dressed so badly that one contemporary described him as a 'subaltern on half-pay'. Behind Cánovas stands the Senate House, a neoclassical work created in 1820 out of a convent dating back to 1581.

V. The Encarnación One of the finest convents in Madrid, and still functioning, is the Convento de la Encarnación, which lies on a quiet square just to the south of the Plaza de la Marina Española. Founded in 1611 by the wife of Philip IV, Doña Margarita, it was built by Juan Gómez de Mora, whose hand is evident above all in the austerely beautiful granite façade of the church. The supremely elegant church interior, with its delicate stucco-work and predominance of whites and pastel blues, was remodelled in the late 18th-century by Ventura Rodríguez, but still retains its original organ, on which wonderful concerts are given every Sunday morning at 11.30. Guides from the Patrimonio Nacional will take you around the rest of the convent, where, among many lesser works of art, are a signed painting by José de Ribera of *John the Baptist* (1635) and two sculptures by the great 17th-century master of polychromed wood, Gregorio Fernández. Also here is a curious Flemish panel representing a marital swap between France and Spain, Louis XII of France receiving Anne of Austria, and the future Philip IV getting in exchange Isabelle de Bourbon, the whole ceremony taking place half way across the estuary of Bidasoa, which lies between the two countries. But all these works, however interesting, are eclipsed by the extraordinary Reliquary that is the Convent's greatest claim to fame. This comparatively small room is lined on every side with smart wooden cases as in an old library, but instead of books the cases display no fewer than four thousand relics, the whole collection bringing together every conceivable anatomical fragment of every conceivable saint. A tiny vial contains the most sacred of these relics, a drop of blood from St. Pantaleon, a fourth-century martyr and doctor whose blood was generously distributed among many reliquaries. However, this particular sample, little bigger than a pin-prick, has a special significance, for, every year, on the anniversary of the saint's martyrdom on 27 July, it regularly de-coagulates, and has only done so at other times of the year to warn of impending catastrophes, such as the First World War, or the Civil War. Sceptics generally, and visitors from Protestant countries in particular, tend to wince in places such as these, but most people will at least be able to appreciate the harmonious refinement of the setting, with its elegantly restrained reliquary cases, its altarpiece of *The Nativity* by Leonardo's follower Bernardo Luini, and its superb coffered ceiling, which sparkles with classical grotesques painted by Vicente Carducho.

Heading northeast from the Convent along the Calle de la Bola (with its famous, old-fashioned restaurant of this name), we pass to our left the short Calle de Guillermo Rolland, where, at No. 7, the great fantasist and lover of the absurd, Ramón Gómez de la Serna was born in 1883. As we emerge eventually into the singularly ugly Plaza de Santo Domingo, the magical aura which hangs over the surroundings of the Royal Palace at last begins to wear off, and we return to a more mundane world, albeit only briefly. At the junction of the square and the unfortunately named Calle de Venereas, once stood the Café Varela, an establishment made famous by the poet and costumbrista Emilio Carrere. Madrid might lose the bodies of its famous poets, but it does not so easily forget their memories, for in the middle of the characterless Galician restaurant which has replaced the Café Varela can be found a memorial plaque touchingly inscribed with the words: 'This is where the great poet Emilio Carrere wrote his finest verses.'

The City of the Enlightenment

THE MUSEO DEL PRADO *to* THE GLORIETA DE ATOCHA

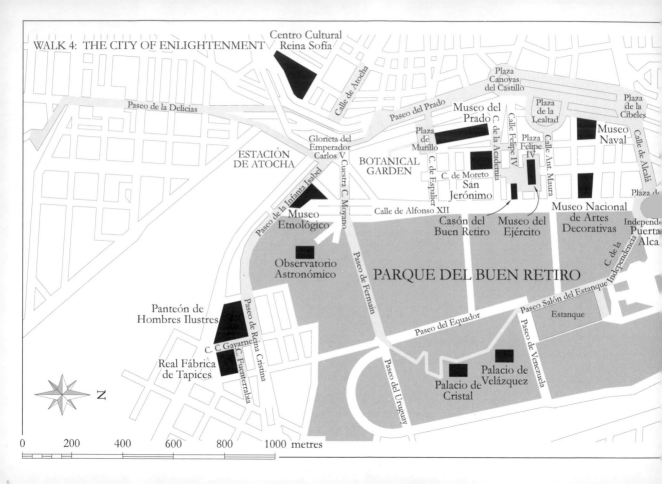

WALK 4: THE CITY OF ENLIGHTENMENT

Centro Cultural
Reina Sofía

Calle de Atocha

Paseo de la Delicias

Plaza
Canovas
del Castillo

Paseo del Prado

Plaza
de la
Lealtad

Plaza
de la
Cibeles

Museo del
Prado

Museo
Naval

Calle de Alcalá

Glorieta del
Emperador
Carlos V

Plaza
de
Murillo

C. de la Academia

Calle Felipe IV

Plaza
Felipe
IV

Calle Ant. Maura

ESTACIÓN
DE ATOCHA

BOTANICAL
GARDEN

C. de Espalter

C. de Moreto

San
Jerónimo

Plaza de

Paseo de la Infanta Isabel

Cuesta C. Moyano

Museo
Etnológico

Calle de Alfonso XII

Casón del
Buen Retiro

Museo del
Ejército

Museo Nacional
de Artes
Decorativas

Independ
Puerta
Alca

Observatorio
Astronómico

PARQUE DEL BUEN RETIRO

C. de la Independencia

Paseo de Fermín

Panteón de
Hombres Ilustres

Paseo del Equador

Paseo Salón del Estanque

Estanque

C. C Gavarne

Paseo de Reina Cristina

C. Fuenterrabia

Real Fábrica
de Tapices

Paseo del Uruguay

Palacio de
Cristal

Palacio de
Cristal

Paseo de Venezuela

Palacio de
Velázquez

N

0   200   400   600   800   1000 metres

The City of the Enlightenment

THE MUSEO DEL PRADO *to* THE GLORIETA DE ATOCHA

'The past is not better than the present, but it is lit by a suggestive, crepuscular twilight both poetic and distinct from the crude and sour reality of the present.' With these words, written at the outbreak of the Spanish Civil War, the elderly Pío Baroja embarked on a nostalgic evocation of the Buen Retiro, the park that forms the main setting of his romantic novel, *Nights of the Buen Retiro.* The world of aristocrats in their finery, parading carriages, and nocturnal brilliance that Baroja evoked might have gone, but a residue of aristocratic elegance, leisurely unconcern, and even poetry lingers on in that beautiful area of Madrid extending from the Retiro gardens down to the Paseo del Prado. This is the showcase heart of Madrid, exceptionally rich in monu-

ments and museums, graced by the smartest of turn-of-the-century apartment blocks (including the one in which Baroja himself lived), and featuring what is still one of the most enchanting of Europe's city parks.

The initial development of the area is due to the presence here of the 15th-century Monastery of San Jerónimo, from which the Buen Retiro Palace of Olivares fame evolved. However, this is essentially the Madrid of Charles III, whose memory will constantly be invoked in the course of the following itinerary, which begins outside the outstanding museum which he founded, the Prado, and ends at what is now the remarkable Centro Cultural Reina Sofia, which is housed in one of the most ambitious buildings of Charles'

enlightened reign. In the painting here Goya was clearly inspired by the royal hunting portraits of Velázquez, but with the difference that Charles III is shown – in true Englightenment fashion – as an ordinary gentleman out to enjoy himself.

I. The Paseo del Prado   The impact of Charles III on the appearance of Madrid is to be felt above all in the broad and shaded thoroughfare of the Paseo del Prado, which runs from the Calle de Alcalá down to the railway station at Atocha. Originally a large poplar-lined walk known as the *prado* or meadow of San Jerónimo, this had enjoyed since the mid-16th century a reputation as a leisure retreat that was warm in winter and cool in summer. Pedro de Medina, in a book of 1560 on the glories of Spain, wrote of this walk that 'it is fascinating and most entertaining to observe the crowds who go there, comprising some of the most splendid women, exquisitely attired gentlemen, and all sorts of lords and ladies in coaches and carriages.' 'Here,' he continued, 'you can savour to the full the freshness of the wind on summer nights and evenings, and hear much good music, without any risk of being attacked, robbed or of suffering any other harm, thanks to the good care and attention of the court mayors.' Medina's account of the original Paseo was an idealized and optimistic one, for other authors of this period mention the fights that often broke out here and the sordid sexual encounters that relied on the density of the surrounding foliage and the various hollows and other natural deformities that pock-marked the terrain. What is more, the beautiful embellishments referred to by both Medina and others amounted to little more than two insignificant fountains fed by a long and stagnant ditch which ran the whole length of the walk.

Reform of the Prado de San Jerónimo and of the adjoining Prados of Atocha and Recoletos had clearly become a pressing necessity by the late 18th century, and in 1775, after seven years of planning, work on a new line of paseos was finally begun under the direction of the engineer José de Hermosilla. The ground was levelled, the ditch filled, new rows of trees planted, and a series of splendid fountains created, the latter all being designed by the great Ventura Rodríguez.

The most elegant and popular part of this new avenue was the stretch between the Calle de Alcalá and the Carrera de San Jerónimo, a stretch which begins at the north with the famous fountain of Cybele seated imperiously in her chariot, and ends with the fountain of the trident-bearing Neptune pulled along by his horses. Known as the 'Salón del Prado', this was where most of Madrid would at times be seen to gather, and certainly all the fashionable young. Mesonero Romanos described it in 1830 as a place 'where amorous intrigues rule the day, where the confusion, the constant social intercourse, the ceaseless civilities, the variety of clothes and faces, the noise of the coaches and horses, the dust, the boys selling water and cinnamon, and, in short, the bustling life which is not to be found in any other of the city's paseos, all combine at first to irritate foreigners, who, however, end up by loving it all.' Even Théophile Gautier, whose snobbish French prejudices prevented him from being able to appreciate the elegance of the Salón del Prado, had nonetheless to admit that 'it was one of the most animated sights that can

167

be seen, and it is one of the most beautiful promenades in the world, not because of the site, which is most ordinary (in spite of all the efforts of Charles III to correct its defects) but because of the astonishing assembly which gathers there every evening, from half-past seven until ten.'

How this assembly looked is shown opposite in a print by another French visitor, Gustave Doré The place, though still keeping its trees, fountains, and general air of sophistication, is very different. By the turn of the century it had lost most of the old palaces that once flanked it, and had acquired its present stone benches and landscaped central reservation. The most significant of the changes is that it is no longer the animated rendez-vous of Madrid, the noise and confusion of the place today being not the result of loitering crowds but of the constant flow of car traffic. Only in the Paseo de Recoletos, to the north of the Cybele fountain, can we experience something of the social vitality of the Salón in its former days, and only then during the summer months, when its pavements are lined with open-air bars that remain packed until the early hours

of the morning.

II. The Museo del Prado The crowds that assemble in the southern half of today's Paseo de Prado are of a different kind from the summer ones on Recoletos, for they have come here not to drink or socialize, but to visit one of the world's most popular museums. This area immediately to the south of the Neptune Fountain was designated by Charles III less for pleasure than for instruction, and specifically scientific instruction. The Prado Museum was conceived initially as a Museum of Natural Sciences, and as a complement to the adjoining Botanical Garden, which was laid out in 1774 by the up-and-coming young architect Juan de Villanueva. The Botanical Garden, which was greatly enriched in its early years by seeds collected in the course of numerous scientific expeditions to Latin America and the Philippines, was badly neglected in the 19th century, so much so that Richard Ford reported that it came to be inhabited by a brood of escaped boa-constrictors that bolted any unfortunate dog or cat that strayed in to study botany. Now restored to its original state, the garden deserves a visit not only for its botanical specimens but also for its elegant terraced layout, and the sophisticated simplicity of Villanueva's buildings, including Palladian-inspired entrance gates and a superlative pavilion and greenhouse.

Villanueva, having consolidated his growing reputation with the Botanical Garden, was entrusted in 1775 with the design of the Prado Museum itself. So as to make the museum a natural extension of the promenade alongside it, he created a structure that is enormously long in relation to its height, and indeed he had even toyed at first with the idea of building in front of it a long covered portico where strollers could take refuge in times of rain. The great scale on which he worked, and his use of granite and the Doric order, could have led, in less capable hands, to a cold and monotonous structure. Instead, the building (opposite) is a most lively composition, incorporating elements of a palace, temple, and rotunda (see page 172) and with a rich interplay of arcades, niches and colonnades. The end result, though dismissed by Hemingway as being 'as unpicturesque as an American High School building', is one of the supreme achievements of European neoclassicism, and a structure which is far too little appreciated by those whose first reaction is to rush inside to see the paintings.

Charles III did not live to see his cherished museum completed, and the place was never to house the intended scientific collections. Work had only begun in 1785 and was to continue until 1808, but no sooner had it been finished than the museum was ruthlessly pillaged by the French, who even stripped the lead from its roof. Left to decay, the building was on the point of collapse when Ferdinand VII decided to have it adapted to house the royal collection of paintings, as previously suggested by his father, Charles IV. The new museum was inaugurated in November 1819 and opened to the public 'except on rainy days and when there is mud around'. After the revolution of 1868 the museum was appropriated by the state, and its holdings greatly increased by the incorporation that year of the Museo Nacional de la Trinidad, which was made up of works of art confiscated from dissolved monasteries and convents. This collection of

æreligious works, combined with the fabulous treasures amassed by the royal family, continue to form the basis of the Prado's collections today, despite numerous later donations. The size of the holdings will be more apparent than ever before when or if the current plans to transform the museum are completed. For much of the 1990's the place was a noisy chaos as the paintings were all rehung, and the structure thoroughly restored and re-roofed in response to such scandalous occurences as water leaking into the room containing Velázquez' *Las Meninas*. Though the renovation of the main building was finished in 1999 (ominously the leak in the Velázquez room recurred immediately after the re-opening), work is apparently yet to begin on the proposed extension of the museum to almost twice its present size. The former monastery church of San Jerónimo was acquired for this purpose in 1998 and is to be joined to the Villanueva building by a controversial glass structure designed by one of Spain's leading architects, Rafael Moneo.

Leon Trotsky, coming to Spain in 1916 after having been expelled from wartime France, paid a salutary visit to the Prado and was reminded again of the 'eternal' element in Art. Reactions to the museum have generally been as gushing as Trotsky's, and, from the time of Richard Ford onwards, a tour of the place has frequently constituted the highpoint of a stay in Madrid. It is unfortunate, however, that Madrid's tourism is concentrated to such a great extent on this one place that if you come here during the summer months the unbearable overcrowding caused by the invasion of huge tour groups is likely to make you reflect less on the 'eternal' element of Art than on the mortal failings of the human body. The congestion is not helped by the special nature of the museum's collections, which do not add up to a balanced survey of western art, but are focused instead on groups of outstanding paintings by a relatively select number of artists, several of whom – such as Hieronymus Bosch, Velázquez and Goya – are represented by most of their best known works.

The unbalanced quality of the collections is to a large extent a reflection of the idiosyncratic and at times obsessive tastes of the Spanish royal family. Isabel la Católica was passionate above all about Flemish art, which is why the museum has such a remarkable collection of early Flemish works, in particular by van de Weyden, whose sense of pathos and drama was especially close to Spanish sensibilities. Charles V had a great affection for Titian, admiring him for the emotional directness of his paintings, as is seen, for instance, in the Prado's magnificent equestrian portrait of the emperor. More Titians were acquired by Philip II, whose interest in the artist was rather different from his father's, being concentrated on mythological paintings featuring female nudes. Most of Titian's later mythologies were commissioned by Philip, who referred to them as *poesie*, which was probably his euphemism for erotica. Despite, or perhaps because of, his bigotry and religious mania, Philip II seems to have had an obsession with the erotic; on one occasion he even requested Titian to send from Italy a female nude seen from the back so as to balance another work in his collection in which the nude was seen from the front. What is undeniable is Philip II's love for the

bizarre, a love that expressed itself most blatantly in the avid way in which he collected the works of Hieronymus Bosch. He is known to have spent hours locked away in his bedroom at the Escorial contemplating such paintings as *The Garden of Earthly Delights*, undoubtedly revelling in its unrivalled wealth of sexual and macabre details. In contrast, an orthodox and distinctly wholesome attitude towards art was shown by his son Philip III, whose greatest contribution to the royal collections lay in his patronage of Rubens, another artist exceptionally well represented in the Prado. Philip IV inherited his father's interest in Rubens, but as a patron he is remembered principally for his extraordinary association with Velázquez, an association between a monarch and a painter that is virtually unique in the history of art. Every day the king would visit the artist in his studio, and as an outcome of this friendship, Velázquez felt emboldened to place himself on the same level as the royal family in *Las Meninas*, the work that attracts the Prado's greatest crowds (see page 29).

For all the public exposure which they have

received, the paintings of Velázquez continue to have a vividness which early writers on the artist attributed to the miraculous. The uniform brilliance of these works certainly highlights the limitations of the Prado's holdings of other Spanish artists, which are surprisingly patchy. The collection of Spanish medieval art, though making for a pleasantly quiet part of the museum, has neither the range nor excitement of Barcelona's Museo de Arte de Catalonia. The El Grecos – mainly acquired at a comparatively late date – will have a muted impact on anyone who has been to Toledo. Trotsky, mysteriously, singled out the Riberas for special praise, but, with the major exceptions of a monumentally powerful *Flaying of St Bartholomew* and a subtly realistic *Jacob's Dream*, there are better examples of his work elsewhere in Europe, as is also sadly true of the work of Velázquez's other great contemporaries, Zurbarán and Murillo. The relative paucity of the 17th-century holdings is a sorry indication of the way in which English and French travellers mercilessly plundered Spain's heritage in the wake of the Peninsular War, when Spanish art reached the height of its popularity.

It is with its vast collection of paintings by Goya that the Prado Museum comes back into its own again, reviving wilting spirits, and ensuring that a visit to this building ends on a note of climax. The numerous loud-mouthed tour guides also seem to perk up at this point, for Goya's works, in particular the Black Paintings, give an opportunity to voice the romantic and very clichéd view of the artist as a tormented soul. Personally I prefer to emphasize instead Goya's love of pigeon-shooting and his financial canniness: he rarely failed to materialize at shareholders' meetings. I have little sympathy too for the idea of Goya as a radically political artist, for, though he depicted the horrors of Spain's War of Independence, he appears to have been quite happy to have worked for anyone who paid him, and indeed was under the pay of the French one moment, and of the tyrannical Ferdinand VII the next. Perhaps the least attractive aspect of the Goya legend, and one peculiar to the Spanish vision of him, is the way in which he has come to symbolize Spanish machismo. As we stand in front of the *Maja Desnuda*, we are almost certain to overhear someone talking gleefully about the affair which Goya is supposed to have had with the Duchess of Alba, who, even less plausibly, is said to have posed for the picture. In fact the only documentation to have come down to us about Goya's intimate life takes the form of a recent and scarcely publicized discovery of a collection of love letters written by Goya to a man. None of this information has of course any relevance to an enjoyment of the paintings, but temples of art such as the Prado tend to enshrine mythologies about artists, and these mythologies need occasionally to be questioned.

III. The Royal Palace of the Buen Retiro

Leaving the Prado by its northern door, we find ourselves confronted by a very pictorial monument to Goya by the turn-of-the-century sculptor Mariano Benlliure, the stone base of which is ridiculously carved with a group of demons hovering over a blissfully oblivious *Maja Desnuda*. At the top of the neighbouring flight of steps is the Calle de la Academia, which gently climbs east towards what was once the Royal Palace of the Buen Retiro. The first building that we come to on the right is the former monastery church of San Jerónimo, which stands on a terrace above the Prado, its gothic spires and pinnacles forming an unusual element in the skyline of a city otherwise little affected by this style. The monastery was founded by Ferdinand and Isabel in 1505, and in 1528 became established as the place where the nobility and Cortes of Castile swore allegiance to the crown princes of Spain. The basis of the future Royal Palace of the Buen Retiro was laid in the early 1560's when Philip II ordered the building here of a Royal Apartment, intended to provide lodgings for the king when he retreated to San Jerónimo for Easter services, or when he took part in the various state ceremonies organized here, such as solemn entries into the city. Badly damaged by the French in the early 19th century, the monastery was dissolved in 1835, and was subsequently used as barracks and a military hospital. The church, and the adjoining ruins of a 16th-century cloister, are all that is left today of the original complex, which was demolished after 1868 together with most of the Royal Palace. Saved, and thoroughly restored and remodelled during the reign of Isabel II, the present church has a strong 19th-century character, but nonetheless retains much of its original appearance, in particular its porticoed west portal, which is in the elaborate late gothic style known as the Isabelline plateresque. The building has continued to be used this century for important royal functions, such as the marriage in 1906 of Alfonso XIII to Victoria de Battenberg, and, following the death of Franco, the religious ceremony that inaugurated the reign of Juan Carlos I.

How the monastery looked in 1656, engulfed in what was then very recent building is seen in the detail from Texeira overleaf, which also gives us a glimpse of the original layout of the prados (de San Jerónimo above, and de Atocha below).

The parallel street to the north of the Calle de la Academia, the broad Calle de Felipe IV, is blocked off at its upper end by the sturdy mass of the Casón del Buen Retiro, an annexe to the Prado Museum. This, and the nearby Army Museum, are the main and much altered archi-

tectural fragments of the Retiro Palace, the grand and fantastical complex which had been dreamt up by Count-Duke of Olivares as a way of consolidating his hold over Philip IV. When work had begun on the building in 1630, the intention had been simply to enlarge Philip II's Royal Apartment in preparation for the ceremony in 1632 of swearing allegiance to Prince Baltasar Carlos. However, almost immediately, Olivares began imagining a vast centre of the arts and recreation, complete with a beautiful series of gardens where plays and pageants would be put on in the summer months. This is the palace we see in Texeira's map. It was put up at great speed under the principal supervision of Juan Gómez de Mora and G. B. Crescenzi, and inspired both extravagant eulogies and the most virulent criticism, the latter being voiced mainly by Olivares' growing number of enemies, who referred to the palace contemptuously as the 'chicken-coop' after an aviary in its gardens (a grandiose openwork affair on the edge of the park, seen in the bottom right hand corner of the Texeira detail). Olivares' eventual fall from favour led to the

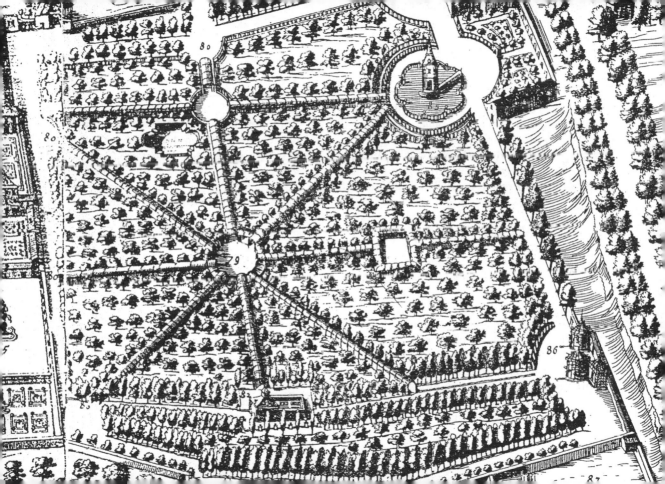

palace being much neglected, but in the 18th-century the Bourbons lived here while the Alcázar was being rebuilt. Left in ruins during the French invasion of Spain and the capture of Madrid by British forces, it was largely pulled down after the collapse of the Spanish monarchy in 1868.

The Casón del Buen Retiro, built by Alonso de Carbonell in 1637 as the ballroom of the palace, was almost entirely remodelled in the late 19th-century and given a neoclassical casing, but we should still be able to identify it on Texeira. The insipid back façade, which dates back to 1877, overlooks the Retiro park, and indeed faces the park's one remaining 17th-century gate. Far more imposing is the main façade, which rises above a monument by Benlliure to Isabel II's mother María Cristina, and was built in 1891 by Ricardo Velázquez Bosco, whose splendid Palacio de Cristal and Ministry of Agriculture will be admired later on this walk. The building is now given over to the Prado's 19th-century holdings, which range from grand historical works of the Romantic period, such as Carlos Luis de Rivera's *Daughters of the Cid,* to delicate turn-of-the-century landscapes by artists such as Santiago Rusiñol. The museum attracts undeservedly little attention and can no longer rely even on the spill-over from the crowds who visited Picasso's *Guernica,* which from 1981 to 1992 was separately and inappropriately displayed in the one part of the building to have survived the 17th century – the ball-room itself. Now that Picasso's emotive block-buster has been removed from this festive setting and taken to the Centro Cultural Reina Sofia, we can give our undivided attention to the room's colourful, triumphant ceiling fresco. This was executed in 1694 by an artist as renowed as Picasso was for the speed with which he painted, Luca Giordano, who was sometimes known as *Fa Presto* – that is, 'works fast'.

Whereas Picasso's *Guernica* chronicled the tragedy of war, its glories are celebrated in the absurdly anachronistic Army Museum (Museo del Ejército), which is situated just to the north of the Casón del Buen Retiro. Housed in the main surviving section of the Buen Retiro Palace, it has miraculously retained one of the grandest of the palace's original rooms, the ceremonial hall known as the Salón de los Reinos. For this room Zurbarán painted ten canvases of the Labours of Hercules, and Velázquez executed five of his equestrian portraits of the royal family, as well as his celebrated *Surrender of Breda*, which formed part of a series of twelve large battle scenes representing the victories of Philip IV. The paintings by Zurbarán and Velázquez are now in the Prado, and the room's oriental carpets, silver lions, and other lavish furnishings have all disappeared. The Army museum will eventually be transferred in its entirety to Toledo's Alcázar, after which the Salón de los Reinos might have all its original canvases returned. However, even without such drastic measures being taken, enough remains to make this room an essential sight for anyone who wishes to understand the context for which some of Velázquez's greatest paintings were intended: some of the pictures by his school are still in place, and, more importantly, the room has kept its magnificent gilded ceiling decoration, comprising the escutcheons of the twenty-four kingdoms of the Spanish monarchy, and elaborate classical grotesques.

The Salón de los Reinos in itself is sufficient reason for visiting the Army Museum, but, sadly, the notion of a military museum in a country which has only recently emerged from a military dictatorship seems to have put off all but school children and die-hard Francoists from coming here. In its present layout, the place is essentially a monument to Francoism, and has numerous busts and portraits of Franco and his generals, and even a reproduction of General Moscardó's horrendous study in Toledo's Alcázar. Yet to anyone with a sense of humour and a taste for the ludicrous, this has to be one of Madrid's most entertaining museums. Confronted, in the empty, gloomily lit halls, with a compressed, symmetrical display of thousands of rifles, medals, swords, and tattered old flags and banners, we have the impression of having inadvertently opened a vast packing-case that has been left undisturbed for years. The necessary note of bathos is provided by the sense of chaos underlying all the would-be military precision, the models of soldiers who appear to be dressed for amateur theatricals, and the piped military music, which accompanies us throughout the museum, eventually depositing us in the cavernous basement, where we reel from the sight of a veritable ocean of cannons. You will be glad to know that the contribution made by women to all this glorious military history has not been forgotten, and there is a tiny vestibule grandly entitled 'Sala de Las Heroinas', featuring a portrait of María Pita, who outwitted '*el pirata Drake*'.

From the Army Museum we should head back east towards the Paseo del Prado, crossing the Calle de Ruiz de Alarcón, where No. 12 is the elegant residential block in which the writer Pío Baroja lived. Despite the grandeur of his home surroundings, Baroja was often to be seen in the company of vagrants, and, during his Madrid years, was described by González Ruano as 'resembling a beggar dressed in a suit snatched from a corpse'. Almost round the corner from Baroja's house, overlooking the Plaza de La Lealtad, is the palatial Hotel Ritz, gleaming in its coat of icing-sugar plaster. Built in 1908 by the French architect of the London Ritz, Charles Mewès, it replaced the Hotel Paris as Madrid's most luxurious hotel, and also served as a model for the many other French-style buildings to be put up in Madrid over the following two decades. Mewès, taking into account the proximity of the neoclassical Prado Museum, was unusually restrained in his design of the building's exterior, reserving his neo-baroque decorative exuberance for the reception hall and adjoining spaces. If we are respectably dressed we will be allowed to wander into the fabulously appointed main bar, where we might even be tempted to slouch into one of the arm-chairs and order a coffee, an experience which acts as a decompression chamber after the noise of the traffic outside, but which is likely to be less relaxing the moment the bill is presented. The young Salvador Dalí, short on funds but with his life-long fascination with the world of the very rich, ordered a cocktail here in 1926, made an impression by telling the barman to keep the very considerable change, and then, having cut his finger on the glass, created a special cocktail of his own featuring his blood and the cotton cherry from the hat of an elegant and bewildered blonde next to him. Afterwards he rushed out into the street, feeling, as he was later to relate in his autobiography *My Secret Life*, 'as greatly moved as Jesus must have felt when he invented Holy Communion... The sky over Madrid was a shattering blue and the brick houses were pale rose, like a sigh filled with glorious promises. I was phenomenal. I was phenomenal.' He began to run, jumping with exaggerated leaps into the air, and shouting at the top of his voice, 'Blood is sweeter than honey.' In this state he tripped over one of his fellow students, who was to tell everyone the next day that 'Dalí is crazy as a goat.'

Making a less dramatic exit from the Ritz, we should walk over to the small shaded garden in the middle of the Plaza de la Lealtad to see the large obelisk designed by Isidro González Velázquez to commemorate the victims of the 2nd of May. The idea for such a monument was proposed by the Spanish parliament in 1814, but it was not until 1840 that the present one was finally completed. Covered all over with stirring words, such as '*¡Honor eterno al patriotismo!*', it even incorporates at its base an urn containing the ashes of those killed by the French. The gilded silver keys to this urn are kept for some reason in Madrid's Municipal Archive.

IV. The Thyssen-Bornemisza Collection
Anyone who has spent part of the day visiting the Prado risks suffering now a surfeit of paintings by crossing over to the western side of the Paseo del Prado to see the Thyssen-Bornemisza Collection. Once much coveted by Britain, this collection is rich in exactly those aspects of western art poorly covered by the Prado, and has turned this part of the city into what is clumsily referred to as a 'golden art triangle'. However, the Spanish government's acceptance of the collection in the 1980's was not universally welcomed in Spain: the elegant early 19th-century Palacio de Villahermosa had to be drastically transformed to house what was – until 1994 – only a short-term, and extremely expensive loan. Further irritation was later caused by the insistence of Baron Thyssen's wife, a former Spanish beauty queen, on having the walls of Rafael Moneo's brilliantly remodelled and cleverly lit interior painted a salmon pink. Doubts about

the Baroness's taste seem confirmed by the embarassing double portrait of her and her husband that stands today in the museum's spacious vestibule and shows her dressed as a Christmas tree fairy.

The recommended tour of the museum begins on the second floor with the old master paintings amassed by the present baron's father, the founder of the collection. Originally hung in the beautiful lakeside setting of the Villa Favorita at Lugano, these make up the most consistently exciting part of the museum, and include important medieval works from Italy and Germany, and a renaissance collection famed for its delightfully detailed representation of *St George* by Carpaccio, and a near unrivalled group of Italian, Flemish and German portraits: an artist little known outside Spain is the Flemish-born court painter to Isabel la Católica, Juan de Flandes, who is represented here by an exceptionally delicate and luminous portrait of a *Spanish Princess* (left), once thought to be Juana la Loca, or possibly Catalina de Aragón. Caravaggio's compelling *St Catherine at her Wheel* helps ensure that the high quality of the collection is maintained into the baroque period, and there are also fine works by French and Italian 18th-century artists such as Boucher and Canaletto. Interest begins only to flag on descending to the first floor, where a dreary and tiring series of rooms devoted to 17th-century Dutch art is barely relieved by some lively portraits by Hals. This is followed shortly by Europe's largest collection of 19th-century American paintings, a welcome relief after the Dutch art, but, as a whole, too specialist in its appeal to deter the general, non-American visi tor from hurrying on towards the largely disappointing holdings of Impressionist and post-Impressionist art. A tour of this floor ends on a much-needed high note with one of the greatest and most extensive collections of German expressionists to be seen outside Germany. Most visitors will have had enough by now, but those who continue into the basement will be rewarded by some good Cubist and early abstract works before finally reaching a ragbag selection of fashionable contemporary art testifying to the indiscriminate and impersonal collecting habits

of Baron Heini.

V. From the Plaza de la Cibeles to the Retiro Park Returning to the other side of the Paseo del Prado, and continuing north, we pass another of the fountains designed by Ventura Rodríguez, this one featuring the god Apollo standing on a plinth surrounded by representations of the Four Seasons. Adjacent to this, at the junction of the Paseo del Prado and the Calle de Montalbán, is the Ministry of the Navy, the modern extension to which houses a Naval Museum (Museo Naval) featuring a chaotically arranged collection of ships' models. The better organized but less entertaining National Museum of Decorative Arts (Museo Nacional de las Artes Decorativas) stands further east along the Calle de Montalbán, occupying a late 19th-century residence at No. 12. Excessive good taste, and an atmosphere of cold sophistication somewhat dull the impact of this museum's wonderful and wide-ranging collection, one of the highpoints of which is a colourful 18th-century Valencian kitchen entirely decorated with illusionistic ceramic scenes featuring servants, kitchen vessels, food, and such delightful details as a cat tugging at a large fish.

The Plaza de la Cibeles, presided over by its famous fountain of the charioted goddess, was peaceful enough in 1862 when Doré made the engraving opposite. Now this intersection of the Paseos del Prado and Recoletos with the equally broad Calle de Alcalá is the nerve-centre of modern Madrid, and it is here, at its southeastern corner, that we find one of the city's most spectacular and eccentric buildings. Gómez de la Serna speculated that one day this building might enjoy a more dignified function than its present one, and perhaps even be taken over as the headquarters of the Ministry of the Interior, as the prominence both of its architecture and situation surely deserved. For the moment, however, it remains what it has always been, namely the city's central Post Office. Designed in 1904 by the great Antonio Palacios, and completed in 1919, its construction signified for Gómez de la Serna the 'official arrival in Madrid of unprecedented structures, built neither for God nor for the pure aristocracy of old.' It was, as he also noted, a curious mixture of the 'hybrid and the rational', a work that was daringly modern for the time, while at the same time outlandishly drawing on Spanish architecture of the past. Conceived as a colossal temple to Progress, its exterior of castellated towers thrown up to a great height earned the building the nickname of 'Our Lady of Communications'. As for the lavish decorative coating of the building, this can best be described as 'neo-Churrigueresque'; it is complemented by a wonderful row of large gilded bronze letterboxes, evocatively inscribed with the main destinations in Spain.

Heading east from the Post Office building towards the main entrance of the Retiro Park, we briefly join the Calle de Alcalá, which was formerly the main road running east out of Madrid. On the other side of the street, at No. 57, is Café Lion, one of the last of the many famous cafés that once lined the street all the way west to the Puerta del Sol. Founded in 1929 as a replacement to the Café Lion d'Or, it attracted the two opposed extremes of the Spanish political world of this period, both of which were

drawn to the café's basement section known as 'The Happy Whale'. One of its regulars was the founder of the Falange, José Antonio Primo de Rivera, who was constantly to be seen here with an admiring crowd right up to the time he was arrested and shot by the Republicans in November 1936. Another habitué was García Lorca, who, with the Chilean Communist poet Pablo Neruda, and members of the travelling theatre company called 'La Barraca', would come both here and to the neighbouring (and still surviving) Cervezería Correos. Higher up the street we emerge into the circular Plaza de La Independencia, part of the perimeter of which is taken up by the gates of the Retiro Park, and the rest by a harmonious group of residential blocks dating back to the 1870's. In the middle of all the traffic stands one of the most beautiful of Charles III's legacies to Madrid, the three-arched city gate of the Puerta de Alcalá, through which – in the words of Gómez de la Serna – 'the dawn threads each morning its golden point'. This was the most important of Madrid's gates, not only on account of its position alongside the Royal Palace of the Buen Retiro, but also because it was the entrance to the city for those travelling here from Barcelona and France. Accordingly, Charles III took particular care in the choice of its design, rejecting no less than five projects by Ventura Rodríguez in favour of the present structure by Sabatini, a perfectly proportioned work of uncluttered simplicity, the sculptural decoration of which is set apart from the rest of the granite monument by being executed in white Colmenar stone. We see it opposite in 1857.

If we were to continue heading east along the Calle de Alcalá we would skirt the northern side of the Retiro Park, coming eventually to the large equestrian monument to the hero of the first Carlist War, Baldomero Espartero, whose well-endowed horse has given rise to the popular Madrid saying, 'to have more balls than the horse of Espartero'. Instead, we enter the Retiro, where we find in front of the main entrance an alley of trees leading up to the large rectangular pond, the Estanque, which forms the the main survival of the original royal park of the Buen

Retiro. The park was inaugurated in the autumn of 1632 with a mythological spectacular recreating the loves of Orpheus and Eurydice, the Estanque being filled with boats carrying members of the court, as well as musicians playing the music of Monteverdi. After 1767 the park was opened conditionally to the public, but it was not to be handed over to the municipality of Madrid until the reign of Isabel II, by which time it had been thoroughly restored following devastation caused by the French. In its first fifty years as the city park of Madrid it acquired its present-day layout, as well as a superb series of architectural and sculptural embellishments, including what may be described as Madrid's answer to Rome's Victor Emmanuel Monument: the Monument to Alfonso XII. This magnificent structure, seen oppposite in the 1950's, consists of a vast oval formed on one side by steps leading down to the Estanque, and on the other by two arms of a colonnade flanking the enormously tall plinth which supports the equestrian bronze of the monarch by Benlliure.

Pío Baroja may have looked back nostalgically to the Buen Retiro park of his youth, but the place today has changed remarkably little over the years, the greatest difference being that today few people other than vagrants would think of coming here at night. But from the late afternoon right up to dusk, a large cross-section of Madrid society swarms around the bosky shores of the Estanque, under the watchful eye of Alfonso XII. Open-air cafés, rowing-boats for hire, the ubiquitous street performers, pavement artists, portrait painters, fortune-tellers, flamenco-strumming gypsies, even an elderly man with a typewriter calling himself a poet, form part of the endlessly absorbing human zoo of the Retiro. Until comparatively recently there was also a real zoo, a legacy of the park's royal menagerie, and a place where miserable polar bears prowled in endless circles trying to avoid a decorative trickle of water and the taunts of a public who ignored the notices not 'to spit or throw sunflower seeds at the animals'. 'It is an indisputable fact,' wrote Nina Epton in 1964, 'that all these cramped animals look contented and the bears are actually frolicsome.' Today the grounds of the former

zoo are taken over every May and June by the hundreds of open-air stalls constituting Madrid's Book Fair, a genuinely frolicsome event marking the arrival of summer, and attracting almost the whole of Madrid, not for the actual books, but for the crowds of parading people.

The Retiro is fortunately sufficiently large and varied to accommodate all tastes. Lovers of peace, or indeed lovers, can escape the worst of the crowds by slipping off into the woods immediately to the south of the Estanque. Here also are two architectural marvels by Ricardo Velázquez Bosco, the first of these – the Palacio de Velázquez – being a large pavillion in glass, brick and iron erected in 1882 for the last of a number of exhibitions that were once held in the park on the lines of London's Crystal Palace. Profusely decorated with ceramics by Daniel Zuloaga, this pavilion is now used for temporary art exhibitions, as is the nearby Palacio de Cristal, the most endearing of Velázquez's works. One of the most stunning examples in Spain of a glass and ironwork structure, with two long sides inspired by the shape of a cathedral apse, this gains an added beauty from its position above a small and picturesquely planned lake, where gliding swans and a great central jet of water further enhance the cool and relaxing atmosphere. Less in harmony with the surroundings is the sculpture by the contemporary Basque artist Chillida on the lake's southern shores, a work which seems at first sight like the emptied contents of a lorry carrying building materials. Numerous other sculptures, of a more traditional kind, are scatterered throughout the park, including, at the end of the main avenue running south from the Estanque, a monument by one Ricardo Bellver entitled *The Fallen Angel*. Though the actual style of this work is traditional, the subject-matter certainly is not, and Madrid is very proud to possess a monument which is claimed to be the only one in the world dedicated to Lucifer.

Lucifer has been condemned to the bleaker, southern half of the Retiro, and from here we would be best advised to head to the park's southwestern exit, noting as we do so Juan de Villanueva's Observatory, a necessary corrective to Satanism which rises on the hill to our left.

Commissioned in 1785 by Charles III, it is a temple to the spirit of the Enlightenment, its central telescope contained within a classical rotunda that sits proudly above a colonnaded portico. Leaving the park, and crossing over the Calle de Alfonso XII, we reach the sloping street known popularly as the Cuesta de Moyano, the railings of which mark the southern edge of the Botanical Garden. In front of these is a long row of recently restored turn-of-the-century book-stalls, where we can buy both new and second-hand books and experience daily something of the animated atmosphere of the annual Retiro Book Fair.

VI. Atocha and the Centro Cultural Reina Sofia   At the bottom of the hill the noise increases as we reach the southern end of the Paseo del Prado, where a whole series of radiating thoroughfares disgorge their traffic into a sprawling and untidy square dignified both by the name of Glorieta del Emperador Carlos V and by the grandeur of the surrounding buildings. In the case of the Ministry of Agriculture (immediately to our left on entering the square) rarely

can a building of such majestic and glorious character have served such an earth-bound function. Built in 1893 by Velázquez Bosco, it features much ceramic decoration by Zuloaga on its vast exterior, and a monumentally-sized porticoed frontispiece which seems almost to be borne on wings, thanks to its crowning allegorical figure of Glory flanked by winged horses.

The history of Madrid itself soars off into flights of fantasy as we approach, on the western side of the Ministry of Agriculture, the neoclassical building housing the Museum of Ethnology (Museo Etnológico y Antropológico). There is nothing remarkable about the actual building – a coldly academic structure – nor about its clearly if unimaginatively displayed collections of Anthropological, Ethnographical and Prehistorical items. However, the building takes on an eerie fascination with a knowledge of the strange story of its founder, Dr González Velasco, one of the most famously eccentric of Madrid's personalities. A distinguished scientist and master surgeon, Dr Velasco assembled in his house a Cabinet of Curiosities, the future nucleus of the present museum, which was built next to his house and inaugurated in 1875, the year of his death. Until the outbreak of the Civil War, when it mysteriously disappeared, one of the objects displayed in the museum's hall was a skeleton belonging to a giant whom the doctor had encountered on a trip to Asturias and had promised free board and lodging in his Madrid home on condition that he could keep his body after his death. The doctor had various other human skeletons in his museum, including those of a 28-year-old mass murderer called Juan Tomás Blanco and of a consumptive young woman. It was the presence of the latter corpse in the doctor's collection which provided material for the best known story associated with him, a story where fact and fiction are difficult to separate, and which indeed has been celebrated in a novella by Ramón Sender entitled *The Daughter of Doctor Velasco*. The daughter in question was a blonde called Gertrude who died young of tuberculosis, inspiring her stricken father to try and preserve her memory by embalming her corpse. There were even reports that the doctor had been seen taking this corpse with him on his carriage rides up the Paseo del Prado, a promenade which he had regularly undertaken with his daughter in happier days. Nothing remains to testify to the doctor's reputed skills as an embalmer, and the best which can be offered to the macabre-minded vistor to the museum today is a battered old camel with its stuffing falling out.

Those in search of memories of the dead will find that a short detour to the east of Dr Velasco's museum leads to the Pantheon of Illustrious Men (Panteón de Hombres Ilustres), which was planned in the 1890's in conjunction with the proposed reconstruction of the ruined 16th-century Basilica and Monastery of Atocha, famous for being the burial place of the missionary and champion of the Indians, Fray Bartolomé de las Casas. This Pantheon, inspired by Pisa's Campo Santo, features a large cloister surrounded by cypresses, and a tall bell-tower built of bands of different coloured stone. It is interesting as the sole important example in Madrid of the influence of Italian medieval architecture, and as a repository of some fine monuments by Benlliure and other fashionable turn-of-the-century sculptors. As a place for honouring Spain's dead, however, it was almost as much of a fiasco as San Francisco had been, most of its corpses – unhappy perhaps in their inappropriately Italianate surroundings – being later removed, leaving only among the ranks of the famous dead a group of political figures which includes the Andalucían lawyer and civilian Unionist Ríos Rosa, and the three assassinated statesmen, Práxedes Sagasta, Eduardo Dato, and Cánovas del Castillo. Funds ran out before the actual Monastery and Basilica of Atocha could be rebuilt, and the present buildings, dating from after the Civil War, are depressing pastiches of the Herreran style. Perhaps the best reason for making a detour to this part of town is to visit the Royal Tapestry Factory (Real Fábrica de Tapices), which is situated further to the east, at the junction of the Calles de Fuenterrabía and Julián Gayarre. The original factory, for which Goya had executed the numerous tapestry cartoons that are now in the Prado, had been founded by Philip V at the beginning of the 18th century, but the present building dates only from the 1880's. It still functions as a tapestry factory, and the fascinating guided tour through its small, decaying rooms will give us much insight into the patient process of weaving tapestries, and also into the sad amount of work that has gone into the generally hideous products of recent years.

The elderly Mesonero Romanos, in one of his characteristic outbursts of nostalgia, concluded a description of the Paseo del Prado by reflecting that the sonorous pealing of the bells of Atocha, San Jerónimo and Recoletos had given way to the whistle of locomotives and to great hisses of steam. He was referring to the recently completed railway station of Atocha, which had been built according to a plan which he himself had proposed on the southern side of the Glorieta del Emperador Carlos V. The original structure, inaugurated with the completion in 1851 of the railway line between Madrid and Aranjuez (the second oldest in Spain), was succeeded in the 1890's by a splendidly elaborate ironwork structure. The latter, full of evocative memories for those who have set off from here down to the south of Spain, has now been made the terminal of the high-speed train service to Seville, the AVE, and given a palm-filled interior resembling a post-modernist glass-house; behind this rises a singularly bleak new station built in the early 1990's by Rafael Moneo, who had come to prominence ten years earlier with his Archaeological Museum in Mérida. Enthusiasts of the old days of railway travel will have today to satisfy their enthusiasm with a visit to the nearby Estación de Delicias, which can be reached by heading south from Atocha down the Paseo de Delicias. This fine ironwork structure of the 1880's was a shunting station which came popularly to be known as the Flea Station, a more appropriate name than its official one of Station of Delights. In keeping with the present universal trend of preserving the past by turning it into a museum or heritage centre, the station is now a Railway Museum, its tracks lined with old engines and carriages, including an old dining-car where we can sit down for a drink in a setting of neo-baroque splendour, an experience which belongs to not-so-distant days of Spanish travel.

A more imaginative transformation of an old building is to be seen at the Centro Cultural Reina Sofia, which stands directly in front of the old Atocha Railway Station. This was originally the Hospital General de San Carlos, which had been founded by Philip II but was later rebuilt during the reign of Charles III, who entrusted the work to his favourite architect, Francesco Sabatini. Sabatini envisaged a building with no fewer than seven courtyards, which would have made it even larger than the Royal Palace. Only one of these courtyards was completed, but this alone is of echoing proportions, as are the marbled rooms and corridors within the former hospital. Converted by Antonio Fernández Alba in the 1980's into the present cultural centre, the building manages to house the city's museum of modern art (Museo Español de Arte Contemporáneo) and still have room to put on some of the most ambitious and spaciously laid out art exhibitions in Europe today. I particularly remember a Giacometti exhibition in which one of this sculptor's tiny striding figures was the sole work placed in a hall over fifty metres long.

The museum takes up only one of the building's five floors, but seems nonetheless to involve as much walking as does the Prado. Though there are foreign school works ranging from an Arp relief to a light installation by Dan Flavin, this enormous collection is largely of Spanish works, beginning with a decorative, nostalgic group of paintings from the turn of the century, and proceeding to the dark and sombre canvases of the Castilian artist Solana, who is seen at his best in the powerful portrait of Gómez de la Serna presiding over one of the famous tertulias at the Café del Pombo that we reproduced on page 19. After this the visitor comes to more familiar Spanish territory with numerous works by Miro, Dalí, Gris, and, above all, Picasso, whose celebrated *Guernica* now provides the museum with its main focus of interest. The story of this enormous monochrome canvas goes back to a commission which Picasso had received during the Civil War to decorate the Spanish Pavilion at the Paris World Exhibition of 1937. Undecided for several months as to what he was going to paint, Picasso was presented with the ideal subject-matter when, in April of that year, German planes of the Condor Division destroyed the Basque town of Guernica, a bombing which was purely vindictive and had no military significance. Picasso, sharing the general sense of outrage provoked by this attack, set about working on the canvas with his characteristic speed and passion, completing the work by late June. After the Civil War he left the painting in the Museum of Modern Art in New York with the proviso that it should go to Spain on the return of democracy to the country. When a stable democracy was finally established, there was much debate as to where in Spain the work should be displayed, with many people arguing in favour of a special museum for it in Guernica itself. The artist's own, modest, wish was that it should hang near the great works of Velázquez in the Prado. So as not openly to defy this, the work was placed in 1981 in the Prado's annexe in the Casón del Buen Retiro, where it stayed until 1992, when it was transferred to its present and far more suitable location, amidst considerable complaints from the artist's family and

197

others. In addition to this continuing controversy, the work still arouses strong political emotions and consequent fears of attacks from right-wing extremists: though gun-carrying members of the Civil Guard no longer protect it, bullet-proof glass does.

The crowds that tend to gather in front of *Guernica* disperse soon afterwards, leaving few foreign visitors to persevere into the long hall containing such figurative Spanish masterpieces of the 1930's onwards as Alfonso Ponce de Leon's *Accidente,* a surreal nocturnal scene in which an elegantly suited man has been ejected through his car window into a thorn bush: with characteristically Spanish black humour he lies dead below a sign reading 'No trespassing'. Spanish abstract artists of the Franco years, so much better known than their figurative contemporaries, are featured in some of the rooms beyond: the bold, dark, and unmistakably Spanish works of such remarkable artists as Saura, Tapiès, Millares and Chillida, are perfectly in key with the monumental austerity of the architectural setting.

Sabatini's building has much in common with the Escorial, and tiredness is liable eventually to set in, for all the distractions of the works of art on show here. Fortunately there is always the reviving excitement of the most recent architectural addition to the building – its exterior lifts. Those who financed the reconstruction of the building in the 1980's were anxious to create a lively structure that would express the optimism of the city as it approached the end of the millennium. Not content with the way Fernández Alba had respected the severe character of the building's original exterior, they turned to other architects to try and lighten this exterior. The solution eventually adopted was the application to the front and back façades of glass lift shafts which shine with dazzling modernity against Sabatini's great expanses of brick. Visitors ascending on these lifts have the sensation of rising in the air above an ever-expanding panorama of Madrid, a sensation also of being effortlessly projected from the world of Charles III into that of the present day.

Parks and Gardens

THE PLAZA DE ESPAÑA *to* EL PARDO

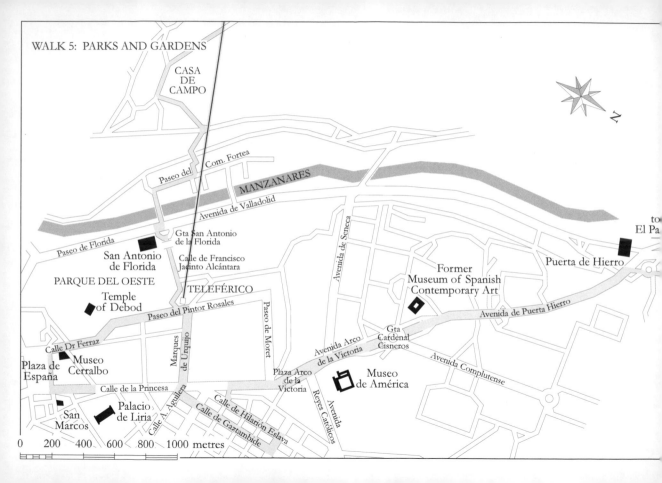

WALK 5: PARKS AND GARDENS

CASA DE CAMPO

N

MANZANARES

Paseo del Com. Fortea

Avenida de Valladolid

Paseo de Florida

Gta San Antonio de la Florida

San Antonio de Florida

Calle de Francisco Jacinto Alcántara

PARQUE DEL OESTE

Avenida de Seneca

Former Museum of Spanish Contemporary Art

Puerta de Hierro

to El Pa

Temple of Debod

TELEFÉRICO

Paseo del Pintor Rosales

Paseo de Moret

Avenida de Puerta Hierro

Calle Dr Ferraz

Marques de Urquijo

Gta Cardenal Cisneros

Plaza de España

Museo Cerralbo

Avenida Arco de la Victoria

Avenida Complutense

Calle de la Princesa

Plaza Arco de la Victoria

Museo de América

San Marcos

Palacio de Liria

Calle A. Aguilera

Calle de Hilarión Eslava

Calle de Gaztambide

Avenida Reyes Católicos

0   200   400   600   800   1000 metres

Parks and Gardens

THE PLAZA DE ESPAÑA *to* EL PARDO

The story of Madrid as it expands at alarming speed from the 1860's onwards is best told as we move into the northern half of the city, progressing through the changing city evoked by Pérez Galdós into a landscape of skyscrapers suggestive of America. A foretaste of Madrid's development since the 1930's will be had in the course of this chapter, which, covering an area that extends northwest of the Royal Palace, passes two of the earliest of the city's skyscrapers, and later heads off through the modern University City. Yet the principal theme of the itinerary is not the city's modern aspects, but its green spaces, which in turn bring back memories of the 17th and 18th centuries. Goya too makes a prominent appearance in these pages, some of

his greatest works being found in the former isolated hermitage between the Parque del Oeste and the vast green expanses of the Casa del Campo. We will arrive finally in the forested grounds of the Pardo, an appropriate conclusion to a chapter intended largely as a rural interlude before the urban onslaught to come. This is the Madrid that Ramón Villaamil, the tragic protagonist of Galdós' novel *Miau*, comes to appreciate only in the sad, closing stages of his life. On the premature summer's day which he chooses for his suicide, he goes to what is now the Plaza de España and stares north towards the distant Sierra, relishing the green and wooded landscape which lies in between. The horse-chestnuts, the plane trees, and the black poplars are on the point of sprouting, the privet hedges are already showing their new leaves, and small pink flowers dot the Judas trees. "'How lovely that is!" he said to himself, loosening the neck of his cloak, which was making him very hot. "It's as if I were seeing it for the first time in my life, or as if the Sierra and those trees and this sky have only just been created.'"

I. The Palacio de Liria, and the Plaza de España Villaamil lived – as will be seen in the following chapter – off the Plaza de Las Comendadoras, and on his way to the Plaza de España would have passed near the Palacio de Liria, which I have chosen as the starting-point of this itinerary. Standing in a large garden off the long and busy modern Calle Princesa, this palace (shown opposite) is an enclave of the 18th-century containing perhaps the richest of the city's private art collections. The building, which recalls in its elevation both the Royal Palace in Madrid and the Bourbon Palacio de La Granja, was commissioned in 1762 by Jacobo Stuart Fitz-James, 3rd Duke of Berwick and Liria, and someone who later married into the house of Alba, one of

Spain's most important aristocratic families. The original architect was the Frenchman A. Guilbert, but he was replaced in the 1770's by Ventura Rodríguez and Francesco Sabatini. The English architect Edwin Lutyens remodelled the interior around 1900, and the whole palace was extensively reconstructed following severe damage in the course of the Civil War. Lutyens is sometimes thought to have been responsible as well for the staff quarters adjacent to the main entrance gates, outside which there gather, every Friday morning, the small groups of people who have made appointments to visit the palace.

These Friday morning tours seem principally to attract those with a hankering for the world of privilege, and clear signs of delight are shown as an elderly liveried retainer takes us across the beautiful lawn and into the marbled vestibule, from where a grand staircase by Lutyens leads up to the lavish suite of first-floor rooms. Amidst all the porcelains, tapestries and gilded furniture, is displayed a collection of paintings of uniformly high standard, including a panel of the Virgin by Fra Angelico, one of the relatively rare oil landscapes by Rembrandt, a superb self-portrait by Mengs, and works by Fra Bartolommeo, Titian, Palma Vecchio, Andrea del Sarto, Guardi and Rubens. Most of Spain's leading 16th- and 17th-century painters are represented, and there is an exceptionally rich group of family portraits, ranging from Titian's portrait of the 3rd Duke of Alba up to portraits of members of the Stuart family by Reynolds, Gainsborough and Raeburn. One room is dedicated to Goya, and features a celebrated full-length portrait of the 13th Duchess of Alba, one of the hands of her puppet-like body pointing to an inscription in the ground bearing the enigmatic words, 'Only Goya'. Among the portraits of more recent members of the family are works by Madrazo, Winterhalter and Augustus John, and a horrendous Velázquez pastiche by Zuloaga showing the present Duchess as a child, seated on horseback, behind a large Mickey Mouse toy.

This apparition will prepare us for the shock of returning to the 20th century the moment we leave the house and make our way south down the noisy Calle Princesa towards the nearby

Plaza de España. Immediately before entering the square we could make a short detour back into the 18th century by turning left on to the Calle de San Leonardo to visit the church of San Marcos, which sits incongruously alongside ugly 1950's apartment blocks. Founded in commemoration of the Battle of Almansa – in which the first Duke of Berwick had taken part – this church is one of the finest ecclesiastical works by Ventura Rodríguez, and a masterpiece of the Madrilenian late baroque. The curved arms of its severe façade pull one into a gilded polychromed interior conceived as a succession of five unequal ellipses, the largest of which has a dome covered in frescoes featuring the Duke of Berwick mounted on a white steed.

The Plaza de España, marking the site of yet another convent pulled down by Joseph Bonaparte, once formed part of land belonging to the Dukes of Alba, who sold it to the municipality of Madrid on condition that a children's garden was built in the middle of it. The long square, sloping down towards the viewpoint admired by Villaamil, is taken up today by a large terraced

garden, though, instead of any attractions for children there is in its centre a huge monument to Cervantes (opposite). With pretensions as soaring as its size, this multi-figured work of the 1920's rises up above a large pool, the centrally-seated figure of Cervantes surrounded by a nightmarish mêlée of his creations, as well as by allegorical figures symbolizing his essential 'Spanishness'. The upper half of this memorably vulgar square is redolent of the 1950's, and is given a strong South American look by its two skyscrapers, at one time the largest in Europe. The earlier and architecturally more interesting of the two is the Edificio España, which was designed in 1947 and occupies the whole of the square's eastern side. A typically megalomaniac product of the early Franco years, it has a grandiose tiered elevation comparable to that of Moscow's University Building, but is unmistakably Spanish in the elaborate neo-baroque ornamentation placed above its entrance portal. The adjacent Torre de Madrid, at the northeastern corner of the square, dates from the mid 1950's, and, with its thirty-two floors, is slightly higher than its neighbour. This was the first of Madrid's truly tall buildings to abandon all neo-baroque trappings, but the end result today is a structure of remarkable tackiness, its futuristic pretensions gone grey and mouldy. The interior, the first in Spain to have air-conditioning throughout, is worth visiting only to take the lift up to its top-floor bar, from where an incomparably extensive view of Madrid can be enjoyed.

II. The Museo Cerralbo and the Paseo Pintor Rosales At the southwestern corner of the Plaza de España is the former building of the Asturian Mining Company, a fine turn-of-the-century structure which has recently undergone a bold conversion inside to create one of the city's many exciting new venues for art exhibitions. The ironwork structure of the original hall, incorporating rows of spindly Corinthian columns, is strikingly contrasted with white tubes for the air-conditioning, curved walls of coloured steel, and gangways in light wood. For an unchanged interior of the last years of the 19th century we must head due north of the square along the Calle de Ferraz, and take the first

turning to the right. Behind the eclectic red-brick exterior at No. 17 Calle Ventura Rodríguez lies the Aladdin's cave of the Museo Cerralbo. This was the palace of the 17th Marquis of Cerralbo, a politician, collector, and pioneering student of archaeology who died heirless in 1922, leaving the house and its contents to the state. The house, virtually untouched since the Marquis' day, was built in the 1880's and decorated and furnished in a style which represents the apogee of the neo-baroque. This is not a place which will appeal to genteel English tastes, though it is difficult to imagine how anyone could be unmoved by its atmospherically-lit rooms, where the sun peers through the gaps between great swathes of heavy drapery, illuminating a gilded profusion of paintings, columns, swollen mirrors, dusty family mementos, marble-topped tables and the restless arabesques of silk and velvet-lined furniture. The *horror vacui*, or fear of empty spaces, that characterizes the decoration of this palace, is balanced by its near-sepulchral silence. This is one of the least-publicised of Madrid's great museums, and the little that is written on it in guide-books gives greater emphasis to the art treasures than to their setting, which is by far the museum's greatest attraction. Few of the works by the many famous artists supposedly represented here are of more than minor interest, and the sole paintings that stand out afterwards in the memory are the wall and ceiling decorations by the eccentric and virtually unknown Máximo Juderías Caballero.

Juderías Caballero, a native of Zaragoza, attracted the attention of the Marquis at an early age, and was a guest in the palace for seven years while engaged in its decoration. He was later offered commissions from other aristocrats, but became disillusioned with Madrid after the elderly Duchess of Castro Enríquez asked him to cover up the nudes on some decorations that he had planned for her house on the Calle del Arenal. Subsequently settling in Paris, he returned to Spain only at the end of his long life, dying eventually in a remote Aragonese village in 1951, by which time he had long been forgotten by the Spanish art establishment. An academic artist who showed no originality either in his style or

subject-matter, Juderías was nonetheless a painter of stunning technical virtuosity, and, as we enter one of the rooms that he decorated in the Cerralbo Palace we suddenly emerge from the all-pervading baroque gloom into the brilliant sunlight of an illusionistic decoration, here portraying peasants at work in the fields. He reserved his greatest technical feats for the palace's extraordinary ballroom, where, competing with a gilded, mirrored and marbled setting of overwhelming lushness, he produced a Tiepolo-inspired ceiling in which historical and mythological figures co-exist effortlessly with people in everyday dress, such as a group of realistically-observed musicians placed directly above the actual Musicians' Gallery.

Returning to the Calle Ferraz and continuing to head north, we skirt to our left the long and very beautiful gardens of the Parque del Oeste, which were laid out at the beginning of this century and have wonderful views towards the Sierra de Guadarrama. If the mind is still dazzled by the Cerralbo Museum we might well feel that we are suffering from an illusion the moment we see, at the southern end of the park, what looks unmistakeably like an Egyptian Temple. This is not a mirage but the Temple of Debod, a structure of the 4th century BC erected during the reign of the Pharaoh Azakheramon of Meroe, and presented to the Spanish Government in 1968 as a gesture of thanks for the efforts of Spanish archaeologists in preserving monuments threatened by the Aswan Dam. This venerable survival from ancient Egypt stands at the heart of what is now, during the summer months, the most fashionable night-time district of Madrid: the parkside promenade which passes directly in front of it, the Paseo Pintor Rosales, lined from June to September with open-air bars or *terrazas* that are thronged until the early hours of the morning by the young and elegantly dressed. The Paseo Pintor Rosales is the northern continuation of the Calle Ferraz, and if we keep walking north along it, we will come, near the junction of the Calle Marqués de Urquijo, to the Estación Teleferico, from which we can descend by cable-car to the distant Casa de Campo. However, if we want to see Goya's frescoes in the Hermitage of San Antonio de

Florida, we should descend instead by foot down the Calle Francisco y Jacinto Alcántara. This will take us through the wooded centre of the Parque del Oeste, and past the Ceramics School where the Zuloaga family once had a studio. Next to this shaded and quietly situated building is a gate through which we can see a short alley of cypresses leading to a distant column. This marks the site of the common grave where forty-three of the Spaniards executed by the French on 3 May 1808 lie buried. The day after the execution, members of the lay confraternity of San Antonio de Florida applied for permission to recover the bodies from the pit in which the French had left them, and bury them in consecrated ground near their church. On the wall besides the grave is a ceramic version of Palmaroli's dramatic painting of female mourners now in Madrid's Town Hall (Casa de la Villa), while Goya's more famous version of the actual execution (reproduced on pp. 44-45) is used to mark the entrance of this intimate and quietly affecting cemetery.

III. The Hermitage of San Antonio de la Florida and the Casa de Campo The railway tracks leading to the Estación del Norte now separate the cemetery from the former Hermitage of San Antonio de la Florida, which stands at the bottom of the hill, within sight of the Manzanares. Since 1927 the original church of the hermitage has not been used for services, which are held instead in the twin building adjoining it. The tiny church, which was commissioned by Charles IV in 1792 in response to the growing cult of St. Anthony, is a neoclassical jewel by the little known architect Francisco Fontana. Its fame, however, is due entirely to its frescoes by Goya, who received the commission from Charles IV in 1798, the year of the building's consecration. Goya took 120 days to complete the work, painting vividly lit angels and ecclesiastical symbols on the spandrels, and covering the whole of the dome with a scene of St. Anthony raising a murdered man to life so as to exonerate the saint's father by identifying the true murderer. This apparently uninspiring scene was set by Goya behind a fictive balcony, around which he portrayed a crowded cross-section of contemporary Madrid society. The general animation and glistening areas of white reveal the influence of G.-B. Tiepolo, but the darkly satirical and boldly expressive quality of some of the figures look ahead to the Romantic era. It is also a remarkably secular depiction of a religious scene, with no heavenly onlookers to balance the realistic world below. The only god to be found in this church today is Goya himself, whose corpse was brought here in 1919 from Bordeaux, and lies where one would normally expect to find the high altar.

The shaded banks of the river Manzanares, where crowds of washerwomen used to gather (as the painting on p. 21), were deprived early this century of all remaining elements of the picturesque by being enclosed in large walls of stone and lined on both sides by characterless buildings. Nonetheless, with the disappearance of the washerwomen, this area emerged as a popular place to spend a leisurely summer's afternoon, and a number of cheap and modest eating establishments grew up along the river's banks. Near

the Hermitage is the only one of these to survive, Casa Mingo, where many Madrilenians come during the summer months to eat roast chicken and the delicious Asturian cheese known as *cabrales*, accompanying all this with a bottle or two of Asturian cider, which is traditionally poured out into the glasses from a great height. Another attraction, now gone, was the nearby swimming-pool of El Lago, quiet and luxuriant and much frequented by transvestite prostitutes during their work breaks.

By crossing the bridge directly in front of the Hermitage and then negotiating the more ominous-looking dual carriageway of the M-30, we now reach Madrid's largest recreational area, the Casa de Campo. Originally a hunting ground acquired by Philip II, this is a vast undulating park, rather frayed at its edges, and containing such attractions as tennis-courts, a fairground, woods, and a large lake for swimming and boating. From the top of one of its mounds we are offered one of the finest views of the Madrid skyline, the cliff-top bulk of the Royal Palace framed on one side by the skyscrapers of the

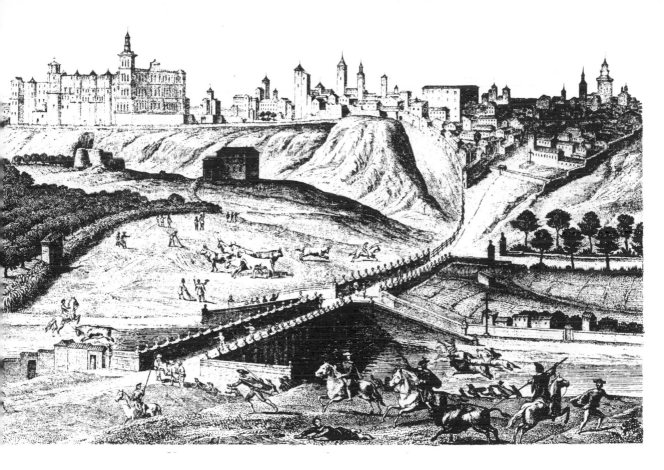

Plaza de España, and on the other by the huge dome of San Francisco el Grande. (We can compare how it looked in the 17th century, previous page, before the Royal Castle was burned down, and while bulls were still put to pasture alongside the Manzanares; and how it was portrayed by Goya in his painting of the romería, pp. 12-13.)

Near the highest part of the park we will find the main terminal (Estacion Teleferico) of the cable-car which we take back up to the Paseo Pintor Rosales, enjoying vertiginous views down to the Manzanares all the way.

IV. Moncloa and the University City Between the Paseo Pintor Rosales and the parallel Calle Princesa extends an oblong grid of streets laid out in the late 19th century but lined today mainly with elegant residential and office blocks dating from the 1920's onwards. Heading east of the Paseo along the broad Calle de Marqués de Urquijo we pass at No. 47 a block marked by a recent plaque to the leading member of the Generation of 27, Rafael Alberti, (left) who lived here between 1931 and 1936, during those years in which his activities as a poet came to be subservient to his involvement in Marxist politics. We eventually come out at the main commercial stretch of the Calle Princesa, where we should turn left. One of the long parallel streets running north of here is the Calle Gaztambide, where at No. 65 is a grey and grimy modern college and residence belonging to the Escolapian Fathers, a teaching order founded in the 17th century by St. Joseph of Calasanz. This unpromising building will now have to feature in the itinerary of anyone seriously interested in Goya's works, for, since 1990, its chapel has housed one of this artist's most powerful religious works. Commissioned in 1819, it represents *The Last Communion of St. Joseph of Calasanz,* a subject of particular significance to Goya, and not only because he had been born, like the saint, in Aragón and had been educated at an Escolapian School. In 1819 he had been struck down by a serious illness, and thoughts of his own last communion must certainly have entered his head. The kneeling saint, illuminated by a solitary beam of light, and with his eyes closed as his lips touch the holy wafer, is a literal and especially moving portrayal of blind faith, frightening in its fanatical intensity and yet also offering a glimpse of hope in the darkness. The following year Goya's mood was to take a more pessimistic turn, the lingering effects of his illness triggering off the first of his 'Black Paintings'.

The last years of Pérez Galdós' life were spent at a red-brick residence which once stood at No. 7 on the Calle Hilarión Eslava, the parallel street to the north of the Calle Gaztambide. Blind, embittered, and virtually insolvent, he died here on 5 January 1920, out of favour with both the political and literary establishment, but still commanding an enormous popular respect among the people of Madrid (as we can guess from the photograph of his funeral overleaf). His house, which had been built in 1910 for one of his cousins, was pulled down as late as 1976, the efforts to save it as a museum to the writer having resulted only in the preservation of its plaque, which now adorns a modern apartment block. The area of Madrid most marked by Francoist architectural ideals is reached as we continue

to walk north along the Calle Princesa and come out into the Plaza de la Moncloa. To our left, rising like a monster above the northern end of the Parque del Oeste, is the Air Ministry, a triumphantly sized monument of which Hitler would have been proud. Its architect, Luis Gutiérrez Soto, had established his reputation in the 1920's as a pioneering representative of functionalism, but later came under the influence of the primitive neoclassicism purveyed by Hitler's architects P. L. Troost and Albert Speer. The architecture of the Nazis was greatly admired by the Falange, and elements from such buildings as Troost's Haus der Kunst in Munich and Albert Speer's Zeppelinfeld in Nüremberg were imitated in the initial design of the Air Ministry, work on which was begun in 1942. The collapse of Nazi Germany, however, led to a major change of plan, and the building ended up in 1951 as such a pastiche of the Escorial that it came popularly to be known as the 'Monasterio del Aire'.

On the opposite side of the Plaza de la Moncloa is a tall rounded temple to Franco's war dead, while the square culminates at its northern end in a Fascist-style triumphal arch bearing a Latin inscription recording Franco's military victory. The arch has at least some practical value, for inside is kept the archive of Madrid's Complutense University, the enormous campus of which begins immediately below the monument, extending far into the northern horizon. The University City, which is spaciously laid out in pleasant verdant surroundings, was founded by Alfonso XIII in 1927, but was severely damaged during the Civil War, and replanned in the 1940's as yet another monument to the greater glory of Franco. The main attraction for tourists is the Museum of America (Museo de América), which is the first large building we come to as we descend from the arch down the broad and busy Avenida Arco de La Victoria. Housed in a neo-Herreran complex incorporating a library and church as well, this museum features a celebrated collection of ancient finds from Latin America, many of which were amassed in the course of the scientific expeditions launched during the reign of Charles III. Further down, just to the west of the intersection which joins the Avenida Arco de Victoria with the Avenida Puerta de Hierro, is the tall block which was built in 1969 to house the Museum of Spanish Contemporary Art. One of the major and bolder commissions of the last years of the Franco regime, this structure was much admired in its time, though it is generally considered today as being more suited for use as a multi-storeyed carpark than as an art gallery. A number of fine modern sculptures lie around its attractive gardens, but the bulk of the collections was moved to the Centro Cultural Reina Sofia several years ago. Unoccupied and of uncertain future, the building stands today as a monumental folly commemorating a bygone era in both politics and architectural taste.

V. El Pardo   Frequent buses starting from near the Plaza de la Moncloa ply the Avenida Arco de la Victoria in the direction of El Pardo, a journey of some fifteen minutes. On the way we pass near the residences of both the prime minister and the King, and also skirt the exclusive residential district of Puerta de Hierro, which numbers among its many luxurious modern villas the colourful hi-tech structure comprising the house-museum of the Moroccan-born millionaire Jacques Hachuel. The Puerta de Hierro itself, sitting today in between the two lanes of the La Coruña motorway, is an elegant baroque gateway commissioned by Philip V to mark the entrance to the hunting grounds of El Pardo. These grounds, which have been used by Spanish kings from at least the early 15th century onwards, are formed of gently undulating terrain covered with what is now a rather threadbare carpet of oaks and junipers, populated by a great variety of game. The nearest area of natural beauty within easy reach of Madrid, the place is very popular with daytrippers, who come here to take their siestas under the shade of trees, preferably after having had a filling lunch of game served in the many bars and restaurants of El Pardo village. The village, founded by Charles III, has a lively appeal at weekends, but would be unremarkable were it not for the large palace which dominates it, and the nearby summer pavilion of the Casita del Príncipe. The Palace has its origins in a hunting lodge built by Henry III in 1405, which was replaced in 1547 by a grander structure commissioned by Charles V, a great enthusiast of hunting. Rebuilt in the early 17th century by Francisco and Juan Gómez de Mora, it was later remodelled and enlarged by Francesco Sabatini for Charles III. Elements of the 17th-century structure, such as the high-pitched slate roofs and the corner towers, are clearly apparent as we stare at the main façade from across a vast forecourt, but the interior has a highly restored 18th-century character, as well as a number of later additions. What the original palace looked like can be guessed from the painting here, which shows the hunting lodge, the Torre della Parada as it was in 1640, with a deer being ceremonially dismembered in the courtyard. It was for this little building that Velázquez painted his famous hunting portraits, now in the Prado, and quite possibly the *Tela Real* reproduced on pp. 30-32. Many of the royal family's Titians were once kept in the palace itself – including the portrait of Charles V at the Battle of Mühlberg also in the Prado. Today the palace contains numerous canvases by the ubiquitous

Luca Giordano, ceiling-paintings by Goya's teacher Bayeu, and a beautiful folding-screen by the most successful Catalan artist of this century, José María Sert. However, the interest of the palace is primarily historical, and, in the course of the guided tour around it, we will be shown the room where Alfonso XII died, and numerous mementos of Franco, who took over the building as his main residence immediately after the Civil War, when it had served as the headquarters of the International Brigade. Among the Franco memorabilia are the heavy desk used by him for the writing of Christmas cards, the neo-gothic chapel where he prayed, and the 18th-century theatre which he transformed into a cinema, complete with an ingenious system of air-conditioning hidden in a row of lions' heads around the cornice.

The Casita del Príncipe lies a few minutes walk to the north of the palace, and is a tiny neoclassical masterpiece, commissioned from Juan de Villanueva in 1782 by the future Charles IV. The exterior is exceedingly simple, but the interior is of exquisite richness, with a central marbled hall and a suite of rooms on either side decorated by the likes of Bayeu and Maella, and with some outstanding portraits by Mengs. Another 18th-century building that can be visited in the grounds of El Pardo is La Quinta, but this is situated three kilometres southeast of the village, and is inaccessible by public transport. Used as an office by the present king, Juan Carlos, before he ascended the throne, the building occupies a fine hill-top position and is covered throughout with a remarkable series of hand-painted mid-19th century wall-papers. Those who have made the walk here from the village can pick up the Madrid bus by heading due west until the main road is reached, a distance of just over two kilometres. The descent through the forest is pleasant enough, but if we are already beginning to long again for the city, we will feel reassured as we suddenly catch sight once more of that by-now-familiar profile of Madrid looming enticingly above the Manzanares.

Churches and Tenements

THE GRAN VÍA *to* SAN PLÁCIDO

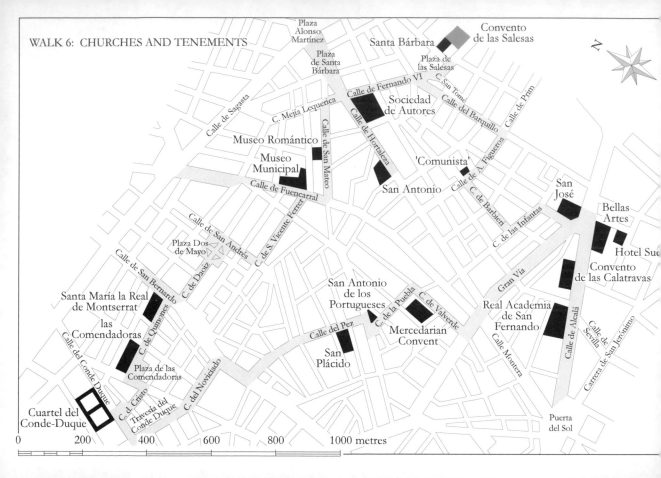

WALK 6: CHURCHES AND TENEMENTS

Plaza Alonso Martínez

Plaza de Santa Bárbara

Santa Bárbara

Convento de las Salesas

Plaza de las Salesas

C. San Tomé

Calle de Fernando VI

Calle del Barquillo

Calle de Prim

Sociedad de Autores

Calle de Sagasta

C. Mejía Lequerica

Calle de San Mateo

Calle de Hortaleza

Calle de A. Figueroa

Museo Romántico

Museo Municipal

Calle de Fuencarral

'Comunista'

San Antonio

C. de Barbieri

San José

Bellas Artes

Hotel Sue

Calle de San Andrés

C. de S. Vicente Ferrer

C. de las Infantas

Plaza Dos de Mayo

C. de Daoiz

Calle de San Bernardo

Gran Vía

Convento de las Calatravas

San Antonio de los Portugueses

Calle de la Puebla

C. de Valverde

Santa María la Real de Montserrat

C. de Quiñones

Calle del Pez

Mercedarian Convent

Real Academia de San Fernando

Calle de Alcalá

Calle de Sevilla

las Comendadoras

San Plácido

Calle Montera

Calle del Conde Duque

Plaza de las Comendadoras

C. d. Cristo

Travesía del Conde Duque

C. del Noviciado

Carrera de San Jerónimo

Cuartel del Conde-Duque

Puerta del Sol

0   200   400   600   800   1000 metres

N

Churches and Tenements

THE GRAN VÍA *to* SAN PLÁCIDO

Back once again at the Puerta del Sol, we will find that there is still much to be seen at the very centre of Madrid, and that we have by no means exhausted even its 17th- and 18th-century monuments. We need only walk down the western end of the Calle de Alcalá to be confronted by a rapid succession of sights from the Golden Age right up to the 1920's. However, what might be described as the heartland of this chapter lies just to the north of this street, in between the vulgar but splendid swathe of the Gran Vía, and the long line of French-style boulevards which extends west from the northern end of the Paseo de Recoletos. This area, relatively little visited by sightseers, contains a remarkably wide range of monuments, but its appeal will be primarily to those who are interested in the Madrid known to Pérez Galdós, and specifically in the world of artisans, shop-keepers and minor officials with which he felt most at home. The more elegant developments that took place in Madrid from the late 19th century onwards will be dealt with in the next and final chapter, but here we shall be looking at a part of the city now characterized by considerable urban decay. The process of smartening up this area will doubtless soon begin in earnest, but until this happens, the visitor who comes here will have the uncanny sensation of walking into one of Galdós' novels, and being faced with the very scenes that he described with affectionate but unflattering realism a hundred years ago.

I. From the Real Academia de San Fernando to the Bellas Artes building The Calle de Alcalá, the longest of Madrid's streets, has its origins in an ancient drover's road along which shepherds from Extremadura, until comparatively recent times, led their flocks towards northern Spain. Its subsequent development was closely similar to that of the nearby Carrera de San Jerónimo, convents and palaces being built along its western end in the course of the 16th century, followed by cafés in the 19th century, and, in more recent times, the headquarters of large banks. In contrast to the Carrera de San Jerónimo, however, this western end of the street has kept many of its old buildings, beginning, at No. 3, with the imposing former Customs House commissioned in 1761 by Charles III. This Italianate structure, with its rusticated basement, was the first of many works built in Madrid by Francesco Sabatini, and one with a design clearly derived from that of a Roman palace.

Further down the street, at No. 13, is the seat of the Real Academia de San Fernando, an institution founded by Philip V in 1752 as Spain's first academy of the fine arts. The building which it occupies, originally the home of the banker Juan de Goyeneche, was built in the 1720's by the baroque architect José de Churriguera, but, following its acquisition by the Real Academia in 1774, was stripped of its baroque embellishments so as to be given an appearance more in keeping with the academy's Enlightenment ideals. Entering through the severe neoclassical portal which replaced an exuberant baroque one by Churriguera we come to a dark vestibule, from which a heavy flight of steps leads up to the museum housing the academy's extensive art collections.

The recently re-hung museum is arranged on two floors around a large stuccoed hall where the academy's official sessions are held, presided over by busts of Philip V and Charles III. The collections, especially rich in 17th- and 18th-century Spanish paintings, were once thrown together in an apparently random manner that seemed ultimately best appreciated as one big joke; today, however, anarchy and the absurd have been sacrificed to chronological clarity. Helpful attendatnts now make sure you begin your tour with the earliest paintings, among which is a witty portrait by Arcimboldo (entitled *Spring*) that was formerly, and mysteriously, surrounded by Japanese netsuke. A sparkling if not altogether convincing canvas by Rubens of *Susanna and the Elders* paves the way for the Spanish Golden Age, which begins with an austerely powerful painting by Zurbarán of the *Blessed Alonso Rodríguez,* and proceeds (in the building's chapel) to a polychromed *Crucifixion* by Gregorio Fernández, one of the greatest of Spain's Baroque sculptors. Further on are a coarsely realistic paintings of the *Ecstasy of the Magdalene* by José Ribera, and a fantastical *memento mori* by Antonio Pereda in which a wealthy young man is shown asleep next to a table piled high with symbols of earthly vanity: this work, recalling the Don Juan legend, might have influenced Goya's famous etching entitled *The Sleep of Reason Produces Monsters,* and hence Goya's own reworking of the idea in his portrait of Jovellanos.

A large oil sketch by Fragonard for his *Sacrifice of Callirhoe* in the Louvre (the work he

La Esposicion de Pinturas.

submitted for the Prix de Rome) features in a room otherwise made up of paintings by artists active in 18th-century Madrid, such as Van Loo, the idiosyncratic Luis Paret, Corrado Giaquinto (the Director of the Academy until his replacement by Mengs in 1761) and Mengs himself, who is represented here by a truly memorable portrait of the Marchioness of Llana dressed as a maja. The last and in many ways most impressive room we visit on the first floor is devoted to Goya, and contains thirteen of his paintings, including two small self-portraits from opposite ends of his career, and the strikingly eccentric portrait of Manuel Godoy (detail p. 43), who, though portrayed with all the usual official trappings, is shown slouching in an armchair. Goya's satirical vision of human folly and fanaticism is evident in a sinister depiction of the popular festival of the Burial of the Sardine, and in three late works representing the Inquisition, a madhouse, and a procession of Flagellants. Only the most dedicated art lovers need continue up into the second floor, where numerous indifferent 18th-century pieces are succeeded by a rag-bag collection of 19th- and 20th-century paintings, of which the most memorable are some oils by Sorolla and his fellow Valencian 'impressionist' Cecilio Plá, and a gloriously overblown Egyptian scene by Muñoz Degrain, more of whose works are to be seen shortly after leaving the building and returning to the appropriately grand Calle de Alcalá.

Among the exuberant early 20th-century buildings that give this street its essential character is the Casino de Madrid, which stands next to the Real Academia, at No. 15. A fashionable French architect called Tronchet won a competition to design this building, but Spaniards protested about the way he had confirmed foreign stereotypes of their nation by including reliefs of castanets and guitars on the façade. In the end the commission went in 1903 to a Spaniard, who produced a very French design with an interior of Monte Carlo-like opulence, featuring a quite magnificent grand staircase that flows down into the hall as if it were a billowing drapery. It is typical of the many contrasts of this idiosyncratic street that only a few doors away from the Casino we will come to the former convent church of Las

Calatravas. Dating back to 1670, this was saved on the intercession of General Prim in 1870, after which its façade was remodelled in a terracotta-pink style imitative of the Lombard renaissance. Of the original church, the finest survivals are the tall dome, and the elaborate altarpieces by José Churriguera, just about visible in the exceptional gloom of the severely planned interior.

The other side of the street is dominated lower down by the soaring Art Deco pile of the Bellas Artes building, which was designed in 1919, and continues to function today as an arts club and cultural centre. It is another work by the extraordinary Antonio Palacios, who abandoned here both the hieratical symmetry and neo-baroque ornamentation of his Post Office building in favour of more solid cube-like forms and a bizarrely asymmetrical composition which culminates in a tall tower intended as an urban light-house casting its beams throughout nocturnal Madrid. The interior, gleaming with dark marble and Tiffany glass, was conceived as a city within a city, and its many floors embrace a series of theatres, exhibition halls, cinemas, conference rooms, and a large and luxuriant bar lined with enormous canvases by Munōz Degrain, an artist sometimes called Picasso's first master. The main entrance to the building is on the short and quiet Calle de Marqués de Casa Riera, where we will also find the luxurious Hotel Suecia, one of the friendliest and most pleasant places to stay in the centre of Madrid. Owing to the presence on its premises of the Swedish consulate, this Swedish-run hotel played an important rôle in the cultural life of Madrid during the Franco era, offering a sort of sanctuary to controversial writers and intellectuals. In its recently refurbished bar, where dissidents once gathered, can still be seen the occasional intellectual from that generation, taking refuge from the younger crowds who favour the bar at the Bellas Artes. The charming former head waiter of the restaurant below, Miguel Fernandez, is a Madrilenian celebrity with numerous stories to tell of the hotel's famous guests: he has a pipe presented to him by Hemingway, and is proud of once having had to lend a tie to Che Guevara. The restaurant itself is famous for its

magnificent smørgasbord, which is inspected periodically by the King of Sweden's own cook.

II. The Gran Vía Directly across the Calle de Alcalá from the Bellas Artes is the opening of the Gran Vía, its slope lined with a further succession of overblown buildings, shielding in their case a number of luxury shops of old-fashioned appearance. The construction of the street in 1910 (inaugurated by the King, photographed here) involved the pulling down of a large area of central Madrid, and aroused considerable controversy; sentimentalists like Díaz-Cañabate felt that the character of the city had been irrevocably destroyed by this 'horrible series of buildings and traffic jams'. However, long before the street had been built, the hearts of many other Madrilenians had been warmed to it by a comic and fantastical zarzuela entitled *La Gran Vía*. The tunes of this enormously popular work by Federico Chueca, though dating back to 1886, are still hummed today by many elderly Madrilenians, and form the *leitmotif* of one of the stories within a story of Felipe Alfau's eccentric novel *Chromos* (1948), a vision of Spanish life through the eyes of Spaniards living in America. It was only a matter of time before the street came to be regarded as representing the quintessential charm of Madrid, one of its greatest enthusiasts being the writer Francisco Umbral, who was reminded by it of New York and Chicago, and daily experienced an enormous elation as he began the slow ascent from the Calle de Alcalá, eyeing the cosmopolitan procession of shops and people as if it were a cinematic spectacle.

The Gran Vía undoubtedly presents its finest profile when seen from just below its fork-like intersection with the Calle de Alcalá (overleaf), the point where the two great thoroughfares meet being marked by one of the most popular of Madrid's buildings, the very name of which is evocative of turn-of-the-century cosmopolitanism, the Edificio Metropolis. Built in 1905 by the French architects Jules and Raymond Fevrier, it celebrates the joining of the two streets with a cylindrical frontage consisting of a ring of paired giant columns, an attic level of richly carved statuary, and a tall crowning dome highlighted in gold and bearing a bronze representation of

Winged Victory. The building, as seen on a grey, empty dawn, is the subject of the painting shown on page 57, a much-reproduced canvas by the most popular Spanish artist of today, Antonio López, who has specialized in meticulously observed Madrilenian scenes, and has recently achieved some international prominence as the protagonist of Victor Erice's haunting film *The Quince Tree Sun* (1992). Another painting of Madrid by López, enigmatically entitled *María y los Embajadores,* is reproduced as the cover of this book and on p. 14.

Tucked away on the side overlooking the Gran Vía is the entrance to the narrow street of the Caballero de Gracia, where, in the words of Alfau, 'a delicate romance still dwelt in wandering shadows...' This street, which gave its name to one of the best known songs from Chueca's *La Gran Vía*, hides at its northern end a quite outstanding neoclassical oratory by Juan de Villanueva, the back of which, overlooking the Gran Vía, has been subject to a drastic modern alteration. Adjoining the Edificio Metropolis, at No. 1 Gran Vía, is a luxuriously appointed shop belonging to the jewellery firm of Grassy, who keep in the basement here a museum featuring a superb collection of Art Nouveau clocks.

One of the longest running and most endearing institutions on the Gran Vía is to be found on the northern side of the street, at No. 12. Called misleadingly the Museo Chicote, this is in fact an elegant bar founded in 1931 by Perico Chicote, a well-known Madrid personality who came to be known as 'the king of the cocktails'. While working as barman at the Ritz, Chicote had been presented by the Brazilian Embassy with a bottle of the Brazilian rum called Paraty, and this inspired him to form a collection of drinks from all over the world, which were displayed in the bar's cellar and gave the place its title of museum. This museum soon came to be known as the most popular in Madrid after the Prado, but, sadly, the collection was eventually sold, reputedly to the Walt Disney Corporation. Even without its 'museum', however, the bar is well worth visiting, both for its architecture and for its evocation of bygone glamour. In the middle of its simple Art Deco façade – designed, inciden-tally, by the Air Ministry architect, Luis Gutiér-rez Soto – is a swing door leading to a perfectly preserved Art Deco interior, gleaming with chrome and mirrors, and with a row of semi-circular alcoves. The courteous elderly waiters who worked here until very recently seemed themselves survivors from the 1930's, when the film director Luis Buñuel would have given them his famously particular instructions for the mixing of a dry Martini. Characterised by the English writer Laurie Lee as exuding in its early days an atmosphere of 'weary eroticism', the bar attracted the likes of Ava Gardner, Gregory Peck and, inevitably, Hemingway before degenerating by the end of the 1950's into what Lee referred to as a 'prophylactic for tourists'.

The travel-writer Archibald Lyall, describing the Museo Chicote in 1960, wrote that 'up to about eight in the evening it is a respectable bourgeois resort but then, by a sort of tacit and accepted convention, the ladies of good society clear out and the ladies of the town come in and take over.' A similar transformation occured from the early 1980's onwards, when the place

was taken over at night by leading members of the Movida, who helped bring back the spirited atmosphere of the bar's heyday. Sadly, in the past few years the Chicote has gone again out of fashion and now has a lugubrious and slightly seedy atmosphere at all times.

III. Chueca   The time has finally come to plunge into the warren of dark and decayed streets that extend to the north of the Gran Vía. To do so we should start off at the lower end of the street, turning left into the Calle del Marqués de Valdeiglesias. The latter street begins around the corner from the church of San José, which has a façade by Pedro de Ribera and a dark interior featuring a plaque commemorating the wedding here in May 1802 of Simon Bolívar. The short street emerges into the Calle de las Infantas, where, on turning right, we see the Casa de las Siete Chimeneas. Though heavily restored and altered over the centuries, this palace is still recognizable as the late 16th-century structure we can see in the detail from Texeira opposite. The name means 'House of the Seven Chimneys', but Texeira for once seems to have slipped up on detail. The house was built by the two architects of the Escorial, Juan Bautista de Toledo and Juan de Herrera. In the 18th century the building was inhabited by Charles III's notorious minister Squillace, but English visitors will prefer to remember this as the place where in 1623 the future Charles I of England stayed, together with the Duke of Buckingham, Sir Kenelm Digby, and Endymion Porter. This mission, to urge his suit to the Infanta María, was not a success but the young prince was set on his course as the greatest collector in Europe by the overwhelming example of the art in the Spanish royal collections.

The area we are now in is filled with restaurants, and we will find at the western end of the Calle de las Infantas a tiny, crowded and once famously cheap Cuban establishment, Zara. This was founded by one of the many refugees fleeing from Castro in the early 1960's, a period when Cuban food began to have a considerable influence on local cuisine. The dish of rice, fried banana and tomato sauce known as *arroz a la Cubana* became one of the staple offerings in

Madrid restaurants, and inspired Francisco Umbral to write a whole page describing how the Gran Vía came to smell of it. One restaurant where we will not be finding *arroz a la Cubana* is the nearby Salvador, which is one of the most traditional of Madrid's restaurants, and a place where the menu has changed little since the time it was opened in 1941. Situated at No. 13 Calle Barbieri, the street running north of the Calle de las Infantas, it has pleasant intimate dining-rooms covered with photographs of the many bull-fighters and other celebrities who have eaten here, Hemingway being of course among them. The founder, Salvador Blázquez, had numerous distinguished friends, and there is even a photograph showing him as a young man in the company of the aged and near-blind Pérez Galdós. The great speciality of the place is breaded hake or *merluza rebosada*, a dish of characteristically Madrilenian simplicity but one requiring considerable skill to achieve the subtle, succulent results to be tasted here.

At the northern end of the Calle Barbieri we emerge into the Calle de Augusto Figueroa, almost directly in front of another famous eating establishment, though of a different kind from Salvador's. Its dirty peeling façade – at No. 35 – simply bears the words 'Tienda de Vinos' (Wine Store), but it is known by everyone as 'El Comunista', supposedly because every dish on offer carries the same cheap price. The establishment, which has been in the same family for over a hundred years, became a renowned literary and artistic meeting-place in the 1950's and 60's, under the ownership of Ángel Miguel, who still runs the place today. Francisco Umbral remembered the restaurant as being 'a bit prison-like and a bit railway station-like' but redeemed by a 'naïve and almost anonymous' decoration and above all by the near-continual presence of a charismatic and enigmatic woman called Sandra, around whom there always gathered a crowd of 'poets, painters and homosexuals'. The look of the place is unchanged today, down to the grime on its high yellowing walls, the wooden panelling below, the simple benches that serve as seats, the poorly washed glasses, and the odd print and amateurish painting with which someone began an attempt long ago to bring some colour to the otherwise bare surfaces. The service is brusque, and the prices remain ridiculously if not uniformly cheap.

The run-down district which we are now in, popularly known as Chueca, was formerly referred to as that of the *chisperos*, which is both the word for 'blacksmiths' and the old Madrid slang for 'underworld characters'. Bronze and iron foundries could once be found here, but this traditionally poor area has also maintained over the years a lowlife atmosphere, and up to very recently was a favourite haunt of drug-addicts and other 'marginal elements' of Madrid society. At the eastern end of the Calle Augusto de Figueroa, however, we come out on to the long Calle de Barquillo, which though dark, dirty and narrow, is an animated thoroughfare with vestiges of grand residences, such as that at No. 34, which was the birthplace in 1756 of Francisco Castaños, whose victory at the Battle of Bailén in 1808 was the first major setback in Napoleon's career. The street was also the route used by royalty on their way to the magnificent Convent of Las Salesas, which was founded in 1747 by Barbara of Braganza – the wife of Ferdinand VI – as a retreat for her widowhood. It forms the centrepiece of a smart residential district which we will reach as soon as we emerge from the northern end of the Calle de Barquillo. The church of the former convent, which was built between 1750-58 to the designs of the French architect François Carlier, is one of the most sumptuous and harmonious in Madrid, combining French classicism with baroque pomp. Rising on steps above a large forecourt, its porticoed granite façade is articulated by a giant order of piers and enriched by statuary in marble and white Colmenar stone, including a central medallion containing a relief of the Visitation. The best time to come here is on a fine late afternoon, when the rays of the sun dramatically highlight the relief carvings on the façade, and give to the dignified interior a warm suffused glow in which the wealth of marbled furnishings acquire an added radiance. The decoration of the interior, which includes altarpieces by the Italian artists Cignaroli and Giaquinto, has a carefully orchestrated unity culminating in a high altar resplendent in green serpentine marble. Later in the century Charles III commissioned Sabatini to design the tombs of Ferdinand VI and Barbara of Braganza, which stand respectively in the south transept and in a side chapel adjoining the presbytery. These flamboyant baroque works, with their richly carved statuary by Francisco Gutiérrez, contrast markedly with the neo-renaissance tomb of the 19th-century military hero, General O'Donnell, which is situated in the north transept. The convent itself, now adapted inside to house the city's Law Courts, was never to be used by Barbara of Braganza, who died before she could become a widow.

From here the Calle de Fernando VI ascends in a northwesterly direction towards the Calle de Hortaleza, passing a fish-shop with its abundant contents arranged like some Rubensian still-life, and an equally enticing fruit-shop, whose tightly packed, symmetrical displays bask in multi-coloured glory under a large sign inscribed EAT A LOT OF FRUIT. As we near the top end of the street, however, our attention will be absorbed entirely by the inflated and fantastical organic forms that ooze down the walls of the remarkable building which appears to our left. With its predominance of undulating lines, and restless overall decoration which appears to have been moulded in putty, this building is one of the few genuine examples of Art Nouveau in Madrid, and by far the most distinguished. Though it is not by Gaudí, as is popularly thought, it is by another Catalan, Grases Riera, who built it in 1902 as both an office and residence for the banker Javier González Longoria. The exterior, with its surrounding Art Nouveau ironwork, has recently had a face-lift, while the interior has been largely transformed for its present use as the headquarters of the Society of Authors. Nevertheless, if we come here on a weekday morning, we should step inside to see the grand staircase, a painted ironwork structure which lies immediately beyond the rounded main entrance, enhancing the building's overall sense of movement with serpentine forms that soar with spiralling elegance up to a stained-glass dome bursting into a kaleidoscope of colours.

At the end of the Calle de Fernando VI the long Plaza de Santa Barbara opens up to our right. Sloping gently, it rises towards the noisy line of boulevards to the north; its shaded central reservation is covered with café tables. To our left meanwhile begins the long Calle de Hortaleza, a dark, narrow and very noisy thoroughfare of little architectural distinction, but with several interesting old shops, and a number of fashionable discothèque bars that cater for the incessant nocturnal flow of people. At this northern entrance to the street is the most exclusive of these bars, Hanoi, where, if we manage to look sufficiently interesting to persuade our way past the doorman, we will find ourselves in a post-modernist marble coffin of a room, where booming music, a row of video screens, and posing groups of design-conscious *yuppís* all compete for our attention. On the opposite side of the street, at No. 104, is the building where Peréz Galdós, fed up with his publishers, bravely decided in 1897 to set up a publishing and printing company dedicated solely to the bringing out of his own works, an ill-fated enterprise which lasted until 1905. Further down the street, at the junction with the Calle de Farmacía, are the late 18th-century college and church of San Antón, the first institution established in Madrid by the Escolapian fathers. This is where Goya's *Last Communion of San José Calasanz* used to hang before it was transferred to the Escolapian College on the Calle Gaztambide (see page 213). In the absence of this work, the only good reason for making a special journey to this singularly lugubrious building is to see the bizarre ceremony that takes place here every year on January 17th. On that day a long procession of mules, horses and other animals files past the church to be blessed by a monk, who doubly ensures that they leave in a state of grace by selling 'holy straw' to the owners.

IV. The Museo Romántico and the Museo Municipal The northern continuation of the Calle Fernando VI is the Calle de Majía Lequerica, where we will find, at the junction with Hortaleza, a building of 1912 with an unusual and grotesque decorative feature in the form of a line of enormous lizards supporting the upper balcony. From here we should take the first turn-ing to the left, leaving the bustle which surrounds the Plaza de Santa Barbara and entering the dark and quiet Calle de San Mateo. Half-way up this street, at No. 13, we come to an attractive palace in dark-red brick, which was built for the Marquis of Matellana by Manuel Martín, a cousin of Ventura Rodríguez. In 1924 this building was transformed into the Museo Romántico, the brainchild of the Marquis of Vega-Inclán, who left to it his own miscellaneous collections, which included minor canvases by Spanish 17th-century artists, paintings of his own after El Greco, and a reproduction of a Toledan interior of the 16th century. Vega-Inclán was a romantic in the popu-lar sense of the world, and his nostalgic view of the past led him to establish the famous El Greco House in Toledo as well, and the equally bogus Cervantes House in Valladolid. The Romantic Museum is as much of a fake as these last two institutions, its principal intention being to recre-ate a typical Spanish house of the Romantic era. Nonetheless it has considerable charm, and, as we walk along its creaking floorboards through a series of mellowed rooms, we might well feel that we have stumbled across an atmospheric survival of the last century. The artistic high-point is a painting by Goya of *St. Gregory*, which hangs in the chapel. But, amidst all the esoterica and heavy dark furniture which take up the rest of the rooms, we will see works by most of the leading Spanish artists of the early 19th century, from the society portraitist Federico Madrazo to the Sevillian costumbrista Valeriano Bécquer. The most genuinely 'Romantic' painting is a small expressive canvas by Leonardo Alenza representing a wild-looking man on the point of plunging a dagger into himself while jumping off a cliff into a landscape that features a man hang-ing from a tree. There is a certain element of bathos as we move from Alenza's witty satire of the Romantic fashion for suicide to the nearby room dedicated to the most famous of Spain's suicide victims, Mariano José de Larra. The ulti-mate object of pilgrimage on any Romantic tour of Madrid must surely be this room's display case containing, among other personal memen-tos of Larra, the pair of duelling pistols he used to shoot himself in 1837.

At the top of the Calle de San Mateo is the long Calle de Fuencarral, which grew up in the course of the 17th century as the city extended its boundaries north to what is now the Glorieta de Bilbao. The street, lined today mainly with turn-of-the-century buildings, has kept an old fashioned commercial character, with numerous small shops that have survived despite growing threats from the large department stores to the south. Its one outstanding monument – to be seen to our right as soon as we emerge from the Calle de San Mateo – is the former Hospicio de San Fernando, a hospital for the poor begun in 1722 by Pedro de Ribera. Even for those who have just seen the fantastically decorated Society of Authors' Building on the Calle de Fernando VI, the shock of being confronted by Ribera's frontispiece for this hospital is a considerable one. By far the most elaborate of Ribera's creations, it displays a baroque exuberance which is not only very uncharacteristic of Madrid, but also worthy of comparison with the extreme examples of the baroque style to be seen in Galicia and Andalucía. A sculptural group of St. Ferdinand receiving the keys of Seville acts as the pivot of a composition bursting with garlands, draperies, shields, urns and every other conceivable ornamental detail, the whole pushing up the entablature of the façade to create a broken pediment of Borrominesque derivation. A characteristic feature of Ribera's work, and indeed of Spanish architecture as a whole, is the placing of such an exceptionally elaborate work in the middle of an otherwise severe façade, built in this case of dark-red bricks. The simplicity of this façade is matched also by the chapel to be seen inside, a typically Madrilenian single-aisled structure, with barrel-vaulting and shallow transepts.

From the late 18th-century onwards the frontispiece of the Hospicio (pictured on page 36) was pilloried by critics, historians and architects, who held it up as the supreme example of bad taste, and would doubtless have loved to have seen it pulled down. An opportunity to do so presented itself early this century, when the building was in such a terrible condition that its remaining inmates had to be transferred else-where pending its demolition. Fortunately the Academy of Fine Arts interceded at this point, and the building was saved for use as Madrid's Municipal Museum and Library (Museo Municipal), the first director of which was the poet Manuel Machado, who is commemorated by a plaque near the entrance.

The museum has a chronologically displayed collection relating to the history of Madrid from medieval times. The most important of its many works of art is an allegory of the city by Goya that had originally featured the portrait of a triumphant Napoleon: it is an indication perhaps of Goya's true character that, at a later stage of the War of Independence, when the French were in retreat, this portrait was hurriedly replaced with the words '2nd of May'.

One large room is given over entirely to the museum's single most remarkable exhibit: an enormous wooden model of Madrid, commissioned by Ferdinand VII in 1828. Madrid was very lucky in its early topographical representations. Pedro de Texeira's plan of 1656, which we have been following through the book, and which can be seen in its entirety here, is considered today as one of the masterpieces of urban cartography. The wooden model, executed over a period of nearly two years by an army officer called Gil de Palacio, is also one of the greatest examples of its kind, and enjoyed such a success at the time that the French ambassador in Madrid invited Palacio to do a similar model of Paris. Peering closely at it, we will be drawn back into the streets of early 19th-century Madrid, observing the city before its dramatic transformation after the second half of the century.

Among the various mementos of the city's rich literary history, our window onto so many of those transformations of the 19th century, are a poignant sketch of Perez Galdós on his death-bed and the wonderfully reconstructed studies of the 'two Ramones', Mesonero Romanos and Gómez de la Serna. That of the former, removed from his house on the nearby Glorieta de Bilbao, has an uncluttered simplicity that contrasts with the fantastical anarchy of Gómez de la Serna's, which dates from his Buenos Aires years and keeps the

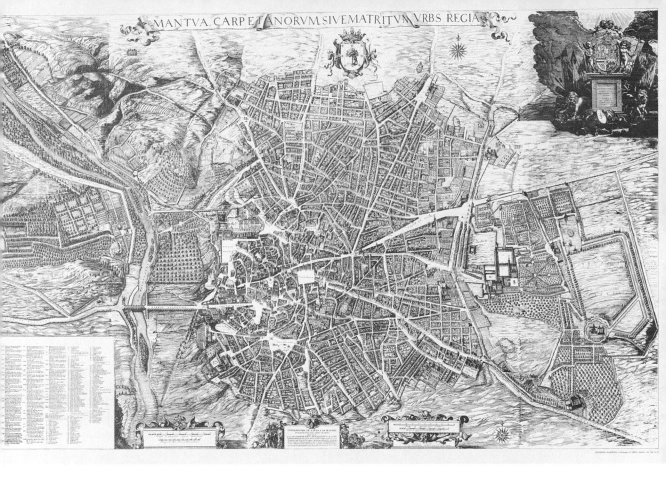

MANTVA. CARPETANORVM. SIVE MATRITVM VRBS REGIA

visitor spellbound with details like convex mirrors, swans flying on the walls, a stuffed leopard, a photographic collage, and even mirrored balls that hang from the ceiling like those of a discothèque.

V. Malasaña After leaving the museum, we should make our way to the back of the building, where we will find a quiet square named after Pedro de Ribera, in whose honour there was transferred here the only one of his Madrid fountains to have survived. Known as the Fuente de la Fama, it is a further reminder of this architect's ornamental genius, and has a lively design of dolphins and angels to support the trumpeting figure of Fame. A short detour to the north of here will take us to the Glorieta de Bilbao, the site of the 17th-century gate of Fuencarral, and now a busy intersection. On its southern side is the cavernous Café Comercial, which became popular with journalists after the Civil War, and was later the scene of numerous literary and political tertulias. One of its habitués in the 1950's and 60's was the writer and costumbrista César González Ruano, who used to arrive daily at nine-thirty each morning, glance at the papers, and then set about writing at least two of his own articles, fuelling himself for the task with constant cigarettes and cups of coffee. Previously he had been a mainstay at the Café Gijón, but he gave up that place supposedly as a result of a quarrel with the owner and of being pestered there by so many people that he had been unable to do any writing. The Café Comercial, as well as being an important testimony to Madrid's cultural life during the Franco period, is one of the city's most popular meeting-places, particularly for visitors from other parts of Spain. An evening's rendez-vous with friends here is likely to end up in the bars of neighbouring Malasaña, a district which is also reached by heading due west of the Museo Municipal on the Calle de San Vicente Ferrer.

Though popularly referred to today as Malasaña, this district was once known as the Barrio de Maravillas ('The District of Marvels'), a poetic name with a certain ironic resonance in view of the terrible poverty which the area has experienced. With its former population of manolos, this has traditionally been a working and lower-middle class district, the life of which in the early years of this century was beautifully evoked by Rosa Chacel in her autobiographical novel, *Barrio de Maravillas*. After the Civil War, the district became increasingly run-down and impoverished, as many of its older members saw their children leaving it in favour of the huge residential blocks on the city's outskirts. Property speculators soon began threatening to demolish it altogether, though their plans were fortunately stopped as a result of intensive neighbourhood protests. These protests had also the effect of drawing this district to the attention of the city's young, who soon began occupying the many empty flats and garrets, delighted to find such cheap accommodation in a quiet central area only a few minutes' walk from the Gran Vía. From the early 1960's onwards Malasaña acquired an increasingly bohemian and student character, and bars and discothèques began to proliferate. Its overall seediness nonetheless remained, and by the mid-1980's the area was in danger of being taken over almost entirely by drug addicts.

Attempts to tidy the place up have only been partially successful, and this is still a poor and decayed area, criss-crossed by dark and narrow streets crammed with 19th-century terraces uniformly streaked in grey. It is still one of the livelier nocturnal districts of Madrid, though the protagonists of this night-life are not so much the smart young businessmen of other areas, but ageing hippies and bohemians, and unshaven, sinister-looking types dressed in regulation black leather. The appearance of Malasaña, however, should not put us off from coming here, for we will also find this district to be a wonderful survival of old Madrid, with a virtually unrivalled range of old shops and bars, and a sense of neighbourly intimacy which is rapidly disappearing elsewhere.

The Calle de San Vicente Ferrer, where Rosa Chacel spent her childhood, is by night one of the more animated of Malasaña's streets, with numerous night-spots such as Manuela, a well-known alternative bar which seems to have remained stuck in the 1960's. As with all this district, however, it is remarkably quiet by day,

barely disturbed even by traffic. At No. 28, at the corner with the Calle de San Andrés, we will come to the Laboratorio de Especialidades Juanse, a pharmacy covered on the outside with some of the most famous of Madrid's surviving ceramic decorations. Dating back to 1925, these highly entertaining and colourful works are all advertisements for the products once sold within, and comprise absurd scenes of people suffering from symptoms ranging from tooth-ache to rheumatism, and even diarrhoea. Next door, marking a shop which once specialized solely in eggs, are some equally spirited if more tasteful ceramics representing hens.

From here we should descend north down the Calle de San Andrés to the Plaza Dos de Mayo, which is at the centre of Malasaña, and was also the site of the most important event in this district's history, which we probably know from Goya's painting, reproduced opposite. The square was at one time occupied by the military barracks of Monteleón, and it was to here, on that fateful day of 2 May 1808, that the young artillery officer Pedro Velarde made his way immedi-ately on hearing the shots fired by the French in their attempts to subdue the uprising centred on the Puerta del Sol. On the orders of the French military government the barracks were firmly closed, but Velarde was able to persuade his way in and convince its commander, Captain Daoíz, of the necessity of distributing arms to the crowd of compatriots outside. A violent skir-mish then ensued as the Spaniards attacked the French garrison stationed here, launching them-selves against the superior forces with a bravery verging on despair (as we can see in Goya's painting opposite, in which Spaniards lash out furiously against Napoleon's squadron of Mamelukes). The fighting, which lasted for several hours, ended with the capture of the barracks, by which time the losses on both sides had been considerable. Velarde was killed outright, and the wounded Daoíz was taken home, where he died a few hours later. The two heroes were buried in the nearby church of San Martín, but their remains were transferred soon afterwards to San Isidro and later to the sarcoph-agus which lies at the foot of the 2nd of May

243

Monument in the Plaza de Lealtad. Their memory was further commemorated by the revolutionary government of 1869, which decided in that year to erect a monument to them in the middle of the Plaza Dos de Mayo. In this they are shown in classical guise, standing underneath the arch which once formed the entrance to the destroyed barracks.

The classical apparitions of Daoíz and Velarde haunt a square bordered by tall rows of greying 19th-century residences, the whole characterized by a seedy charm which can take on a more sinister aspect late at night, when the square is frequented by a dark and dissolute-looking crowd spilling over from the surrounding bars. One of the older of these bars is the mirrored and intimate Dos De on the square's eastern side, where a strange and solitary Californian known as El Pollo Colorado is regularly to be heard giving the most entertaining renditions of flamenco that you are ever likely to hear. Brought up among the gypsies of Granada, he is now one of the well-known personalities of Malasaña, living the life of a vagrant and singing flamenco in a way which seems at first to be a parody but becomes deeply moving. There are few other *payos* or non-gypsies who have managed to capture so well the complex rhythms of flamenco.

IV. In the world of Galdós' *Miau* The western limits of Malasaña are marked by the wide and ugly Calle de San Bernardo, which is reached by walking due west of the Plaza Dos de Mayo on the Calle de Daoíz. The buildings at this street's northern end are mainly modern, the principal exception being the monastery church of Santa María La Real de Montserrat, which rises up directly in front of us, its exterior distinguished by the crowning bulbous forms of a splendidly elaborate tower, a baroque structure of the early 18th century generally attributed to Pedro de Ribera. Continuing west from here along the narrow Calle de Quiñones, we enter a district with much of the grimy 19th-century look of Malasaña, and with much of the latter's fascination. The street which we are on skirts the southern façade of the Montserrat Monastery, a building which in Galdós' day served as a women's prison. It was directly in front of this façade that Galdós situated the house of Don Ramón de Villaamil, the tragic protagonist of one of his greatest novels, *Miau*.

Written in 1888, immediately after *Fortunata and Jacinta*, this book is the story of an unremarkable civil servant who, only a few months before becoming entitled to a pension, loses his post as a result of one of the many falls of government which Spain experienced in the late 19th century. The 'Miau' of the title, so evocative of the pathetic and ineffectual cries for help of its hero, is also a reference to the cat-like features of his wife, sister-in-law and daughter, with whom he is irrevocably saddled but who are too absorbed in their own mediocre lives to show much of an interest in or understanding of his. The one member of his family with whom he enjoys any closeness is his young and sickly grandson, Luisito, who suffers from blackouts during which he has conversations with God. Reflections on the cruelty of divine providence punctuate the narrative, which ends, as we have seen, with the deranged Villaamil shooting himself near the present Plaza de España, telling himself that the gun would not go off:

> The shot echoed in the solitude of that dark and deserted place. Villaamil gave a terrible leap, his head plunged into the shifting earth, and he rolled straight down into the gulf. He retained consciousness only for enough time to say: 'Well... it did....'

Miau lacks the panoramic vision of Madrid shown in *Fortunata and Jacinta*, but as a telescopic view of a particular area of the city it is perhaps without equal in Galdós' work. Almost every street and monument in that evocative district which extends to the west of the Calle de San Bernardo features in the novel, an especially important role being played by the churches of Montserrat and Las Comendadoras, the latter being situated at the opposite end of the Calle de Quiñones, overlooking the square named after it. These are the places where the pious womenfolk of Villaamil's family regularly attend mass, where Luisito has his visions, and where Villaamil vainly attempts to find some consolation for his plight. Whereas the Montserrat church is described as having a 'cold and bare' interior, that of Las Comendadoras is referred to as 'one of the most beautiful and serene in Madrid'. This latter building, dating back to the 1660's, has retained its original appearance, even though the convent to which it is attached was remodelled by Sabatini in the middle of the 18th century. Its porticoed brick façade is flanked by two Herreran-style towers, behind which rises a large and elegantly simple dome. Once inside we find ourselves in the south transept of a building shaped like a Greek Cross and covered all over in grey and white stucco. The harmonious interior – the ornamentation of which is largely concentrated on the consoles supporting the elaborate entablature – has a fine high altar by Luca Giordano of *St. James the Moor-Slayer*. Meetings of the Knights of Santiago (whose patron saint he is) are still held in the church, and the numerous banners of this Order that are hung inside not only give this place an added solemnity, but also provided on one occasion a distraction for the restless Luisito.

Playing children and elderly people seated on benches are the main signs of life on the homely if slightly faded Plaza de las Comendadoras, from where we should head west on the short Calle del Cristo, setting off in the same direction in which the by now confused and paranoid Villaamil embarked on the last jouney of his life. The small Plaza Guardia de Corps, known in Galdós' time as the Plazuela del Limón, is where *Miau* begins, with a devilish rush of school-children out of which emerges the shy and unfortunate Luisito. The square reappears again in the closing pages of the book, as Villaamil resolutely approaches it with a mounting hatred for his family that borders on frenzy. He would certainly have been in no mood to appreciate the magnificent and profusely ornamented main portal of the Barracks of the Conde Duque. Commissioned from Pedro de Ribera in 1720 as a barracks to house the newly formed bodyguard of Philip V (a regiment to which Manuel Godoy was later to belong), the Conde Duque is one of the largest of all Madrid's buildings and consists of three enormous courtyards of an essentially austere character. Partially destroyed by fire in 1869, the building was left to fall down, but was restored in the 1980's by the Municipality of Madrid to serve as a library, archive and cultural centre. The work of transformation was entrusted to Julio Cano Lasso, who came up with an eccentric, post-modernist solution for the half-destroyed frontispiece to be seen inside the main courtyard. Instead of restoring it back to its original condition, he strengthened its appearance as a ruin by applying brash modern elements such as large cubes of glass to a structure which has been left with cracks, exposed sections of masonry, and even a half-broken urn from which weeds have been allowed to grow.

Descending to the southern corner of the former barracks, and turning left on to the Travesía Conde Duque, we come out again on to the Calle de San Bernardo, next to an austere classical building that marks the site of a Jesuit College. With the decision made in 1842 to transfer the Complutense University from the nearby town of Alcalá de Henares to the centre of Madrid, this former Jesuit College was rebuilt as the main university building, which it remained until the creation of the University City from 1927 onwards. Across the street from it, at No. 44, and immediately below it, at No. 45, are the two remaining palaces of a street once lined with aristocratic palaces of the 17th and 18th centuries. A similar decline in fortunes characterizes the Calle de la Pez, which runs west of San Bernardo from a point immediately below the palace at No. 44. This was until the 1930's one of the liveliest and smartest streets in central Madrid, inhabited by a remarkable cross-section of the city's society, from the aristocracy down to the lower middle-classes. Its animation stemmed both from the nearby presence of the University and from its numerous shops, which made it a popular place for strolling, as Galdós suggested in *Miau* when he described how Luisito came here one day to browse in its tantalizing shop-windows. The departure of the University in 1927 initiated the decline, and the calle later became absorbed into the area of urban decay centred upon Malasaña. Near its eastern end it crosses a narrow and attractive sloping square, overlooked by one of the more interesting and least visited convents in the centre of the city.

The Benedictine convent of San Plácido was founded in 1623 by Doña Teresa Valle de la Cerda under the patronage of Philip IV's secretary of state, Jerónimo de Villanueva. Almost immediately the place came to acquire a scandalous reputation, due initially to rumours that numerous nuns, including Doña Teresa herself, had come to be possessed by the devil and had had to be exorcized by their confessor, Juan Francisco García Calderón. Under torture Calderón confessed to having indulged in sexual practices with his spiritual daughters, and was subsequently condemned by the Inquisition to life imprisonment. Doña Teresa was released without punishment, doubtless thanks to her friends in high places. The story of the convent's corruption does not end there, however, for shortly afterwards Philip IV fell in love with one of the nuns, and connived to see her with the help of Villanueva, who lived in an adjoining house. Thanks to a secret tunnel built expressly for the purpose, the king managed to gain entry into the convent, but his plans to seduce the nun were to be thwarted by Doña Teresa, who having had previous warning of the nocturnal visit, had persuaded the nun to lie on a funeral bier and pretend to be dead. News of all these doings came nonetheless to the attention of the Inquisition, and eventually to the Pope, who demanded to see the documents relating to the case. This time the Count-Duke of Olivares came to the rescue, and arranged for henchmen to arrest and throw into prison the messenger whom the Inquisition had sent to Rome. Philip IV meanwhile, repenting his misdeameanours, commissioned Velázquez to paint for the convent church the beautiful canvas of *Christ on the Cross* that is now in the Prado.

Though it no longer possesses this painting by Velázquez, the convent church has several other impressive works of art, including a superb high altar of the *Annunciation* by Claudio Coello, a cupola painted by Francisco Rizi, and a polychromed statue of the dead Christ by Gregorio Fernández. These works gain greatly from their harmonious setting, which has been barely disturbed since the early 17th century. An almost undecorated brick wall characterizes the entrance façade on the Calle de San Roque, and a similar sobriety and simplicity are to be found inside, where we are guided around by nuns of a more respectable kind than those of Doña Teresa's time. The restraint of the interior contrasts markedly with the decorative brilliance of that in another 17th-century monument nearby, which we can reach by walking to the very end of the Calle de la Pez and joining the narrow and descending Corredera Bajo de San Pablo. A large group of dishevelled people, very much in keeping with the character of this street, are to be seen daily outside the building at No. 16, which has been, since the 18th century, a charitable institution devoted to the feeding of the poor. Originally this was a Portuguese hospital founded by Philip III in 1603, but of this institution there survives only the Church of San Antonio de los Portugueses, on the corner of this street and the Calle de la Puebla. This centrally planned structure, designed by Juan Gómez de Mora in the 1620's but remodelled in the late 19th century, seems from the outside like an elegant gasometer, but the recently cleaned interior is coloured all over with some of the most extensive fresco decorations to be seen in Madrid. The walls, painted at the end of the 17th century by Luca Giordano, feature scenes from the life of St. Anthony, whose apotheosis is represented on the dome in an elaborate Bolognese-inspired illusionistic decoration executed in the 1660's by Francisco Rizi and Juan Carreño.

The Calle de la Puebla, another important street of Hapsburg origin which has recently fallen into decay, heads east towards an austere Mercedarian convent of the early 17th-century. Ramón Gómez de la Serna lived for many years in a first-floor apartment at No. 11, while the convent itself features in Galdós' *Miau* as the place where the exhausted Luisito sits down on one of its cold steps and experiences another of his visionary blackouts. From the convent the narrow Calle de Valverde sweeps southwards like a roller-coaster towards the tall silhouettes marking the Gran Vía. Emerging on the Gran Vía, we see in front of us what must be Europe's most elegant Macdonald's, situated in a former jeweller's lavishly adorned inside with marble and mirrors and fringed on the exterior with an iron-work canopy from the turn of the century. To our left meanwhile is the famous skyscraper built by Ignacio de Cárdenas in the 1920's to house Spain's national telephone company. Based on a design by the New York firm of Lewis S. Weeks, but modified with ornamental elements of the Spanish baroque, the Edificio de la Telefónica, seen in the distance on page 228, was the building that inspired Alfonso XIII to proclaim in 1929 that Spain had finally entered the modern world.

WALK 7

The Expanding City

THE CAFÉ GIJÓN *to* THE CAPRICHO DE OSUNA

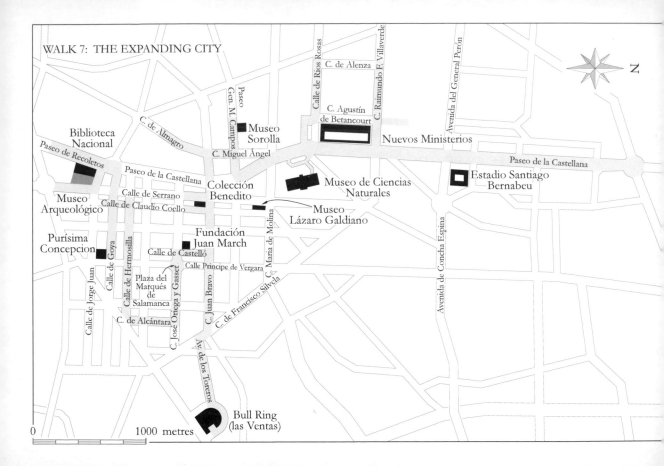

WALK 7: THE EXPANDING CITY

Biblioteca Nacional

Paseo de Recoletos

C. de Almagro

Paseo Gen. M. Campos

Museo Sorolla

Calle de Ríos Rosas

C. de Alenza

C. Raimundo F. Villaverde

C. Agustín de Betancourt

Avenida del General Perón

N

Nuevos Ministerios

C. Miguel Ángel

Paseo de la Castellana

Museo Arqueológico

Calle de Serrano

Colección Benedito

Museo de Ciencias Naturales

Estadio Santiago Bernabeu

Paseo de la Castellana

Calle de Claudio Coello

Museo Lázaro Galdiano

Purísima Concepcion

Fundación Juan March

Calle de Castelló

Calle Principe de Vergara

C. Maria de Molina

Avenida de Concha Espina

Calle de Jorge Juan

Calle de Goya

Calle de Hermosilla

Plaza del Marqués de Salamanca

C. José Ortega y Gasset

C. Juan Bravo

C. de Francisco Silvela

C. de Alcántara

Av. de los Toreros

0   1000 metres

Bull Ring (las Ventas)

The Expanding City

THE CAFÉ GIJÓN *to* THE CAPRICHO DE OSUNA

The transformation of Madrid into the modern city of today, though symbolized for many by the creation of the Gran Vía, had begun in earnest with the laying out after 1860 of the vast and regular grid of streets extending north and east of the Paseo de Recoletos. From the muddle of mean dark streets which characterizes much of the centre of the city we emerge into the spacious and elegant districts of Salamanca and Chamberí, where the distances become greater and the buildings taller. Grand residences of the turn of the century, spectacular modern blocks, and several outstanding museums are featured in this last itinerary, but the scale and monotony of the grid which we have to cross might deter all but the most hardened walkers from attempting

to follow all the route on foot. The enormous size of the area which I am covering will become even more apparent as I continue hurtling north along the Paseo de la Castellana, passing from José María Castro's urban plan of 1860 to Bigador's of 1944. Logically I should have ended the book with some of the more recent and beautiful clusters of skyscrapers that punctuate the northern end of the Castellana, but, instead of finishing on this note of urban progress, I have left the reader amidst the wastelands of the so-called Outer Belt, reserving for this final moment one of Madrid's greatest surprises.

I. The Paseo de Recoletos The broad and shaded Paseo de Recoletos, with which I have begun this itinerary, serves as a last farewell to the Madrid of Charles III, the thoroughfare having been conceived in the 1770's as one of the series of paseos adorning the eastern border of the city. This avenue, which was not to be given a definitive form until the middle of the 19th century, also contains two monuments of particular relevance to the history of the city in modern times. One of these is the palace of the banker and property speculator who gave his name to the district of Salamanca, while the other – on the opposite, western side of the road – is the Café Gijón, the last of the city's great literary cafés, and a place through which most of the recent protagonists of Spain's cultural and intellectual life have passed.

The Café Gijón, situated in between the Calles de Prim and Almirante, was founded in 1888 by Gumersindo Gómez, who came from the Asturian town of Gijón, but had accumulated his money while working as a young man in Cuba. His establishment soon attracted a distinguished clientèle, among the earliest of whom were Pérez Galdós, José Canalejas and the pioneering neurologist Ramón y Cajal. The veiled

Mata Hari entered the café one day in 1914 to ask for a *peppermint frappé,* while in the 1920's the place was the scene of tertulias frequented by such poets as the brothers Antonio and Manuel Machado, Rubén Darío, García Lorca and Rafael Alberti, and by the painter of sultry Andalucían women Julio Romero de Torres, who had a studio off the nearby Calle de Fernando VI. But the café's heyday came after the Civil War, when, with the closure of of the Pombo and other such celebrated institutions, it became the city's unrivalled literary café, rejected only by Hemingway, who once refused to go in on the grounds that he hated all literary tertulias, and that the people who attended them were just 'a load of show-offs'. The tertulias were not just literary ones, however, for there were daily discussion groups of every conceivable kind, from those attended by painters to others frequented by army officers, the café forming a neutral territory where political and intellectual differences could be absorbed. The late Buero Vallejo, one of the bright stars of post-war Spanish drama, once talked to me of the Gijón in those years, and, while standing in the café itself, was able to point out the very tables where each of these various groupings had sat. The most significant of the various coteries was the group of young artists and writers known as *Juventud Creadora*, among whose members was the recent Nobel Prize-winning novelist Camilo José Cela. It was at the time of his daily visits to the Café Gijón that Cela wrote one of the most controversial and influential novels of the early Franco years, *The Hive* (1951), an episodic work centred on a Madrid café and dealing with the petty hopes and aspirations of the many who gravitated in its orbit.

The present decoration of the Café Gijón, a large and gilded mirrored space, with red-plush seating around the walls, and wooden chairs and tables in the middle, dates from the refurbishment of 1948, the main survival of the original institution being the elaborate clock under which Galdós is reputed to have sat. Under the management for many years of the white-haired men known as 'the two Pepes', and with an appropriately dignified and long-serving staff, the café is still haunted today by many of its habitués of the past, though the majority of those who come here now are either businessmen who enjoy the elegant setting or else tourists who have heard of the café's former reputation as a meeting-place for artists and writers. Gone forever are the days when aspiring writers from the provinces, such as Francisco Umbral, made the café the base from which – in the words of González-Ruano – they set out 'to conquer the Puerta del Sol'.

The Marquis of Salamanca, whose grandiose palace is one of the main adornments of the eastern side of the Paseo de Recoletos, was one of the most flamboyant and successful of Madrid's conquerors from the provinces. 'He was', wrote his biographer and apologist, the Count of Romanones, 'above all a conqueror of wealth. To conquer wealth, to create it, to amass a fortune, seems rather brutal and even prosaic, but this is not the case when the achievement is that of a genius...' Born in Málaga in 1811, the son of a distinguished doctor, he became actively involved in Liberal politics, and fell in love in Andalucía with the future heroine Mariana Pineda, whose execution for having sewn a

Liberal flag was in the 1920's to inspire a famous play by Lorca. He settled in Madrid in 1837, and through various financial ventures ranging from banking to speculating in the projected Aranjuez railway, soon became one of the wealthiest men in the city, as well as the first person in Spain to have a private bathroom. According to Romanones, his 'ostentatious life-style did much to break the monotony and miserliness which then reigned in Madrid', and he encouraged the hitherto easy-going Madrilenians to 'indulge furiously in speculation on the Stock Market', and to spend their money lavishly rather than to hoard it. However, his use of inside knowledge to speculate in government securities led in 1845 to financial ruin and a brief period of exile in France. Returning to Madrid in 1849, he quickly remade his fortune, but was forced to flee Spain again in 1854, when, after a series of financial scandals associated with the Liberals, Carlists sacked his house, and destroyed his gold-plated private railway coach. A remarkable survivor, Salamanca was soon back in Madrid and sufficiently wealthy again to bring to completion his palace on the

Pasco de Recoletos, where he hung a remarkable art collection which included works by Goya, Brueghel and van Dyck, as well as some of the first paintings by El Greco to enter private hands. The revolutionary events of 1868-74, combined with massive financial investment in what is now the 'Barrio de Salamanca', led to his third and final financial ruin, from which he was never fully to recover. After what he described as fifty years 'without a single day of rest or for taking breath', he died in 1883 in a suburban retreat which has now become enveloped by the ugly sprawl of Carabanchel. His caricature is opposite.

Salamanca's palace, an Italianate structure in a verdant enclosure at No. 10 Paseo de Recoletos, was extended in the early years of this century, since when it has served, appropriately enough, as the headquarters of a bank. We are now on the edge of the district which bears Salamanca's name, but, before heading off into the heart of it, we should walk to the northern end of the Paseo de Recoletos, where we will find, to our right, an enormous neoclassical block entirely dominated by a columned and pedimented fron-

tispiece. The largest building of the reign of Isabel II, it was begun in 1865 and completed in time for the celebrations in 1892 commemorating the fourth centenary of the discovery of America. The part of the building overlooking the Paseo de Recoletos houses the gloomy halls of Spain's national library (Biblioteca Nacional), while its eastern wing, entered from the Calle Serrano, contains the archaeological museum (Museo Arquéologico Nacional) which was founded by Isabel II in 1867. The museum's extensive collections, worthily displayed in an old-fashioned but lacklustre setting, cover Spain's archaeology from prehistoric times up to the medieval period, and even includes rooms devoted to ancient Egypt, Etruria, Greece, and the Middle East. Among the greatest treasures are the finds from Roman Spain, and, above all, such fascinating testimonies of ancient Iberian civilization as the three bejewelled and impassively staring female heads known as the *Damas* of Elche, Baza and Cerro de los Santos.

Immediately to the north of the building is the Plaza de Colón, the western side of which is dominated by a series of tall modern blocks, one of these housing the exceedingly tacky waxworks museum, where lovers of bad taste can enjoy – for a considerable fee – a wax tableau depicting Romero de Torres painting *La Piconera*, a crudely suggestive canvas featuring a young woman stirring the ashes of a brazier. The eastern side of the square is bordered by the large verdant space known as the Gardens of the Discovery, above which soars a neo-gothic monument of 1885 commemorating Columbus. Contained below the gardens are a car park, the airport bus terminal, and a cultural centre, the entrance to which is startlingly marked by a wide and powerful fall of water shooting out mysteriously from underneath the Columbus Monument.

II. The Barrio de Salamanca Heading east from here along the busy Calle de Goya, we enter the great grid of Salamanca, a succession of smart but interminable blocks where we could easily lose any sense of orientation. On the Calle de Goya itself, the one monument to break the monotony is the church of the Purísima Concepción, a turn-of-the-century neo-gothic structure with art nouveau elements. A tall open-work spire, flanked by angels and garishly lit at night, gives considerable drama to the building's exterior, but the interior is more theatrical still, thanks to the pierced star-shaped vault above the crossing, a work inspired by Burgos Cathedral. The building is a popular meeting-place for the conservative and elegantly dressed people who make up a large proportion of the Salamanca district, as is the ground-floor café of the American-style drugstore known as California, which stands on the other side of the street, at No. 47. Recently revamped in a style described as a cross between a Moroccan *souk* and a New York hamburger joint, California exposes itself to the street with a huge and outwardly sloping glass frontage, the upper half of which shields a high-tech bar eerily flooded with red light.

Madrid's high temple to modern design is to be found one block to the north, at the junction of the Calles Hermosilla and Claudio Coello. Known as Teatriz, this is a bar, restaurant and night-club which has been created inside the former Teatro Beatriz by the fashionable Frenchman Philippe Starck. The bar table, a free-standing transparent block lit from inside, has been placed at the centre of the actual stage, which, apart from the addition of an enormous mirror, has otherwise been left largely untouched, and even has its original stage mechanism and a back wall of unadorned brick. The restaurant tables cover the floor of the former auditorium, which is cut off at the back by a massive fall of drapery parted in the middle to reveal a glimpse of an upstairs bar, from which one can peer at those eating and drinking below. Conscious all the time of taking part in a spectacle, one cannot even descend into the reddish-blue penumbra constituting the washrooms without escaping from onlookers, who marvel here at the curious marble slabs over which water pours as one's foot touches a button.

The exorbitantly-priced Teatriz, with its crowds of *yuppís* and *pijos* (the spoilt young rich), is an institution more typical of Barcelona than it is of Madrid, and those in search of a cheaper, friendlier and more authentically Madrilenian experience should head towards the eastern end of the Calle Hermosilla, where at No. 99, we will find the old-fashioned night bar called El Avión. Consisting of little more than a single dark, narrow, and smoke-filled room, it serves cheap beer always accompanied by bowls of *pipas* or sunflower-seeds, the husks of which are spat out on to the ground. The main attraction of the place was until very recently the gaunt and pallid 73 year-old pianist known by everyone as Don César. Though a winner at the age of fifteen of a national piano competition, he devoted the greater part of his life to playing on the modest piano of El Avión, thumping out, with a cigarette constantly on his lips, lively and heart-warming Madrilenian melodies of the past.

Three blocks further north of the Calle Hermosilla is the Salamanca district's central artery, the Calle de José Ortega y Gasset, which is usually referred to by its former and shorter name of the Calle Lista. At its exact centre is a round intersection named after the man whom Galdós considered the most fitting symbol of his age, none other than the Marquis of Salamanca himself, whose statue crowns the traffic island in the middle. One block to the east, near the junction of the Calles Padilla and Castelló, is the smoothly rounded marble and glass block of the Fundación Juan March, situated in a garden adorned with sculptures by Chillida and other modern masters. March, a Catalan businessman who had spent time in prison for embezzlement, atoned for his misdeameanours by presenting to the people of Madrid this remarkable cultural centre, where leading exhibitions of modern art can be seen free of charge, accompanied by excellent catalogues and posters at give-away prices. Round the corner, at No. 38 Calle Padilla, rises a palatial residential block of the 1920's, with pedimented windows and coats of arms. This was the home of the poet and Nobel Prize-winner Juan Ramón Jímenez, commemorated here by a stone inscription carved with one of his lyrical homages to the expanding modern city of Madrid.

Continuing north along the Calle Castelló we come to the broad, landscaped Calle de Juan Bravo. If we were to go to its eastern end and then continue east along the Avenida de los Toreros we would reach Madrid's splendid neo-Moorish bullring, an enormous brick structure built between 1929 and 1932, and containing an excellent museum devoted to the sport. Madrilenians, like Hemingway, claim that this ring (seen opposite with a great hero, Dominguín, in a tight spot) is the most beautiful in Spain, and that the best fights in the country are put on here, though people from Seville would heavily dispute this. Ignoring the taurine distraction and heading instead west along the Calle de Juan Bravo, we pass, at the junction of the Calle de Velázquez, the elaborate iron-work gates surrounding one of the grandest of this district's turn-of-the-century mansions, a lightly coloured neo-baroque building that was originally the home of the Marquises of Amboage, and is now the Italian Embasssy. Further west we cross the Calle Claudio Coello, where, just to the south, at No. 91, we will find a plaque marking the site of the apartment block where the Galician-born Camilo José Cela lived immediately after the Civil War. The lengthy inscription records that he wrote here his first collection of poetry, his first short story, and,

more importantly, his first novel, *The Family of Pascual Duarte* (1942), a work of sensationalist realism which gave rise to the literary movement known as *tremendismo*. Cela, who fought for Franco in the Civil War but was frequently in trouble with the authorities afterwards, has always loved to shock and criticize. However, the poem of his quoted on the plaque shows him in one of his rare complimentary moods:

Madrid
Gateway of Friendship
Chamber of Wisdom and of Genius
Granary of the most diverse situations
And of the most extravagant adventures.

It is difficult to know in which of these categories should be placed the Benedito Collection (Collección Benedito), which is situated at No. 4 of the Calle de Juan Bravo. One of the least known of Madrid's art galleries, it consists of an extensive series of canvases by the Valencian painter Manuel Benedito Vives (who died in 1963), and can be visited by appointment. We will be greeted at the forbiddingly austere entrance portal by the diminutive Doña Vicenta Benedito, one of the artist's nieces, who is convinced that her uncle's work deserves a position in the 'Chamber of Wisdom and of Genius'. The building itself was originally his home, though Doña Vicenta had to sell off most of it to create the enormous space constituting this museum, the walls of which are covered all over with a dark-green velvet such as one might find in a seedy night-club or on the lid of an extravagant box of chocolates. The artist himself, now almost entirely forgotten in Spain, enjoyed a considerable success in his day, as a landscapist, genre-painter, and above all as a society portraitist. His works, ranging from the slick to the embarassingly kitsch, have an undeniable nostalgic charm, though perhaps their primary value is to make us appreciate the more the genius of his teacher Joaquín Sorolla, whose museum is one of the forthcoming attractions of this itinerary.

Immediately to the west of the Benedito Collection the Calle de Juan Bravo intersects with the busy Calle de Serrano, which marks the western limits of the Salamanca district. If we were to head south down this street we would pass a crowded series of shops and banks, as well as the turn-of-the-century block at No. 72 where the composer Manuel de Falla lived between 1901 and 1907. His fourth-floor flat here was the scene every Saturday night and Sunday afternoon of lively meetings with his piano-playing friends, but its principal claim to fame is for having been the place where Falla composed *La Vida Breve*. The northern end of the Calle de Serrano has a quieter and more spacious character, and we should make a detour along it to visit the Museo Lázaro Galdiano, which stands in a garden at No. 122, occupying a tall classical-style building of the early years of this century. This was originally the private residence of Don José Lázaro Galdiano, who named it the Parque Florido in honour of his Argentine wife, Doña Paula Florido. The museum, inaugurated in 1951 following extensive remodelling, consists entirely of Lázaro's remarkably varied collections of fine and applied arts, among the richest and most extensive amassed by a Spanish private collector. Arranged on four floors around an elaborate staircase well, this place is Madrid's answer to London's Wallace Collection, with sculptures and gold-framed paintings displayed in settings crammed with furniture, suits of armour, fans, medals and a plethora of other objects. The paintings include Flemish and Spanish primitives, works by El Greco, Goya and Murillo, and – reinforcing the snobbish 18th-century pretensions of the whole place – portraits by Reynolds, Gainsborough, Ramsay, Raeburn and Hoppner. Among the high points, if you can find them, is a *Self-portrait* by Pedro Berruguete, a *St. John on Patmos* by Bosch, the well-known portrait by Velázquez of Góngora, and a *Portrait of Saskia* by Rembrandt. The great marvel of the applied arts collections is an exquisitely engraved goblet which belonged to Philip II's mad cousin, Rudolph II of Prague.

West of the Calle de Serrano the Calle de Juan Bravo merges into a broad overpass which spans the Paseo de la Castellana. In the squalid spaces below this construction is to be found what is euphemistically refered to as 'The Open-Air Sculpture Museum' (Museo de Escultura al Aire

Libre) an apparently haphazard collection of monumental sculptures by modern masters such as Miró, Julio González and Subirachs. Next to one of the piers on the western side of the Castellana is a large bronze by Henry Moore, miserably sited and almost universally ignored. Continuing west on the Paseo Eduardo Dato, we enter the district of Chamberí, which was built at the same time as that of Salamanca, and has much the same character, if rather less of the latter's monumental uniformity. Almost immediately beyond the Castellana, we will see to our right the beautiful neo-Moorish palace of the Instituto Valencia de Don Juan, while shortly afterwards comes the intersection comemorating the Nicaraguan poet and diplomat Rubén Darío, who worked in the nearby Nicaraguan Embassy. This is the area of Madrid with the greatest number of embassies, a particularly large concentration being found around the Calle de Almagro, which runs south from the Glorieta Rubén Darío. The magnificent French-style mansion built between 1899 and 1902 for the Dukes of Santo Mauro at No. 36 Calle de Zurbano was the

Philippines Embassy until 1991, when it was transformed into Madrid's most luxurious hotel, the Hotel de Santo Mauro. The chandeliered and dazzlingly bright interior features a stylish restaurant built into a library still lined with leather-bound books.

III. The Museo Sorolla   The Calle Miguel Angel runs north of the Glorieta de Rubén Darío, soon reaching the Paseo General Martínez Campos, where we find, on turning left, the much altered building at No. 8 that once housed the Institución Libre de Enseñanza. This experimental educational establishment, founded in 1876 by Francisco Gíner de los Ríos, came to be associated with most of the leading members of the Generation of 98, and paved the way for the Residencia de Estudiantes, which we will shortly be visiting. On the other side of the street, nearer the junction with the Calle Miguel Angel, is the charming house at No. 37 built after 1910 for the painter Joaquín Sorolla. Born in Valencia in 1863, Sorolla studied in Rome and Paris, and later received the First Prize in the Paris Universal Exhibition of 1900. By 1910 he was at the height of his fame, fêted not only throughout Europe but also in America, where he was shortly to receive the prestigious commission to decorate the library of the Hispanic Society of New York with a series of large canvases representing all the regions of Spain. The latter commission occupied him for over eight years, and he had only just finished it when he suffered a hemiplegia, dying soon afterwards, in 1923. Two years later his widow, who features in so many of his paintings, left the house and much of its contents to the nation.

As with the Danish artists Anders Zorn and P. S. Krøyer, with whom he can be closely compared, Sorolla was a painter who went very much out of fashion after his death, and it is only in recent years that he has begun to enjoy a revival in popularity, aided in his case by the bogus description of him as the 'Spanish Impressionist'. His art, which owed little if anything to that of the French Impressionists, evolved from the late 19th-century obsession with painting large-scale figure scenes in the open-air, a tradition popularized by the French painter Bastien-Lepage. Sorolla shared the general concern of the time with vanishing rural traditions, but was at his best when painting members of his family in sunlit settings observed near his seaside homes at San Sebastian and Valencia. His virtuosity, even if degenerating on occasion into mere slickness, was also responsible for creating effects of invigorating freshness. Whatever your opinion of his works, however, you should make every effort to visit his house, if only to recover from the Madrid sun and traffic by sitting in the cool Moorish-style garden. The ground-floor rooms, where the studios are situated, have been left very much as they were in the artist's time, with Sorolla's paintings jumbled together amidst the ceramics, jewellery and other objects that he collected compulsively in the course of his extensive travels around Spain. A particular delight is the dining-room, which Sorolla decorated with an illusionistic frieze of cornucopias and smiling members of his family. A gallery of his works from his student days onwards has been arranged in the upper rooms, while a changing selection of his vivid oil and other sketches can be seen in the tasteful modern extension outside.

IV. The Paseo de la Castellana   From the Sorolla Museum we should head east back to the Paseo de la Castellana, rejoining this grand thoroughfare at the monumental intersection centred on Benlliure's stone and bronze memorial to the 19th-century politician Emilio Castelar. An especially striking group of modern blocks is to be found around this Glorieta, the most recent of which, at the entrance to Calle de Martínez Campos, is Federico Echevarría's Banco Europa building, an irregularly shaped structure with rounded corners and an overall dark-blue glow. An earlier building by Echevarría, with postmodernist elements such as a false upper arcade, houses the offices of the Compañía Nacional Hispánica on the opposite side of the Castellana. Next to this, and most impressive of all, is Rafael de la Hoz's headquarters of the Compañía de Seguros Catalana Occidente, a tall, suspended block of exceptional lightness, magically composed of two superimposed prisms. Heading north up the Castellana, we soon pass to our left, at No. 61, the La Caixa building, another arresting structure, conceived in this case as an inverted chrome pyramid dripping with icicle-like formations. Further up, on the right-hand side, verdant slopes support a long, domed pavillion built as the centrepiece of the 1881 Exhibition of Industry and the Arts, and subsequently transformed into the city's natural history museum (Museo de Ciencias Naturales). The interior of this neo-renaissance building has recently been radically revamped, but in a way that shows off the tall ironwork columns of the original structure, the whole providing an appealingly elegant postmodernist setting in which large elephants and other stuffed animals can happily roam.

The young Luis Buñuel spent a year working at the Natural History Museum under the guidance of a world-famous orthopterist, Ignacio Bolívar, thanks to whom he was able to boast in later life of a gift for identifying insects at a glance and of giving their Latin names. Buñuel was living at the time in the Residencia de los Estudiantes, which lies immediately behind the Natural History Museum, spread out over what Juan Ramón Jímenez refered to as 'the hill of poplars'. Owing to a line of dreary modern buildings in front of it, the Residencia is hidden today from the Castellana, and there are many Madrilenians who think that this legendary institution of the interwar years has long since disappeared.

Founded in 1910 by Alberto Jiménez Fraud, a visionary educationalist and Anglophile, the Residencia was transferred to its specially built quarters on the 'hill of poplars' in 1915. Intended as a progressive cultural and scientific centre, it took as its model the campus of an English university, and had cheap residential quarters for students and teachers, as well as laboratories, lecture-halls, and a theatre. The Residencia played a vital role in the intellectual life of Spain, and acted as a point of contact between the Generation of 98 and the budding Generation of 27, a place where the likes of Juan Ramón Jímenez, Unamuno and the Machado brothers could exchange ideas with budding young talents such as Rafael Alberti and García Lorca. (In the photograph of the Residencia students on this page, Dalí and Lorca are seen at the extreme right; overleaf we see them at roughly the same period, hand in hand, and opposite is Dalí's

portrait of their friend Buñuel.) Buñuel described the Residencia as a place where 'you could study any subject you wanted, stay as long as you liked, and change your area of speciality in mid-stream.' Some idea of its intellectual range can be had from the list of distinguished foreigners who were invited to lecture here in the interwar years, among whom were such diverse talents as Einstein, Gropius, Marinetti, Le Corbusier, Louis Aragon, Bergson and Madame Curie. Moreover, thanks to the creation by Jiménez Fraud in 1923 of the Hispano-English Committee, this list included a particularly large number of English speakers, such as G. K. Chesterton, Maynard Keynes, H. G. Wells, Sir Edwin Lutyens and Howard Carter, the discoverer of Tutankhamen.

After the Civil War, the Residencia, with its strong Republican sympathies, was put to other uses. Its theatre was turned into a church, and the balconied laboratory building known as the *Transatlántico* was even converted into a home for an Egyptian sultan. In recent years, however, the place has been revived, and its tall but homely brick buildings – one of which was scaled by the athletically-inclined Buñuel – serve today for a wide range of cultural events, as well as a residence both for a select group of young artists, writers and scientists, and for visiting academics from abroad. Its present directorship is determined to bring back some of the institution's former intellectual character, and is also slowly restoring the buildings and surrounding gardens back to their original state. The now ruined Transatlántico will be rebuilt to house a García Lorca foundation, and there is even talk of pulling down the modern structures that block the view towards the Castellana. In the meantime we can see the charming 'Garden of the Poets', laid out by Ramon Jímenez in the space between the wings of the main block, and also – inside this block – the room and piano used by Lorca and his friends for musical evenings. Not least we can read the lively account of the place featured in Buñuel's autobiography, which, apart from various stories relating to the antics of his friends Salvador Dalí and García Lorca, includes a famous anecdote about Alfonso XIII suddenly appearing outside Buñuel's window to ask direc-

269

tions. Buñuel, taken by surprise, obsequiously adressed the king as *Majestad*, and realized only afterwards that he had forgotten to remove his hat. Thus was the honour of an anarchist saved.

Across the Castellana from the Natural History Museum begins the stately Calle de Ríos Rosa, where, at No. 54, we find the austere apartment block where Camilo José Cela lived between 1949 and 1954, writing in those years his great novel of Madrilenian life, *The Hive*. Near the top of the street, at No. 21, is another of the outstanding turn of the century structures by Velázquez Bosco, this one housing the Academy of Mining Engineers, and distinguished on the outside by huge ceramic murals by Daniel Zuloaga. Returning to the Castellana and continuing north along this thoroughfare we skirt to our left the enormously long, De Chirico-like arcading that guards the forecourt of the Nuevos Ministerios. The deep recesses of this arcading provide today a convenient hiding-place for lovers, while the inhumanly sized complex behind it now houses three Ministries. Conceived during the last years of Miguel Primo de Rivera's dictatorship, it was

given its monstrous scale and bleak severity under Franco, whose equestrian statue stands on its southern side. The northern side of the complex overlooks the broad Calle de Raimundo Fernández Villaverde, the upper end of which is dominated by a characteristically fantastical structure by Antonio Palacios, the Hospital de Maudes. Built in the second decade of the century as a hospital for the poor, it later fell into disuse, and has only recently been startlingly transfomed inside for use as office and library space for the Comunidad de Madrid. Planned in the shape of a large cross, it presents a variegated profile of turrets and pinnacles, the whole being sometimes described as being in a 'Windsor' style. The overall effect is in fact distinctly ghoulish, and the coarse detailing and textured stone give the building the look of something taken from either a zoo or a horror film. The chapel, on its northern side, is now a parish church worth visiting for its lurid stained-glass.

In terms of sheer numbers of skyscrapers, the Castellana reaches its architectural climax just to the north of the Calle de Raimundo Fernández

Villaverde, in the area to our left known unappealingly as the Azca Urbanización. Shopping arcades, teenage discothèques, cafeterias, restaurants and brash offices are centred here around a futuristic space called the Jardines Picasso, the dominant monument of which – indeed the highest building in Madrid – is the Torre Picasso, a sleek white structure built in 1988 by the Japanese architect Minoru Yamasaki. The northern boundary of the Azca Urbanización is marked by the Avenida General Perón, where we can admire, at the junction with the Castellana, a colourful and large mural by the Catalan artist Miró. On the other side of the Castellana is a monument of interest both to football and architectural enthusiasts, the Bernabeu Stadium, a building dating back to the late 1940's, but given a dramatic concrete casing in 1982, when this home ground for Real Madrid became the main stadium for the World Cup.

V. The Capricho de Osuna Beyond the Bernabeu Stadium the sense of architectural exhilaration which accompanies us for so much of the Castellana begins to diminish, to be revived only in the newly revamped Plaza de Castilla, where a dreary monument to the right-wing politician Calvo Sotelo has now been replaced by the stunningly eccentric Puerta de Europa – two enormous leaning towers that form a spectacular, arch-like conclusion to Bigador's great thoroughfare. From here, it is a short walk to the modern railway station of Chamartín, which for many travellers represents their first and last glimpse of Madrid. Let me leave you instead near the international airport of Barajas, a journey involving a huge leap to the east, across the dual carriageway of the M30 and into what in Cela's day was one of the 'villages of the Outer Belt'. The concluding lines of Cela's novel *The Hive* are those of an unfortunate young man laughing to himself as he reads the latter expression in a newspaper. "'Ha, ha! The villages of the Outer Belt. What a funny expression! The villages of the Outer Belt!'" Alighting at the metro station of Canillejas, the last stop on Line 6, you might indeed feel that I am having a joke at your expense as you confront a sad group of modern blocks facing a motorway junction and an apparently endless vista of wasteland. And now you must enter this wasteland, using the footbridge in front of you to cross the A-2, and heading northeast from here along the narrow Paseo de la Alameda de Osuna. Small encampments of gypsies can be seen, and there are even flocks of sheep grazing in front of modern warehouses. However, the quiet shaded road which you are following is a vestige of an aristocratic past, for it leads to what was once one of the finest summer residences in the vicinity of Madrid.

Known as El Capricho de Osuna, it dates from 1783 and was the creation of one of the most powerful Spanish women of her age, the Duchess of Osuna. She built the place in a way which was clearly intended to impress her two main rivals at the Court, the Duchess of Alba and Queen María Cristina, both of whom she far outstripped in the range and depth of her cultural and intellectual interests. A Francophile who preferred to speak in French rather than in Spanish, she invited to El Capricho numerous musicians, actors and academicians from Paris, and assembled here a renowned library of works in French

translation. (She is seen opposite in a detail from Goya's portrait, where she is surrounded by her children, in the best tradition of Rousseau.) It is for its park, however, that El Capricho is best remembered today, and for this the Duchess secured the services of the designer of the Petit Trianon gardens near Versailles, Pierre Mulot, who was contracted to the Duchess on the understanding that he would work for no-one else in Spain. The laying-out of the park continued into the 19th century, the work being taken over by a Spanish theatre designer called Tadey. El Capricho experienced its Indian Summer under the 10th Duke of Osuna, Don Mariano, who inherited the property in 1844 and died heirless and bankrupt in 1882 after a lifetime given almost wholly to the pursuit of pleasure.

After numerous changes of ownership, El Capricho was acquired by the Comunidad de Madrid in 1974, who have attempted to restore the palace and its park to their former glory. The elegant neoclassical palace, with traces inside of Pompeian-style frescoes, was commandeered during the Civil War as the headquarters of the

Republican defense of Madrid led by General Miaja. The large underground bunker which Miaja built next to it still survives, and there was once talk of turning this evocative labyrinth into a Republican Civil War monument to counteract the gruesome office of General Mascardó in Toledo. Beyond *El Bunker* extends a classical French parterre, offering views to the south of a recently replanted maze. A large 'English Garden' lies further on, its undulating verdant slopes covered with a wonderful range of follies, including a miniature citadel from which an automaton dressed as a soldier used to fire gun salutes, on one occasion accidentally killing a gardener. A winding river, spanned by the first iron bridge in Spain leads from the citadel to a boating lake, where we will find a charming boat-house built in wicker and painted inside wih illusionistic landscapes. From here boating parties of costumed guests once set off on their journey to a neoclassical ballroom, passing on their way an island adorned with a monument to the 3rd Duke of Osuna. The culminating folly is a half-timbered and quaintly skew-whiff rustic

cottage, through the windows of which automata of peasants at work could once be seen. Though the mechanical peasants have gone, those days when aristocrats pursued dreams of rural simplicity spring back to life as we enter the cottage's magical interior, with its balustrade made from the branches of a tree, and its delightful trompe-l'oeil decoration of kitchen utensils, dangling pimentos, rows of washing, and old prints pinned to the walls.

The constant roar of planes from Barajas airport, barely a mile away from El Capricho, brings us back to reality while also perhaps reminding us of a much-quoted saying – reduced in the language of bumper stickers to the enigmatic words *De Madrid al Cielo* – that Madrid is the gateway to the skies. 'From Madrid to the Skies,' runs the saying in full, 'and from the Skies a Telescope to look back at Madrid.' Sometimes, on leaving Madrid from Barajas airport, I have tried to catch a glimpse of El Capricho from the ascending plane, but the site, like so many of this city's attractions, remains obstinately hidden, lost in an urban sprawl, which disappears in turn, absorbed by a crumpled arid landscape of intimidating proportions.

Books about Madrid

The best starting-point for anyone wishing to read further on Madrid has to be Hugh Thomas's *Madrid, A Traveller's Companion* (1988), which has an excellent introduction to the city's history followed by an anthology of travel writings that includes the famous appraisals of Madrid featured in George Borrow's *A Bible in Spain* (1844), V. S. Pritchett's *The Spanish Temper* (1959) and Hemingway's otherwise tedious *Death in the Afternoon* (1932); the only other such anthology dedicated specifically to Madrid was published by the Comunidad de Madrid under the title *Viajeros impeninentes: Madrid visto por los viajeros extranjeros en los siglos XVII, XVIII and XIX* (1989). This has now been supplemented by the novelist Michael Llamanzares' lively *Los viajeros de Madrid* (1998). (Unless stated otherwise, all English books are published in London and all Spanish books in Madrid.) Nina Epton, a now forgotten writer who published prolifically on Spain in the 1950's and 60's, is the author of the lively if rather gushing *Madrid* (1964), which is filled with memories of her childhood in the city. Steuart Erskine's *Madrid, Past and Present* (1924) is in a similarly romantic vein and is as much of a period piece as Archibald Lyall's *Well Met in Madrid* (1960), a slim and highly amusing book, and the best of his guides. Apart from Hugh Thomas's work, the only recent English introduction to Madrid that can be warmly recommended is the elegant and intelligent essay featured in David Gilmour's *Cities of Spain* (1992).

Nothing in English, however, matches in verve and eccentricity the obsessive writings on Madrid by Ramón Gómez de la Serna, a slim selection of which has been assembled in *Descubrimiento de Madrid* (ed. Tomás Borras, 1986). The nearest present-day equivalent to him is Francisco Umbral, a maddening, repetitive and highly polemical author whose *Amar en Madrid* (Barcelona, 1977) is nonetheless one of the finest literary evocations of the modern city. On a more mundane level, there are almost as few good general books on the city in Spanish as there are in English. Among these few is Antonio Cabezas's *Madrid* (Barcelona, 1971; 3rd edition), which forms part of Destino's *Guías de España*, a series remarkable for their evocative black and white photographs of the 1950's; Cabezas is also the author of the *Diccionario de Madrid* (1989), which supplements and brings up to date Pedro de Répide's standard reference work, *Las Calles de Madrid* (1971). The admirably cheap *Alianza Cien* series has reissued the concise and stimulating *Madrid* (1995) by the Catalan author Luis Carandell. Wonderful pictorial records of the city, with good accompanying texts, are contained in *Madrid Pintado: Madrid a través de la pintura* (ed. Alfonso E. Pérez Sánchez, 1993) and Pedro Montoliu's *Madrid 1900* (1994).

The detailed historical accounts of Madrid have tended to be turgid and highly specialized, and, only recently, with the publication of *Historia de Madrid* (ed. Antonio Fernández García, 1993) has a modern work superseded in comprehensiveness the classic four-volume study by Amador de los Ríos, *Historia de la Villa y Corte de Madrid* (1860-64). The more popular and readable historical studies include Nestor Luján's *Madrid de los ultimos Austrias* (1989) and C. E. Kany's *Life and Manners in Madrid, 1750-1800* (New York, 1932). The rare combination of scholarship, flair, and compulsive readability, is to be found in Jonathan Brown's and J. H. Elliot's *A Palace for a King: the Buen Retiro and the palace of Philip IV* (1980), an essential work for anyone interested in the Hapsburg city.

Madrid, 1. La ciudad (1983), published by the Ayuntamiento de Madrid in the series *Guías provinciales de España* (Editorial Tania, S.A., ed. Javier Gómez-Navarro), is by far the best general guide to the city, though it is now complemented in English by Annie Bennett's detailed and enthusiastic *Blue Guide to Madrid,* which is especially strong on historical anecdotes and practical recommendations. Also good, but concentrating mainly on art and architecture, is Chueca Goitia's *Madrid and Toledo, A Cultural Guide* (1972); Alastair Boyd's successful but stuffy *The Companion Guide to Madrid and Central Spain* (1st edition, 1974) has a relatively short section on the city, and is out of touch and sympathy with many of the modern aspects of the place. Copious practical information, combined with a lively treatment of the modern city, can be found in the reliable and regularly reprinted *Time Out Guide to Madrid.* Facsimile editions can be purchased of Ramón de Mesonero Romanos' two classic guides, *Manual de Madrid* (first published 1831) and the more nostalgic *El Antiguo Madrid, Paseos historico-anecdóticos por las calles y casas de esta villa* (first published 1861); another of the great 19th-century guides, also in facsimile edition, is Ángel Fernandez de los Ríos, *Guía de Madrid, manual del madrileño y del forastero* (1837). For bizarre and unusual information see José del Corral, *Curiosi-dades de Madrid* (1990).

An excellent two-volume architectural guide, *Guía de arquitectura y urbanismo de Madrid* (1984) is published by the Colegio Oficial de Arquitectos de Madrid, and includes illustrations of every building discussed. This is supplemented and brought up to date by the numerous and beautifully illustrated architectural guides to the city written and published by Ramón Guerra de la Vega. The standard work on the city's churches remains Elías Tormo's *Las Iglesias del antiguo Madrid* (1927; facsimile edition, 1985), an austere publication filled with useful information but with only a handful of ground-plans and sad black-and-white photographs.

Ediciones La Librería publish the useful and enjoyable *Recorridos didácticos por Madrid,* a series of booklets which includes *Madrid Literario* (1990) and *Madrid Galdosiano* (1990). For a detailed analysis of Pérez Galdós in Madrid, see the exhibition catalogue *Madrid en Galdós, Galdós en Madrid* (ed. Julio Rodríguez Puertolas, Palacio de Cristal del Retiro, 1988); the difficult task of writing a biography of this secretive figure was ably undertaken by Chanon Berkowitz in his exhaustive but readable *Pérez Galdós, Spanish Liberal Crusader* (1948). Among the numerous but generally lightweight books on Madrid published by Ediciones El Avapiés are Juan Luis Cebrián, *El Madrid de Larra* (1992), and Mariano Tudela, *Aquellas tertulias de Madrid* (1984); slighter and shorter still, but with a strong period charm, are the ten volumes of Antonio Velasco Zazo's *Panorama de Madrid* (*c.* 1943), among which are the volumes *Florilegio de los cafés, fondas y mesones*, and *Tertulias literarias*. Not until 1992, with the publication in Madrid of Lorenzo Diaz's *Madrid, tabernas, botillerías y cafés*, were the city's tertulias and café life the subject of an historical survey of any seriousness; particularly good are this book's numerous illustrations and lengthy bibliography. Useful information, amateurishly compiled, can also be gleaned from *Café Gijón, 100 años de historia* (ed. Mariano Tudela, 1988) and José Altabella's *Lhardy, Panorama histórico de un restaurante romántico, 1839-1978* (1985).

But the most enjoyable way of finding out about cafés and Madrid life in general is to turn to the many lively memoirs that this city's writers have produced. In this long list are Ramón Mesonero Romanos' *Memorias de un Setentón, natural y vecino de Madrid* (1880), Ricardo Baroja's *Gente del 98* (1935), Rafael Cansinos-Assens' *La Novela de un literato, 1882-1923* (2 vols., 1985), Ramon Gomez de la Serna's *Pombo, biografía del celebre café y otros cafés famosos* (Barcelona, 1960), and his *Automoribundia* (Buenos Aires, 1948), Antonio Díaz-Cañabate's *Historia de una taberna* (1947) and *Historia de una tertulia* (Valencia, 1952), Cesar González-Ruano's *Mi medio siglo se confiesa a medias* (*c.* 1961), Arturo Barea's *Forging of a Rebel* (1946), Francisco Umbral's *La noche que llegué al Café Gijón* (Barcelona, 1977), and Rosa Chacel's *Barrio de Maravillas* (1980).

One of the hopes of this present book is that the English reader will be curious to discover not only more about Madrid but also about Spanish fiction, many of whose greatest classics, so little known abroad, are set in this city. I envy those who have yet to read Pérez Galdós, whose works form altogether one of the most intimate portraits of a city ever written. Many, such as the *Fontana de Oro* (1875), have yet to be translated, but fortunately the greatest are available in good English editions, notably *Miau* (1888), *La de Bringas* (1884; translated by Gerald Brenan's wife Gamel Wolsey as *The Spendthrifts* and more recently by Catherine Jagoe as *That Bringas Woman)*, *Tormento* (1884), the *Torquemada* quartet (1889-1895), *Misericordia* (1897), and the superlative *Fortunata y Jacinta* (1886-87), the most important Spanish novel after *Don Quixote*. Of the post-war Spanish novels dealing with Madrid, two of the best known are Camilo José Cela's *La Colmena* (1944; translated as *The Hive*), and Luis Martin-Santos' *Tiempo de Silencio* (Barcelona, 1962), the English translation of which (*Time of Silence*) sadly does scant justice to the linguistic pyrotechnics of this experimental author who worked as the director of a psychiatric home up to his early death in a car crash in 1964. A writer as brilliant as Martín-Santos, and more interesting and reflective than the better known Cela, is Rafael Sánchez Ferlosio, whose *El Jarama* (Barcelona 1956; translated as *The One Day of the Week*) is a memorably cynical and poetic portrayal of the boredom of everyday Madrilenian life. Snappy, instantly forgettable, but highly entertaining are Pedro Almodóvar's *Patty Diphusa y otros textos* (1991; translated as *The Patty Diphusa Stories and Other Writings*), irreverent sketches of Madrid written at the time of the *Movida*. Also set in Madrid are the fashionable Muñoz Molina's *Beltenebros* (1989; translated as *Prince of Shadows*) and *Los misterios de Madrid* (1994), and Manuel Vázquez Montalbán's enjoyable detective novel *Asesinato en el comite central* (1981; *Murder in the Central Committee*), which gives an interesting insight into a Catalan's view of the city, in particular its food, dismissed here as consisting of no more than 'a stew, an omelette and a dish of tripe'.

The subject of Madrid's gastronomy is perhaps best investigated in the field than in the library, but those in need of reassurance and food for thought should read Manuel Martínez Llopis' and Simone Ortega's *La cocina tipica de Madrid* (1987), a scholarly and mouth-watering book of recipes and culinary history into which has been stirred a generous dose of information about the city's gastronomic traditions and establishments.

Places to Stay and Places to Eat

Places to stay A high proportion of Madrid's luxury hotels are in the vicinity of the Prado, including the **Ritz** (Plaza de la Lealtad 5; tel 91-521 2857; fax 91-532 8776; see p. 182), the recently opened **Villa Real** (Plaza de las Cortes 10; tel 91-319 6900; fax 91-420 2547) and the **Palace** (Plaza de las Cortes 7; tel 91-429 7551; fax 91-429 8266; see p. 117), which has recently dropped a star so as to lower its prices. Far more endearing than any of these places is the **Suecia** (c/ Marqués de Casa Riera 4; tel 91-531 6900; fax 91-521 7141; see p. 225), which has an intimate atmosphere, the friendliest bar staff in town, and an ideal situation on a quiet street within easy walking distance both of the Prado and of the city's bustling nocturnal heart. Further afield, and more suitable perhaps for business travellers than short-stay tourists, is the **Santo Mauro** (c/Zurbano 36; tel 91-319 6900; fax 91-308 5477; see p. 264), where the chandeliered magnificence of the turn-of-the-century setting clashes occasionally with the ultra-self- conscious modern refurbishment of the bedrooms.

Lovers of kitsch who are on a more limited budget might appreciate the red velvet gloom of the now gone-somewhat-to-seed **Paris** (c/Alcalá 2; tel 91-521 6491; fax 91-531 0188; see p. 75) and, above all, the wonderfully decadent **Monaco** (c/Barbieri 5; tel 91-522 4630; fax 91-521 1601; in the Chueca district, which is described on pp. 230ff), a former 1920's brothel with ceiling mirrors in some of the rooms. Many of the cheapest places to stay in town are in and around the Plaza de Santa Ana (see pp. 125ff), including such basic but clean establishments as the **Jaén** (c/Cervantes 5; tel 91-429 4858), **La Rosa** (Plaza de Santa Ana 15; tel 91-532 7046), the **Mocelo** (c/Prado 10; tel 91-429 4963) and the **Vetusta** (c/Huertas 3; tel 91-429 6404).

Places to eat Anyone coming to Madrid for the first time will want to try at least once one of the city's many traditional establishments of unchanging decor that serve the sort of hearty Madrilenian food described on pp. 62ff. The oldest and most famous of these is the tourist-loved **Casa Botín** (c/Cuchilleros 17; tel 91-366 4217; see p. 88), which specializes in lamb and suckling pig roasted in a wood oven. The attractively tiled **Casa Paco** (Puerta Cerrada 11; tel 91-366 3166; see p. 88) is well-known for its steaks and *sopa de ajo* (garlic soup), while the **Casa Ciriaco** (c/Mayor 84; tel 91-548 0620; see p. 94) has as one of its specialities *pepitoria de gallina* (chicken in almond sauce). Breaded hake (*merluza rebozada*) and squid in its ink (*calamares en su tinto*) are among the perennially popular dishes at the friendly if now

slightly over-priced **Salvador** (c/Barbieri 12; tel 91-521 4524; see p. 232), where it is difficult to get a table out of sight of Hemingway's bearded features. A good place to try a *cocido* (see p. 63) is **La Bola** (c/Bola 5; tel 91-547 6930; see p. 162); but the best *cocido* in town is generally said to be served in the grand and unlikely setting of **Lhardy** (Carrera de San Jerónimo 8; tel 91-521 3385), a restaurant I personally find more interesting for its atmosphere than for its food. My own favourite restaurant specializing in Madrilenian dishes is the homely and modestly priced **El Puchero** (C/Larra 13; tel 91-445 0577), which is well-situated for those indulging afterwards in a drinking binge in Malasaña (see pp. 240ff).

Madrid's top-ranking, Michelin-favoured gourmet restaurants are those serving modern Spanish or the highly-sophisticated Basque cuisine. Among these places are **El Amparo** (Callejón de Puigcerdá 8; tel 91-431 6546), **El Cenador del Prado** (c/Prado 4; tel 91-429 1561), the **Jockey** (c/Amador de los Ríos 6; tel 91-319 2435) and **Zalacaín** (c/Alvarez de Baena 4; tel 91-561 4840), all of which are slightly daunting in

atmosphere and not always deserving of their high reputations.

If you are going to spend a lot of money on food I recommend you do so at the intimate **Lur Maitea** (c/Fernando el Santo 4; tel 91-308 0350) – a Basque restaurant whose light fish specialities make a good change after the predominantly meat-based Madrid diet – and the splendidly eccentric **Viridiana** (Juan de Mena 14; tel 91-523 4478), the owner and chef of which, Abraham García, prepares a limited but constantly-changing menu of imaginative and at times revolutionary dishes.

Those wishing to taste the cuisine of other Spanish regions should try the down-to-earth **Extremadura** (c/Libertad 13; tel 91-531 8958), where the copious helpings of food are followed by a huge array of homemade liqueurs and aquavits, including one whose bottle famously features a pickled snake; excellent but undeservedly little-known is the homely **Algarabía** (c/Union 8; tel 91-542 4131), which is run by two charming sisters from the Rioja, a famous gastronomic region with a cuisine mingling elements from that of

Castile and the Basque Country. Of the various international establishments that have become veritable Madrilenian institutions, mention should be made of the simple, cheap and perpetually crowded Cuban restaurant **Zara** (c/Infantas 5; tel 91-532 2074; see p. 231) and the scarcely less popular **Edelweiss** (c/Jovellanos 7; tel 91-532 3383), where you can eat large portions of *codillo* (shoulder of pork), sauerkraut, and other German specialities, as well as similarly fattening Madrilenian fare.

Finally, anyone interested in forsaking conventional restaurant meals in favour of eating *en plan de tapas* should immediately purchase a copy of José Carlos Capel's excellent *De Tapas por Madrid* (Madrid 1995), one of the best of this series of guides published by El País Aguilar, and so clearly laid out as to be useful even to those who do not understand Spanish. Among the many bars featured in Capel's book is the **Casa Labra** (c/Tetuan 12), a long-established institution off the Puerta del Sol where the *tapas* of salt cod (*bacalao*) are particularly good. The finest Andalucian *tapas* are to be found at the **Bocaíto** (c/Libertad 6), while snails (*caracoles*) are the inevitable speciality of **Los Caracoles** (c/Toledo 106). Rightly listed by Capel as three of Madrid's most outstanding *tapas* bars are the **Taberna de San Mamés** (c/Bravo Murillo 86), and the Barrio de Salamanca's neighbouring **La Taberna del Buey** (General Pardiñas 7), and **La Taberna de Daniela** (General Pardiñas 21): apart from preparing *tapas* of extraordinary refinement and sophistication, these three establishments are also among the best places in Madrid to try out, respectively, such classic Spanish *tapas* as *callos* (tripe), *albóndigas* (meat balls) and *tortilla* (potato omelette). Not featured in Capel, but which I include here out of loyalty to the delightful owners, is the imaginative, lively and exceptionally friendly **De Pura Cepa** (c/Fuente del Berro 31).

Opening Times of Museums and Galleries

Most of the principal churches are open at standard hours, but are closed to tourists during services. Most museums are closed on Mondays, and some also on holidays and during August; winter hours, too, often differ from summer. All opening times, including some of those given in the following list, are periodically liable to alteration, and it is always advisable, therefore, to check before planning a visit.

Armería see Palacio Real

Casa de Lope de Vega, Calle de Cervantes II: Mon-Fri 10-2.30, Sat 10-1.30. Closed Sun and from 15 July to 15 September.

Casita del Príncipe. El Pardo, Mon-Sat: winter, 10-1 and 4-6; summer 10-1 and 4-7; Sun 10-1.

Casón del Buen Retiro, Calle Felipe IV: Tue-Sat 9-7, Sun and holidays 9-2. Closed Mon.

Centro Cultural Reina Sofía, Santa Isabel 52: daily 10-9. Closed Tue.

Convento de las Descalzas Reales, Plaza de las Descalzas Reales: Tue-Sat 10.30-12.30 and 4.00-5.15; Sun and holidays 11-1.30. Closed Mon and Fri afternoons.

Convento de la Encarnación, Plaza de la Encarnación: daily 10.30-1 and 4-5.30. Closed Mon and Fri afternoons. Wed free.

Ermita de San Antonio de la Florida, Paseo de la Florida: 9.30-2 and 4-8; Sat and Sun 10-2.

Museo Arqueológico Nacional, Calle Serrano 13: Tue-Sat 9.30-8.30; Sun and holidays 9.30-2.30. Closed Mon.

Museo de Carruajes, Paseo Virgen del Puerto, Palacio Real, Campo del Moro: daily summer 10-12.45 and 4-5.45; winter 10-12.45 and 3.30-5.15; Sun and holidays 10-1.30.

Museo de Cera, Paseo de Recoletos 41: daily 10.30 - 1.30 and 4-8.30.

Museo de Ciencias Naturales, José Guitiérrez Abascal 2 (at the top of Paseo de la Castellana 80): daily 10-2. Closed Mon.

Museo Cerralbo, Calle Ventura Rodríguez 17: daily 10-3. Closed Mon and August.

Museo del Ejército (Army Museum), Calle Méndez Núñez 1: daily 10-2. Closed Mon.

Museo Lázaro Galdiano, Calle de Serrano 122: daily 10-2. Closed Mon, holidays and August.

Museo Municipal (Hospicio de San Fernando), Calle de Fuencarral 78: Tue-Fri 9.30 -8; Sat and Sun 10-2. Closed Mon and holidays.

Museo Nacional de Artes Decorativas, Montalbán 12: daily 9.30-2.30, Sat and Sun 10-2. Closed Mon and holidays.

Museo Nacional de Etnología, Alfonso XII 68: daily 10-6; Sun 10-2. Closed Mon and holidays.

Museo del Prado, Paseo del Prado: Tue-Sat 9-7; Sun and holidays 9-2. Closed Mon, 1 January, Good Friday, 1 May and 25 December. Free Sat 2.30-7 and Sun

Museo Romántico, Calle San Mateo 13: daily 10-3. Closed Mon, holidays and August.

Museo Sorolla, Gral. Martínez Campos 37: daily 10-3. Closed Mon, holidays and August.

Museo Thyssen-Bornemisza, Palacio de Villahermosa, Pl. Cánovas del Castillo (Neptuno): daily 10-7. Closed Mon.

Palacio de El Pardo, El Pardo (15 km from Madrid):10-1 and 3.30-6. Closed Sun afternoons.

Palacio Real, Plaza de Oriente: daily 9.30-5.45; Sun and holidays 9.30- 2. Closed when in use for royal and official functions.

Panteón de Goya, Gta. San Antonio de la Florida: daily 10-3 and 4-8. Closed Mon and holidays.

Panteón de Hombres Ilustres, Julián Gayarre 3: weekdays only 9.30-1.30, closed holidays.

Real Academia de Bellas Artes de San Fernando, Calle de Alcalá 13: Tue-Sat 9-7; Sun and holidays 9- 2; Mon 9-3.

Real Basílica de San Francisco el Grande, San Buenaventura 1: winter Tue-Sat 11 -1 and 4-7; summer daily 11-1 and 5-8.

Real Oficina de Farmacía see Palacio Real

Rulers of Spain

Castile

1454-74	Enrique IV el Impotente
1474-1504	Isabel la Católica (who had married Fernando II of Aragón in 1469)

Aragón

1458-79	Juan II
1479-1516	Fernando el Católico

Castile and Aragón

1504-16	Juana la Loça, with Philip of Burgundy Regent as Philip I

Spain

House of Hapsburg

1516-56	Charles I (Holy Roman Emperor Charles V)
1556-98	Philip I
1598-1621	Philip II
1621-65	Philip IV
1665-1700	Charles II

House of Bourbon

1700-24	Philip V (abdicated)
1724-25	Luis I
1725-46	Philip V (reinstated)
1746-59	Fernando VI
1759-88	Charles III
1788-1808	Charles IV
1808-14	[Joseph Bonaparte]
1814-33	Fernando VII
1833-68	Isabel II (abdicated)
1868-70	[interregnum]
1870-73	Amadeo , of Savoy
1873-75	[Republic]
1875-85	Alfonso XII
1886-1931	Alfonso XIII (abdicated)
1931-39	[Republic: President Zamera 1931-36 President Azaña 1936-9]
1939-75	[Gen. Francisco Franco]
1975-	Juan Carlos I

Einzug des Printzen . . . . von Engellandt. so . . . . den 23. Martij Anno 1623 zu MADRILL in
Spanien geschehen.

Konigs Pallast

Der Statt Scep-
terdrager.

Höffrich-
ter.

Capitan der
Leibguar.

Trabanten

Ihrer Maiestet Scep-
terdrager.

Die Spanische Leib-
Guard. Leutenant.

Grosse Herra von Spanien oder Titulati

Der Printze von Gales

Graff von Oliuares

Graff von
. . . . .

Extraordin.
. . . . . .

Die vier Herolden
oder Wapen Konige

Der Statt Madrill Obrigkeit so den hummel dragett.

Ihrer M. Trabant-
scher Trabanten

Konig Jacob in Engellandt.
Frid zu stiften in allem Landt.
Seinen Sohn Printz Carln hochgeborn
Zur gemahlin hat aufferkoren

Die Infantin in Spanien,
Derhalb auß groß Britannien
Hochgemelter Printz gantz vnbekandt
Gezogen ist aus seinem Landt,

Sein verheissen Braut selbst zu sehn
Wie dan in Merteri ist geschehn.
Die zeit thet man Celebreren
Mit ringelrennen vnd Thurniern

Da hochgemelter Printz zu Madrill
Dahin Er kommen war gantz still,
Gantz Koniglich zu hoff wird bracht
Gott geb daß Frid dadurch werde gmacht.

Chronology

1702-13 War of Spanish Succession involves most of Europe

1759-88 Reign of Charles III, one of Spain's most prosperous periods; he does much to beautify and improve Madrid

1767 Expulsion of Jesuits

1805 Destruction of Spanish and French naval power at Trafalgar

1808 Charles IV abdicates to Ferdinand VII and both are lured to France, and replaced by Napoleon's brother Joseph
Madrid rising of 2nd of May against the French marks beginning of Peninsular War (British under Wellington supporting Spanish and Portuguese guerrillas; French decisively beaten at Vittoria in 1813)

1812 Constitution of Cádiz, marking birth of liberalism and anti-clericalism in Peninsula

1814 Ferdinand VII returns to Spanish throne and abolishes constitution

1819 Prado opened to the public

1823 French army helps Ferdinand VII restore absolutist rule

1833-39 First Carlist War

1868 Abdication of Isabel II. Search for a successor leads to the Franco-Prussian War.

1871-73 Amadeo of Savoy rules as King

1872-76 Second Carlist War

1873 First Spanish Republic formed

1874 Bourbon restoration (Alfonso XII)

1898 Spanish-American War over Cuba marks the end of empire for Spain, with loss of Cuba, Puerto Rico, and Philippines

1914-18 Spain neutral during First World War

1922-30 Dictatorship of Miguel Primo de Rivera

1931 Fall of Alfonso XIII, and establishment of Second Republic

1936-39 Spanish Civil War, ending with victory by the Nationalists under Franco over the loyalist Republicans after the capture of Madrid following a 29-month siege. Beginning of Franco's dictatorship

1939-45 Spain neutral during Second World War

1947 Franco declares Spain a kingdom, with himself as regent

1975 Death of Franco; Juan Carlos, grandson of Alfonso XIII, proclaimed king. Centre right wins elections in 1976

1981 Attempted military coup collapses on personal intervention of Juan Carlos

1982 Socialists, under Felipe González, return to power for first time since Civil War

1996 Socialists defeated in elections; José-Maria Aznar becomes Prime Minister

Artists, and where to see their works
by Ian Chilvers

Bayeu, Francisco (1734-95) Spanish painter, the teacher and brother-in-law of Goya: Casita del Príncipe; Pardo Palace; Royal Palace.

Benlliure, Mariano (1862-1947) Spanish sculptor, responsible for many of Madrid's monuments, including those to Alfonso XII, Alvara de Bazán, Goya, María Cristina, and the Pantheon of Illustrious Men.

Bosch, Hieronymus (c. 1450–1516) Netherlandish painter, admired and collected by Philip II: Museo Lázaro Galdiano; Prado.

Chillida, Eduardo (b. 1924) Spanish abstract sculptor: Buen Retiro Park; Fundación Juan March

Churriguera, family of Spanish architects and sculptors, of whom the most important was José Benito de Churriguera (1665-1725): former convent church of Las Calatravas; Royal Academy of San Fernando; San Cayetano.

Coello, Claudio (1642–93) Spanish painter, the leading painter in Madrid in the late seventeenth century: Convent of the Descalzas Reales: Convent of San Placido.

Fernandez, Gregório (c. 1576–1636) Spanish sculptor, one of the greatest masters of the painted wooden figure: Convento de la Encarnación; Convent of San Placido.

Giaquinto, Corrado (1702-65) Neapolitan decorative painter, active in Spain (1753-62: Convent of Las Salesas; Royal Palace.

Giordano, Luca (1639-1705) extremely prolific Neapolitan decorative painter, active in Spain 1692-1702: Casón del Buen Retiro; Church of Las Comendadoras; El Pardo.

Gómez de Mora, Juan (1586-1646/8) Spanish architect, the most prolific in Madrid in the early 17th century: Capitania General; Casa de la Villa (Town Hall); Casita del Príncipe; Convento de la Encarnación; Court Prison; Plaza Mayor; Retiro Palace; San Antonio de los Portugueses.

Gonzalez Velázquez, Isidro (fl. 1810) neoclassical Spanish architect: 2nd May Obelisk; Teatro Real (Opera House).

Goya, Francisco de (1746-1828) Spanish painter and print-maker, one of the greatest European artists of his era:College of Escolapian Fathers; Museo Lázaro Galdiano; Museo Municipal; Museo Romántico; Prado, Royal Academy of San Fernando; San Antonio de Florida; San Francisco el Grande.

Greco, El (1541-1614) Cretan-born artist (his real name was Domenikos Theotocopoulos and his nickname means 'the Greek') who settled in Toledo in 1577 and became the first great painter of the Spanish School: Museo Lázaro Galdiano; Prado, San Ginés.

Gutiérrez Soto, Luis (1890-1977) Spanish architect: Air Ministry; Museo Chicote.

Herrera, Juan de (1530-97) Spanish architect, whose strong, solemn, severe style won official approval during Philip II's reign: Casa de las Siete Chimeneas; Royal Palace.

Madrazo, Federico (1815-94) Spanish painter, mainly of portraits, a member of a distinguished family of artists: Museo Romántico; Palacio de Liria.

Mengs, Anton Raffael (1728-79) German painter, active in Spain 1761-9 and 1773-7, an artist important as one of the pioneers of Neoclassicism: Casita del Principe; Palacio de Liria; Royal Palace.

Murillo, Bartolomé Estebán (1617-82) Spanish painter mainly of religious subjects appealing to popular piety; his work was enormously popular in the 18th and early 19th centuries and endlessly copied and imitated: Museo Lázaro Galdiano; Prado.

Palacios, Antonio (1876–1945) the outstanding Spanish architect of the early 20th century: Bellas Artes Building; Hospital de Maudes; Post Office Building.

Picasso, Pablo (1881–1973) Spanish painter, sculptor, graphic artist and designer, the most illustrious artist of the 20th century: Casón del Buen Retiro, Royal Academy of San Fernando.

Ribera, José de (1591–1652) Spanish painter, active in Naples (a Spanish possession at the time): Convento de la Encarnación; Prado.

Ribera, Pedro (c. 1683–1742) the most prolific architect of the early 18th century in Madrid, working in a lavishly ornamented Baroque style: Barracks of the Conde Duque; Fuente de la Fama; Hospicio of San Fernando; Mariblanca Fountain; Palace in Calle de Las Huertas; palace in Carrera de San Jerónimo; portal in Calle de La Magdalena; promenade and hermitage, Pasco Virgen del Puerto; San Cayetano; San José; Toledo Bridge.

Rodriguez, Ventura (1717–85) the leading Spanish architect of the late 18th century: Convento de la Encarnación; fountains in Paseo del Prado; Palacio de Liria

San Isidro, San Marcos.

Rubens, Sir Peter Paul (1577–1640) Flemish painter and designer, one of the greatest and most influential artists of the 17th century; he twice visited Spain – in 1603–4 and 1628–9 – and became friendly with Velázquez: Convent of the Descalzas Reales; Palacio de Liria; Prado.

Sabatini, Francesco (1722–97) Italian architect, active in Spain from 1760, the favourite architect of Charles III: Centro Cultural Reina Sofia; church of Las Comendadoras; Customs House; Palacio de Liria; Puerta de Alcala; San Francisco el Grande; tombs of Ferdinand VI and Barbara of Bragauza, Convent of Las Salesas.

Sacchetti, Giovanni Battista (1700–64) Italian architect who was called to Madrid in 1736 to continue work on the Royal Palace, for which his master Filippo Juvarra (1678–1736) had made designs: Royal Palace.

Tacca, Pietro (1577–1640) Florentine sculptor: statues of Philip III (completion of work by his master Giambologna) (1529–1608) and Philip IV.

Tiepolo, Giambattista (1696–1770) the greatest Italian painter of the 18th century: he settled in Madrid in 1762 at the invitation of Charles III: Royal Palace.

Titian (*c.* 1485–1576) Venetian painter, one of the supreme artists of the 16th century; Charles V and Philip II were among his most important patrons: Palacio de Liria; Prado.

Toledo, Juan Bautista de (d. 1576) Spanish architect: Casa de las Siete Chimeneas; Convent of the Descalzas Reales.

Velázquez, Diego (1599–1660) the greatest of all Spanish painters, one of the supreme geniuses in the history of art: Museo Lázaro Galdiano; Prado.

Velázquez Bosco, Ricardo (1843–1923) Spanish architect: Academy of Mining Engineers; Casón del Buen Retiro; Ministry of Agriculture.

Villanueva, Juan de (1739–1811) Spain's outstanding Neoclassical architect, brother of the architect Diego de Villanueva (1715-74), who published a book attacking the Churrigueresque style in 1766: Casa de la Villa (Town Hall); Casita del Príncipe; Observatory; Oratory in Caballero de Gracia; Plaza Mayor; Prado; Royal Academy of History; Teatro Espanol.

Zuloaga y Boneta, Daniel (1852–1921) ceramicist, noteworthy for his decoration of the buildings of Ricardo Velázquez Bosco: Academy of Mining Engineers; Ministry of Agriculture.

Zurbarán, Francisco de (1598–1644) Spanish painter, mainly of powerful, sombre, religious works: Prado; Royal Academy of San Fernando; San Francisco el Grande.

Illustrations

Index

Most street names are grouped under Calle, with
    some under Avenida, Carrera and Paseo.
Bars, barracks, battles, churches, hospitals, hotels,
    museums, palaces, parks, railway stations and
    theatres are grouped by category.
Birth and death dates are given for selected writers
    and artists.
Numbers in *italic* indicate illustrations.
Numbers in **bold** indicate the principal reference.

Index

PALLAS GUIDES

Other books by Michael Jacobs

Andalucía

The best one-volume introduction to the region *Rough Guide*
Take no other *Cosmopolitan*

464 pp including colour plates, illustrations and maps.
Practical information and full index ISBN 1 873429 43 6 £15.95

The Road to Santiago

Packed with historical as well as architectural goodness *The Guardian*
280 pp including 90 pp plates, maps and diagrams
Practical information, full index ISBN 1 873429 42 8 £12.95

In the Glow of the Phantom Palace

It justifies travel writing. *Felipe Fernández Armesto, TLS*
224 pp including illustrations and maps. ISBN 1 873429 36 3 £12.99

PALLAS GUIDES

Other Pallas for Pleasure guides

Venice for Pleasure

The greatest guidebook to *any* city ever written *Bernard Levin, The Times*
One of those miraculous books that gets passed by hand, pressed urgently on friends
Sean French, New Statesman

275 pp including 32 colour plates, 55 illustrations and maps. ISBN 1 873429 40 1   £14.99

Brussels for Pleasure

One quickly develops enormous respect for his knowledge *Low Countries Yearbook*
425 pp including 100 pp plates, maps and diagrams   Practical information, full index ISBN 1 873429 14 2   £14.99

Flemish Cities Explored

Superbly informative *RA Magazine*
A labour of love. Be sure to pack this one *Sunday Times*
320 pp including 50 illustrations and 7 maps Practical information, full index ISBN 1 873429 30 4   £12.95

This is a Pallas for Pleasure guide book, published by Pallas Athene.
To find out more about other books in this series,
and about our other books, please or write to us at
42 Spencer Rise, London NW5 1AP
or visit
WWW.PALLASATHENE.CO.UK

Series editor: Alexander Fyjis-Walker
Series design consultant: James Sutton
Editorial assistants: Lynette Quinlan, Barbara Fyjis-Walker and Ava Li
Maps by Ted Hammond

Special thanks go to Peter Khoroche, Mona Megalli and Jenifer Otwell

Set in Monotype Baskerville

Printed in China for
Pallas Athene (Publishers) Ltd
42 Spencer Rise, London NW5 1AP

ISBN 1 873429 24 X